Deborah Heckert

Semiotics of Visual Language

Advances in Semiotics
General Editor, Thomas A. Sebeok

Semiotics of Visual Language

Fernande Saint-Martin

Indiana University Press | BLOOMINGTON AND INDIANAPOLIS

Published in French as *Sémiologie du Langage Visuel*
© 1987 by Presses de l'Université du Québec
This translation © 1990 by Indiana University Press

The paper used in this publication meets the minimum requirements of
American National Standard for Information Sciences—Permanence of Paper
for Printed Library Materials, ANSI Z39.48-1984.

 ™

MANUFACTURED IN THE UNITED STATES OF AMERICA

Library of Congress Cataloging-in-Publication Data

Saint-Martin, Fernande
    [Sémiologie du langage visuel. English]
    Semiotics of visual language / Fernande Saint-Martin.
        p.   cm. — (Advances in semiotics)
    Translation of: Sémiologie du langage visuel.
    Includes bibliographical references.
    ISBN 0-253-35057-3 (alk. paper)
    1. Visual communication.   2. Semiotics.   I. Title.   II. Series.
P93.5.S2613   1990
302.2—dc20   89-45920
                                                                             CIP

1 2 3 4 5 94 93 92 91 90

Contents

Figures

Preface

Since the dawn of time and with a profusion that still inspires awe, creative men and women have inscribed configurations of lines, marks, and colors on the most diversified surfaces imaginable, providing for their transmission down to the present time. But these visual representations still remain enshrouded in the mysterious aura surrounding the semi-abstract, semi-figurative engravings on stones or the drawings wrought on the immense walls of obscure grottoes. They are as intriguing in their own way as any of the compelling transformations that mark the art of our own century. It could be said, after these millennia of production of visual representations, that the nature of this language and its modes of functioning still escape us.

Despite widely scattered efforts throughout the centuries, we can attribute to a scholar of our own century, Ferdinand de Saussure, a new awareness of the need to develop a general science of all the various systems of signs, that is, a 'semiology' in which verbal linguistics would constitute one element among many others.

In this perspective, where analyses effected upon other signs (verbal, gestural, mathematical, and so on) would be completed by a theory of visual signs, visual semiotics would contribute to the completion of this general theory of semiology, as uniquely capable of shedding light on the fundamental mechanisms of the symbolic function.

However, the extraordinary developments of verbal linguistics itself, from phonology to generative grammar and the first levels of grammatical formalization in the 1950s and 1960s, paradoxically, placed at risk this whole semiological project, specifically in relation to visual semiotics. The many difficulties encountered, as well as the contradictions surrounding this endeavor, have already been enumerated, notably by Hubert Damisch (1974) in an article summarizing arguments for and against the possibility of producing a semiology of painting.

At its most fundamental level, a semiology of visual language postulates that visual representations are signifying practices constituting a language. This concept retains the minimal definition of language set forth, for example, by Iouri Lotman: "By language, we mean any system of communication which uses signs arranged in a particular way" (1973; 34). Although any communication implies a speaker and a listener, Lotman stipulated that the communicative function can be exercised by any one individual alone, who is simultaneously the sender and receiver of the message which he generates and which "he speaks" in order to inform himself about an internal or external experience.

From the first tentative steps toward constructing visual semiotics, it is this specific linguistic function of visual language which was called into question. This problem resulted from comparisons between visual structures and those newly discovered structures of verbal language, construed as an absolute paradigm for any notion of language and a model for any semiotics.

The program was clearly defined by Roland Barthes: "The point is to draw analytical concepts from linguistics which we think a priori are sufficiently general to permit semiological research to be initiated" (1967). We can better surmise today, a quarter of a century later, the dangers inherent in borrowing various concepts of verbal grammar, which may appear valid at a given moment but not some time later, and in applying them *volens nolens* to visual language. Unfortunately, certain significant, if somewhat 'unconsidered' borrowings, as Luis J. Prieto (1976; 106) astutely pointed out, were made at that decisive moment when it was necessary to establish the basic concepts of a visual, that is a nonverbal, semiology.

It was readily apparent that analytical concepts so selected a priori could not ensure the construction and development of a semiology of nonverbal languages. As pointed out respectively by Damisch (1976), Eco (1976), Metz (1977), Greimas (1979), and Floch (1985), the research inspired by Barthean positions, while claiming the name 'visual semiology' or 'visual semiotics' (both terms interchangeable, for the purpose of this discussion) did not mark the beginnings of a new discipline, but simply perpetuated the iconology instituted by Erwin Panofsky in 1939.

These first attempts to formulate a theory of visual language established a dependence of its basic elements, as well as its syntax and semantics, on the constitutive categories of verbal language. The main preoccupations were the following: Did visual signs possess a double articulation? Were they constituted by 'isolated and isolatable' elements of a finite number, as were the characteristics of verbal phonetic elements? What about certain signs called iconic, that argue against the arbitrary character of the sign linked to verbal units by Saussure and appear to be motivated? If visual signs did not possess the characteristics of verbal language, they were thought as not constituting a bona fide language but rather a sort of secondary and restricted one, interpretable only through the mediation of verbal language.

The consequences that followed were that visual figures could only be determined and stated through the efficiency of words, and that the regions of the visual field which remained unnameable were excluded from any analytical visual discourse. Ignoring the syntactic interrelations which construct these visual figures, this icono-semiology conferred on them merely denotative meanings through their connections with verbal lexicology, or connotations, as Panofsky intended, at the level of intertextuality, that is, the ensemble of textual sources: literary, philosophical, religious, political, and so on.

The strict dependence of this icono-semiology on verbal linguistics placed it in the same impasse as the one confronting verbal semantics which has failed to attain the same maturity or scientific validity as did phonology or syntactic theory. Even before the advent of contextualism and the influence of the cognitive sciences on linguistics, visual semioticians experienced the same fearsome dread that Hjelmslev observed among linguists, when the time came to analyze the contents of verbal language: ". . . confronted by an unrestricted number of signs, the analysis of the content appeared to be an insoluble problem, a labor of Sisyphus, an impassable mountain" (1963; 67).

The research was sidetracked momentarily by more or less fortuitous games of association in the face of visual images, following the hypothesis that Umberto Eco accredited in *L'Oeuvre ouverte* (1965), but drawn now from a modernized iconologic discourse resulting from the development of human sciences (anthropology, psychoanalysis, Marxism, rhetoric, and so on). But soon one became aware of the epistemological fragility of these most varied interpretations of visual images, be they photography, advertising illustrations, or artworks. Toward the end of the 1970s, many investigators no longer believed in the possibility of constituting a semiology of visual language on relatively scientific grounds.

The main reason for this epistemological failure is tied to the refusal to recognize the inability of verbal language—through its links with Aristotelian metaphysics and logic as well as by its mode of production of two-dimensional, discrete signs—to conceive of spatial experiences and to account for the functioning of a spatial, three-dimensional language such as visual language.

This discrepancy between the "surface" levels of verbal and visual languages, which was duly recognized by Saussure, had never been considered fully significant. In a civilization dominated by the *Logos* this oversight has largely contributed to excluding from human consciousness the proper correlative of visual language, namely the experience of space. Succinctly, spatiality can be defined as the apprehension of a simultaneous coexistence of multiple elements in an autonomous form of organization, which is considerably different from that of the temporal order of these elements.

We know that Freud (1979; 285) linked the experience of space to the phenomenon of the unconscious. Just as temporality is unacknowledged by the unconscious, so space would be 'nonexistent' to the conscious mind.

Moreover, whereas the human being has two implements, undoubtedly necessary, to achieve access to consciousness, these being the representation of words and the representation of things, the contribution of the latter is misapprehended, being reduced to a temporal and linear succession of iconic objects, that is, of figures resembling some objects of external reality and identifiable by words. In this orientation, the spatial dimension of things, that is, their mode of integration and function, is entirely lost in an ensemble where their meaning would depend on interactions between spatial coordinates.

Basically, the notion of space, which is preeminently pluralistic, must be thought of as anterior to any notion of the object or the construction of the object. M. Merleau-Ponty (1968; 234) suggested this view when he wrote that space is "a communication with the world older than thought." R. Thom (1972; 327) suggested also that one should consider spatial thought as the basis of man's conceptual thinking. He advocated a much wider use, in natural and human sciences, of diverse geometrical intuitions as basic to the understanding of a fundamentally spatial reality.

This proposition is not altogether new in the field of art theory. The essential message of P. Francastel (1965), an art historian and the initiator in France of the sociological approach to art, has been that artistic representations of each epoch are indissolubly wed to the geometrical hypotheses of different societies. In following the path thus opened, we have laid down some foundations for a semiology or science of visual signs which finds its basic spatial intuitions in the geometrical discourse of topology (Saint-Martin, 1980). This allowed for the present development of a general syntax describing the modes of functioning of visual language.

Topological relations not only constitute the first mediation by which a human being constructs his notions of reality and space, as described by Piaget (1956, 1960), but they also offer, he showed, the means for modeling fundamental organic spaces. These sensorial, concrete perceptual spaces constitute the fluctuating and pluralistic field to which every spatial representation specifically refers. As has already been well demonstrated by the works of Kurt Lewin in the 1930s, topological models seem to be the most appropriate for the representation of human psychological behavior relating to perceptual activities, affective organizations, or linguistic processes of representation.

In particular, topological models allow us to think of the visual-spatial field as a field of forces or dynamic tensions that are in a state of continual change. In addition, they permit us to account for the material energies transported by plastic elements in the context of the dynamic processes that animate perceptual activity itself. In this respect, it would appear necessary to reappraise the contribution of Gestaltian theory, which has been too often reduced to the phenomenon of recognition of the 'figure-on-ground' or the drive for 'good form' (Saint-Martin, 1990). Gestaltian research has in fact described visual perception as being realized through a series of 'visual movements' of expansion and contraction, of interactions between percepts, which continuously modify already established configurations in the visual field (Köhler, 1940). It provides an essential framework for the elaboration of a visual grammar based on the specificity of visual perceptual processes.

Since the aim of any grammar is to study how a given ensemble of signs is organized in order to convey meaning, the syntactic theory of visual language that we propose here, if far from constituting a genuine semantics, could not be constructed without basic assumptions about the very meaning of visual language. These assumptions also necessarily question the phonocentric dogmatism which has dominated semantics as well as visual syntax in the recent past.

We allude, in particular, to the developments of "visual semiotics" by Thürlemann and Floch, which remain anchored in the structural semantics of Greimas (1966) and his "semiotics of the natural world" (1979). Following the productive research undertaken by Umberto Eco (1970) and R. Lindekens (1971), this semiotics acknowledges the existence of a "plane of expression" in visual representation, in the sense that Hjelmslev defined it as different from the "plane of content." This visual plane of expression is markedly dissimilar to the verbal plane of expression and thus necessitates an autonomous description of a relatively syntactic order. This description is still in a rough-draft stage of development. Such a syntactic orientation, which must take into account all existing regions in visual representations and their specific interrelations, has in this context no precise function, insofar as it does not contribute to the interpretation of meaning. Indeed the interpretation of the contents of a work is there defined as being essentially tied to the "figurative," that is, to a verbalized iconic form. This recourse to a natural world, conceived as only furnished by identifiable, nameable forms, overlooks, on the one hand, the decisive analysis of Eco against the use of the iconic sign as a basic element of visual language (1976). It confirms, on the other hand, the hegemony of verbal linguistics with respect to nonverbal semiotics.

Certainly, visual semiotics uses, it its very constitution, the instrumentality of verbal language as well as that of graphic models, but this natural language is no longer a language which refers to natural objects. It is rather a metalanguage, a language which talks about another language. The notions that it develops, the hypotheses and vocabularies that it uses, do not concern the same objects as those referred to by visual language. Those objects of visual representation which are, in some way, marked out by words, are in fact placed between parentheses and observed from points of view and levels of abstraction different from those which constitute them in visual language.

The essential characteristic of a visual language, a language of space, renders it suitable to modelize a large variety of distinct perceptual spaces by which human beings construct their relations with reality (tactile, kinesthetic, thermic, auditory, and so on). Though related, these spaces regroup stimuli quite different from those constructing strictly visual space. These spaces are not denoted or connoted by signs which would resemble, in a mimetic fashion, objects isolatable in the natural world. They are, on the contrary, manifested by structural interrelations of elements, revealed by syntactic analysis of visual texts as representations of nonvisual experiences and constructs.

This syntactic theory allows us to understand how visual language represents, in presenting them in the strict sense, and in "reproducing" them, those dynamic processes linked to our sensory, emotive, and conceptual experience, preverbal or paraverbal as the case may be, in order to render them accessible to a level of linguistic representation which makes consciousness itself possible.

It is, in effect, through the spatial constructs of visual speakers, that human beings can directly recover contact with, deepen, or master their nonverbal experiences. Through them, they can experiment with new modes of integrating the internal/external objects and drives. As new equilibria are attained, the visual spatial constructs can operate upon energies and tensions which, having never been "spoken" at the substratum of being, remain dormant, fixed, and largely unconscious.

We hope that, in opening the way to a more adequate comprehension of one of the most important nonverbal languages—namely, visual language—visual semiotics will bring to it a credibility that can provide a strong balance to the one-dimensional tendency of the Occidental Logos and, in this way, promote the development of a more humanistic civilization.

Acknowledgments

This work is an outgrowth of many years of research in the field of contemporary art theory and criticism which led to the founding in 1980 of the Groupe de recherche en sémiologie des arts visuels (GRESAV) at the Université du Québec à Montréal. A preliminary version was published in English by the Toronto Semiotic Circle Pre-publication series in 1985. Published in French in 1987, *Sémiologie du langage visuel* was translated with the financial help of the Université du Québec à Montréal. I wish to extend my deepest thanks to all of these, as well as to those who assisted me in the most critical task of translation, James D. Campbell and Eileen B. Collins. I am also in debt to colleagues and students in GRESAV whose passion for the problematics of visual representations and timely criticisms has helped this grammatical theory of visual language to take form. Naturally it would seem utopian to try to assess the contribution to this research of more than thirty years of exchanges and discussions with my husband, the artist Guido Molinari.

Chapter One

The Basic Elements of Visual Language

Visual language does not share the privileged position enjoyed by verbal linguistics when it started, at the beginning of this century, to develop a more rigorous approach to the study of verbal language.

The latter was able to draw from a long tradition of theoretical and pragmatic concerns with verbal expression to construct its phonological foundations and develop more adequate syntactic hypotheses. As the linguistic status of visual representations still remains in doubt, visual semiotics presents itself as an altogether new scientific discipline which has to define in the general context of contemporary theories of language the very object it proposes to study.

Given the structuralist or systematic approach adopted quite widely by verbal linguistics, some theoretical difficulties arose in the process of describing visual language as a system where, in a similar way, basic elements are interrelated according to certain laws or regularities. As Ferdinand de Saussure had already pointed out, the definition of an element presupposes that of the system. Paradoxically, the discovery of the fundamental units of visual language, which had evaded observers for a long time, could only be made once the system of internal relations of that language was known. Inversely, the potentialities of a system are determined by the structure of its elements. This apparent circularity is nevertheless superficial as the study of any system is a continuous process of observation of more global and more regional phenomena.

The development of a grammar of visual language seemed in fact dependent on the determination of the traits of the primary elements which permit them to evolve as a system of variations capable of carrying meaning. While these elements are constituted through perceptual processes, they had to be defined in relation to their potential for interrelating as linguistic elements. Once these basic elements are determined, semiotic syntax must provide the laws which regularize their combinations and transformations in the production of multiple statements.

We could cite in this connection the model of verbal linguistics, such as that defined, for example, by Noam Chomsky: "A language is defined by giving its 'alphabet' (i.e. the finite set of symbols out of which its sentences are constructed) and its grammatical sentences" (1957; 21). While agreement can be reached about the need to produce a formal model shared by any type of language, visual semiotics will question the specificity of this definition, as derived from the unique consideration of a digital type of language. For instance, how can visual language possess an "alphabet" made up of "symbols" and constituting a "finite set"? And how would the "grammaticality" of a visual proposition be recognized? As demonstrated by the discovery of forms of representations produced by ancient or foreign cultures, as well as by the evolution of contemporary artistic production, it seems hazardous to invoke a linguistic authority capable of differentiating between grammatical visual sentences and nongrammatical ones. In the absence of a theory of visual grammar indeed, neither intuition nor "competence" of a speaker can decide what belongs to a correct use of visual language.

Several visual "speakers," mostly artists, have been preoccupied in the past with this lack of theoretical foundations for their practice. They have attempted to determine the basic elements of pictorial or sculptural language which could serve as minimal units in the development of a grammar governing their interrelations.

From the beginning of this century, artists like Kandinsky, the Russian formalists and Klee, as well as Mondrian and Albers, questioned the nature of these fundamental elements which, through their "ordered arrangement" as Maurice Denis put it (1964; 13) produce a meaningful discourse. We will use some of their propositions, even if they appear fragmentary and more heuristic at the syntactic level than in relation with the problem of basic units. Artists should not be held accountable for this shortfall in what are properly semiotic concerns. In the visual area, as in any other field, an immediate experience of a reality does not necessarily lead to an easy understanding of its basic constituents. Most native speakers of a language learned through practice, in a suitable environment, would be at loss to identify its basic elements or its syntactic structures.

It remains a fact that the determination of the basic elements of visual language has been, until now, the stumbling block in the construction of a visual semiotics. The semiotician F. Thürlemann could still write, a few

[handwritten marginalia: is there an "alphabet" in visual arts? problems using verbal model for the visual]

years ago, that "a 'plastic phonology'—which aims at describing the first units of the plane of expression and their role in the constituting process—is still lacking. And it is not certain that this lack can one day be made good" (1982; 7).

There have been many arguments about the difficulty of determining a small number of minimal units in painting that can act as an alphabet, following the model of the phonemes which serve in verbal language to constitute morphemes (or words) and which regroup to form propositions. According to the formulation of Louis Marin: "Are there, in painting, elements equivalent to phonemes, to distinctive traits which do not have meaning in themselves but are, in some way, the constituents of meanings that the units of the first level obtain by the integration of their constitutive elements?" (1976; 137). This sort of question seemed important at the time, since it was thought that structures of verbal language had to be shared by all languages and 'double articulation' seemed an essential feature of that language. Soon thereafter, a number of works, notably those of Luis J. Prieto (1966) demonstrated that some languages existed which did not possess this double articulation, but functioned on only one or more than two levels of articulation.

Another obstacle remained in the presupposition that the basic units of visual language had to possess similar characters to those of verbal language. They ought to be simple, autonomous, isolated and independent, constituting a finite set. Obviously, the categories of elements composing visual language are quite numerous and each category offers an almost infinite possibility of proliferation. The chemical industry has already identified more than 60,000 different hues and these shades vary according to quantity, texture, and so on. Similarly, the combination of points, lines, and planes can produce an endless variety of forms and no repertoire of all possible images is conceivable.

Given this situation, it is reasonable to question whether the spoken, linear, and irreversible chain of words in verbal language does offer the best model for the understanding of a visual, spatial and tridimensional language. Like concrete matter, this language seems to present itself through agglomerates of stimuli more than through isolated and independent units. Different models could be obtained from the experimental sciences which had to diversify their notion of 'minimal units' in order to pursue their own development, whether in genetics or physics.

It has been more than thirty years since Bachelard (1951) observed that "chemical atomism" (which instituted differentiated nonhierarchical elements) had to be replaced as an elementary model by another closer to the pluralistic "physical atomism." This new unit juxtaposes different levels of reality in a dynamic structure the boundaries of which are more diffuse. It allows for a better description of interparticle relations, a preoccupation that has replaced the ancient phenomenological concern with the 'substances'. Bachelard's efforts were oriented toward making philosophy of science understand that "the particles of contemporary physics are, in fact, more precisely centres of force than centres of being. They do not resist a mutual becoming, compositions which are above all dynamic compositions" (Bachelard, 1951; 128).

Considering the agglomerates of matter which constitute the semiotic carrier of visual language, visual semiotics has every reason to abandon previous paths and to adopt an epistemology which is more in agreement with the dynamisms of observed phenomena. It will recognize that matter is not inertness, but energy. As Bachelard expressed it:

> It is energy which becomes the fundamental ontological notion of any modern doctrine of matter, even the principle of individualization of material substances. Any atomistic philosophy must, because of this fact, be reformed. One must decide whether the real has a structure in relation to its qualities or whether it produces dynamic phenomena as a result of its structure. (1951; 135)

More recently, René Thom (1981; 308) has also pointed out that in contemporary sciences, "a recent trend seems to be against this reduction to the element," if one is to understand element to be a clearly individualized entity. With particular respect to 'spatial forms', Thom stated that the principle of individualization is realized not through isolated/ isolable elements, but under the forms of "lumps" of elements: "They are topological *lumps* (cells)." While possessing linings and an internal morphological structure, these masses are sometimes barely or not at all visible. These agglomerates themselves, which have a topological structure, must be posited and perceived as elementary units if one wishes to account for the structure of the spatial tissue itself.

On the one hand, this raises the question of the type of geometry best suited to describe a given set of different spatial data. As far as visual language is concerned, we have proposed earlier that Euclidian geometry had to be complemented by topology (Saint-Martin, 1980). But this recognition leaves unsolved the question of the "size" a basic spatial unit should possess to be considered as an element.

Methodologically speaking, as Kurt Lewin (1936; 61) expressed, it would be incorrect "to presuppose in the analysis smaller subparts than those that actually exist." If, for instance, mathematics and physics subdivide their basic elements into virtual infinity, they constitute themselves as sciences in determining certain quantities as guidelines for the analysis, whether the real number or the atom. In the same way, given the crucial role played by perceptual processes in the construction of the visual field, we propose that the dimension of semiotic visual units should be determined in accordance with the specific structure of visual perception.

In a certain sense, the basic element of visual language can only be a psychophysical entity defined by both the subjective and objective aspects of a percept. But to be observable in the visual text itself, it should first be determined by its possibility of being *an objective correlative of a perceptive act*, that is, constituting the external facet of a given percept.

The definition of a basic element of visual language is the result of an abstractive process required for the purpose of analysis, the validity of which can only be demonstrated through its subsequent explanatory powers. It is not to be considered as some panacea which immediately renders possible the development of a syntax or a semantics of visual language. These three levels do not belong to the same epistemological network and each requires different analytical hypotheses.

This has been emphasized by Noam Chomsky, among others, with respect to verbal linguistics: ". . . it would be absurd, or even hopeless, to state principles of sentence construction in terms of phonemes or morphemes, but only the development of such higher levels as phrase structure indicates that this futile task need not be undertaken on lower levels" (1957; 59). Similarly, it would also be absurd and hopeless to try to apply syntactic modes of organizations to elements unable to carry over their requirements.

These considerations have led us to the following conclusion that no endeavor to describe visual language can assume the name of 'visual semiotics', if it does not provide a preliminary level of description, analogous to phonology in verbal linguistics, that can explain how primary elements are joined together to form larger units. Only then can the study of their syntactic rules of association be undertaken, both fields being necessary parts of a "grammar" of visual language.

It will soon appear that basic insights can be gained at that primary level into the conditions of emergence of visual language and some light is shed on the nature of syntactic organization. The analysis of elements offers a coherent system to which one can return from more complex strata, through a reversal of the laws of formation.

1.1. The Coloreme

Following considerations of both the structure and the mechanisms of visual perception, we have defined the basic unit of visual language as the *coloreme*. It corresponds to that aggregate of visual variables perceived in the visual representation by way of an ocular fixation, or focus of the gaze. One might compare it to an area corresponding to the "point of ostension" of a finger directed upon the opaque surface of the same representation.

A coloreme is defined, therefore, as the zone of the visual linguistic field correlated to a centration of the eyes. It is constituted by a mass of energetic matter presenting a given set of visual variables. This primary element of visual language is made up, from a semiotic point of view, of a cluster of visual variables, the properties of which will be described and elaborated upon in a later chapter.

Through the perceptive mechanism of ocular fixation (Arnheim; 1971), the coloreme is immediately structured as a topological region. Visual perception is realized through a positioning of the eye in the direction of the visual field, called an ocular centration or fixation. This fixation can obtain different visual information according to the specific mechanisms of vision it borrows: the fovea, the macula, or the peripheral vision.

The *fovea centralis* is a small pit or depression at the back of the retina furnished by the strongest condensation of *cones*, or receptors of colors, forming the point of sharpest vision, but within a distance of 15 feet and along a small arc of one to two degrees. The *macula* is a yellowish region surrounding the fovea, possessing a lower amount of cones, but covering a wider arc and a further distance. The *peripheral vision* is the name given to the rest of the retina, quite poor in cones but rich in *rods*, or receptors of tonality values; it lacks precision and susceptibility to colors, but can apprehend a wider portion of the field (over 90 degrees) as well as quite subtle movements in that field (Hall, 1966).

It should be noted that a viewer can at any moment use one or the other of these mechanisms of vision, or change from one to the other, thus modifying the visual information he is getting from the world. And in spite of apparent contradiction in terms, an ocular fixation may resort to peripheral vision and produce a blurred interpretation of the visual field when trying to encompass a larger and more distant area. Peripheral vision may also serve other purposes, as can be inferred from A. Ehrenzweig's propositions (1967), which will be discussed later.

Given the richer visual potentialities of the two central sources of vision, we have defined as a coloreme the area of the visual field which is the product of two interrelated zones: (1) a central area more precise, dense and compact, corresponding to foveal vision; and (2) some peripheral layers, less dense, but still rich in colors, corresponding to macular vision.

On the objective plane of representation, the coloreme corresponds to *stupid?* any colored quantity located at the termination point of an ocular fixation and contributing to the formation of a visual percept. The very definition of a percept as an entity structured as a field of forces (Gurvitsch, 1957; 114) requires that the minimal unit ascribed by semiotics to visual language be: *a material zone sufficiently large for perceptual mechanisms to be realized.* In other words, it cannot be microscopic or in any way inaccessible to normal perception. On the other hand, it cannot be too large, so as to permit an efficient realization of foveal and macular vision.

Invariable in its structural properties of interrelating a harder core to surrounding layers, the coloreme offers the topological characteristic of 'elasticity' in its dimension (and form) which excludes the very notion of static metric measurement. This unit reflects the functional dynamism of the organ of sight which is capable of amplifying or reducing the dimensions of the foveal percept within its proper limits of an arc of two degrees, as well as of integrating some of the scope of macular vision.

It is to be expected, however, that the characteristics of a coloreme will be modified when larger portions of macular vision are jointly used to consider the former stimuli of the foveal zone. In the same way the use of peripheric vision will greatly modify the experience of the visual field. While the latter will play a most important role in establishing relations among wider combinations of coloremes, it is not involved in the perception of the basic unit of visual language.

This definition of the element of visual language as a continuous and spatialized topological entity, endowed with somewhat fuzzy boundaries, would appear incompatible with the accepted view of the phonemic unit of verbal language, only if one neglected to consider the actual elasticity of this latter notion. In effect, the phoneme is constituted by a cluster of auditory variables within extended limits, and it can also, according to the individual case, play the role of a morpheme or even of an entire phrase. As put forth by L. Hjelmslev (1963; 63), a verbal phrase is seen:

> . . . to consist of only one clause and a clause of only one word. This phenomenon is constantly turning up in the most various texts. In the Latin imperative "i" / "go" or in the English interjection "ah" we have an entity that may be said to be at the same time a sentence, a clause, and a word. In each of these cases, also, we find a syllable that includes only one part of a syllable.

In the same way that the acoustical analysis of sounds provides little information as to the nature and function of the basic units of verbal language (the phoneme), theories of optics are only a prerequisite to the understanding of visual language. They have to be complemented by a definition of visual variables out of which visual semiotics can be constructed.

In regrouping a finite and specific ensemble of visual variables, the coloreme offers itself as an autonomous—and by its structure, a differentiated—unity, constructed by perception. Its global characteristics are quite different from those of the individual visual variables that constitute it. When one variable is modified, the coloreme is itself entirely transformed along with its interrelations with other coloremes. Visual variables themselves offer a wide potential for differentiation, but no single one among them can play the role of a basic element, since they are all inextricably bound up in any given percept.

If one can consider and analyze them as abstract categories, their behavior and functions within the perceptual process can only be known through the observation of what is concretely qualified and quantified in the visual field. It is the concrete and simultaneous conjunction of variables which constitutes the material structure of each of the coloremes. Once regrouped and energized by perception, these plastic units will enter into interrelations with others, according to a specific group of organizational laws, still totally dependent on the nature of the variables perceived.

In the past, there have been attempts to elevate one of these visual variables over another or to conjugate two of them, as the basic element of visual language. This very temptation has, in fact, and for a considerable time, slowed down the development of visual semiotics.

The historical record is replete with arbitrary choices made in this domain. One may recall the efforts of André Lhote (1967; 91) to determine the constants in the midst of visual variables he called the "plastic invariants." He first listed: "the design, color and value," but added subsequently: "rhythm, decorative character, reversal on the plane and monumentality." In a pioneering work, R. Passeron (1962) identified the "technical elements" as being color, value, line, and "la pâte." For his part, Kandinsky (1976) made the point, the line, and the plane the basic elements of his "grammar of creation." We will return to this latter proposition in our study of the Basic Plane.

More recently, Félix Thürlemann (1982; 20), while denying the possibility of determining the primary elements of pictorial language, did not hesitate to identify them with the duality of color-form, which Vasarely (1970) had previously identified as the very basis of his system of production of visual representations. But the indecision as to the clear definition of what should stand as color or form caused Thürlemann to retain as minimal units of the plastic discourse only the "well-formed" aggregates. These "color-endowed forms" will harmonize eventually with a list of verbal labels, since both proceed from the same reservoir of mental iconic images.

One could ask, given the omnipresence of the visual variable of color, as any line, form, or texture, possesses a color, why it has not been retained as the fundamental element of visual language, superseding all others. In effect, visual perception can be realized only by the mediation of colors which correspond to different quantities of reflected light. Essentially an energetic phenomenon, the chromatic dimension, as we will see further on, is also totally dependent (within the perceptual process) upon the dynamics of the other visual variables. For this reason, the term 'coloreme', which underlines in its formation the importance of color in visual reality, is used as a means of designating the minimal ensemble which regroups, together with the diverse qualities of color, all the other visual components in every point of the visual field.

The attempt to isolate a given visual variable, or even a handful, as basic elements cannot be fruitful. It would be equivalent to a decision in verbal linguistics to undertake the study of a chosen acoustic variable among those which constitute the phoneme (the sound's pitch, tonality, timbre, harmony, etc.) as the basic unit of verbal language. Furthermore, in contrast to the sequential and often isolated mode of presentation of each phoneme, visual variables are immersed in a simultaneous predicament where their perceptual aspect is constantly being modified.

The case is the same within a coloreme or between coloremes. In regrouping these, one should not minimize or ignore the action of some visual variables to the benefit of others. One region cannot totally oppose another by the sole specificity of one variable, its size, color or texture, and so on. Sometimes separated by contrasts within one visual variable, regions may be joined by liaisons produced by other variables.

One should be particularly careful not to isolate from the visual context those regions which can be endowed with the characteristics of a "good form," without due consideration of the nature of those variables which constitute it besides that of form.

One should be constantly aware that abstract considerations relating to the nature of the visual variables can be misleading, as none can exist independently of the others and none can be apprehended in an identical way in two places of the visual text or at different moments. As each coloreme, by necessity, regroups the totality of a set of visual variables, any process of junction/disjunction in visual language is a dialectic equilibrium realized between two or several coloremes and not between different aspects of a unique visual variable.

size of centration.

By definition—the coloreme being the correlative of foveal fixation on a small zone of the visual field—it is impossible to perceive several coloremes through one single centration. As a consequence, given the unique resources for vision of color of the foveal or macular instruments, it is deemed impossible to perceive adequately a large expanse of the visual field through a unique ocular fixation.

In order to perceive such a large expanse adequately, one must effect several successive centrations of the visual field (Saint-Martin; 1988). The different percepts resulting from this circuitous action in time and space, and stored in memory, will act one upon the other at the cortical levels. These will influence the nature of subsequent percepts which will, in turn, be integrated together with the first ones. The very first ocular fixations, which have not been re-equilibrated by subsequent centrations, are particularly deformative of the objective reality of the visual field. In general, as confirmed by K. Lewin (1936; 157): "The first reactions to stimuli are the nondifferentiated reactions of the global organism." In other words, these first reactions result less from sensorial relations with objective stimuli than from reflexes linked to acquired schemas, to anterior structuring habits of the organism, assimilating the new to the already known, in order to secure conceptual or emotional equilibrium.

It is nevertheless true that the spontaneous conduct of most perceivers in front of a visual representation seems to be an active searching, rapidly scanning the entire surface in order to "recognize" some of its parts and obtain a global reaction to the ensemble. This hasty mixing of peripheric vision with a few foveal and macular liaisons leaves most of the visual field literally unperceived.

behavior

This spontaneous trajectory using mainly the scanning of peripheric vision, and recognizing groups of coloremes which lend themselves easily to iconic interpretations, is not to be confused with the sort of scanning advocated by A. Ehrenzweig (1967) which tends more to counteract the hegemony of closed forms within common perceptive habits. Through a deliberate use of intense foveal fixations and peripheric vagueness, Ehrenzweig tries to counteract the pressure toward the "good form" which Gestalt psychology has observed as being a common feature of perception.

What can be called the "normal" perceptive behavior of most subjects in front of a visual field of representation corroborates, in fact, the conclusions of Rorschach (1947) in the application of his noted test on perception. Global responses to a visual field are the result not of an extensive sensorial perception, but rather of a process of interpretation which extrapolates to the totality the meanings extracted from major or minor details, in liaison with mnemonic visual images.

Visual semiotics may also retain from Rorschach's work the fundamental distinction between what can be revealed from *observation*—namely the description and classification of perceived events according to certain clear analytical categories—and what is added as an *interpretation*.

Given the inadequate and arbitrary character of most spontaneous behavior in visual perception, as revealed by Rorschach, visual semiotics will propose that any representation be observed in a systematic way and according to all parameters constituted by visual variables. It will thus aim at an awareness of the dynamics of each centration and will enlarge them sufficiently so as to take into account the effective interactions between all the parts.

In the course of this constitution of the visual text, through a perceptual investment in one coloreme after another and their innumerable interrelations and regroupings in *supercoloremes*, it becomes apparent that any description of a visual text as a whole refers to a specific moment in time, following a decision to put an end to the perceptual process. This temporal closure is deemed legitimate only if the observer has related himself in an adequate fashion to the multiple components of the visual field. The temporary synthesis he achieves should be an integration of the results of this attentive perceptual experience. But this pause is also illusory since the observer, already transformed by his perceptual syntheses, would be able, at the very next moment, to perceive the work anew through new equilibria and felt intensities. This would render him susceptible to experience the dynamic factors at play in the text very differently.

Semiotic analysis is thus conceived as an intense subjective experience calling for the conceptual and emotive resources of the individual and not as a distribution of verbal labels. It does not immobilize or tear apart the visual representation, but rather gives it flesh and blood. It is in no way reductive as, say, the work of the physician is, of whom Lewin (1951; 157) speaks, who cuts up a radiography of a fractured leg into minute pieces and classes them according to their degree of gray tonality. Visual semiotics has to relate to an eminently performative language which is not only dynamic in its material constituents but which cannot be constituted as a text without constant changes in the internal experience of the observer.

1.2. Spatialization and Topology

what remains invariant despite transformation

The intuitions of topological geometry seem to be most fruitful for the definition of the spatializing process proper to visual language. But other conceptual means must be called upon, such as the notions of vectors, intensities, equilibria, and so on, in order to describe the energetic behaviors of visual variables and the perceptual process itself.

This point has been recognized as essential by the topological psychology of Kurt Lewin (1936), which has wed to topological concepts a hodological geometry allowing some calculations, even if it remains nonmetric. The importance of topology has been demonstrated by its possibility of being used efficiently in mathematical applications to vectorial, set theories, and metric spaces (Berge, 1966). Even in the context of tridimensional Euclidean volumes, topology seems eminently successful by virtue of its fidelity to its own intuitions:

> Topology cannot, in fact resolve equations. What it offers is a mathematical vocabulary—adjectives and nouns—which allows solutions to be discussed on a general plane, without them actually being specified, under the condition that the theoretic manipulation does not imply any laceration, cut, excavation or cavities in the volume under consideration. (Thurston, 1984; 108)

In the same way, we have seen the necessity to interpret the concrete visual space as a continuous and undulating mass constituted as a field of forces, the orientations or vectors of which are spread out in three dimensions: height, width, and depth.

These characteristics are present in each and all of its constituents, the coloremes, defined as masses possessing a general nonspecific configuration, as well as a certain thickness or interior volume. But as a dimension of a topological object, interior volume has characteristics quite different from its definition in an Euclidean context, where it is wholly dependent on the stable metricization of the "external volume." We will try presently to clarify this point, which may represent one of the most fundamental intuitions of topology.

1.2.1. The topological volume

It is fundamental for visual semiotics to understand the distinction between the notions of internal and external volume, which was established in Jean Piaget's early works, notably in *The Child's Conception of Geometry* (1960). The internal volume is defined as the quantitative perception of the matter that constitutes the object. As for the external volume, it corresponds to the "place occupied in the environment" (470), measured from a point of view exterior to the object. Knowledge of the external volume necessitates a relation through metric measurements between the object and that which surrounds it. This point of view tends to make the object "an undeformable solid, in the sense of being uncompressible and undilatable" (449).

The internal volume has opposite characteristics. It is perceived as a nonmetric quantification, as the "filling up of envelopments" which constitute the object. If one considers any visible object as offering external surfaces, acting as frontiers or envelopments for the internal mass, the internal volume is perceived as "that which is enveloped by an ensemble of frontiers constituted by the visible surfaces of the exterior" (458). This type of volume can be transformed in its dimensions without losing its quantification.

It can change its external frontiers or contours without modifying the quantity of matter constituting its internal volume. For instance, a quantity of modeling clay always maintains its internal volume, corresponding to the given quantity of clay, even if its external volume adopts the form of a sphere, a cylinder or a surface plane.

There is, therefore, an invariance of the internal volume even if there is a modification of the external one, and this is the basis for the topological notion of a polymorphic, extensible mass, not definable by its external contour, as is the case in Euclidean geometry. In the genetic evolution of the child, as well as in the general culture, the opposition between these two notions of volume has generated a persistent conflict and many misunderstandings. In the domain of visual representations, this conflict was constantly active as seen, for instance, in the difficulty to understand the introduction by baroque art of the notion of a fluid matter and of "deformations" of external volumes (Deleuze, 1988).

From Piaget's research (1952, 1960), it is suggested that topological intuitions are a priority in the experience of external reality and that the ulterior Euclidean notions will evolve from that basis without eliminating them. But the Euclidean intuition of space will attempt to substitute for a dynamic intuition of matter, one of "stable objects" that are substantial, autonomous, isolated each from all others, and unchangeable in time.

In a correlative manner, the topological notion of surface will diverge from that provided by Euclidean geometry, emphazing its function of envelopment: "A surface, in effect, from the point of view of elementary topological relations, is only a part of space enveloped by a line closed on itself and a volume is, from the same point of view, only a part of space enveloped by the frontiers of surfaces, equally closed on themselves" (Piaget, 1960; 490). The surface understood as a boundary will envelop a mass then considered as a full and dense volume, and not a hollow, empty volume or an unfilled expanse of space.

On its smaller scale, the coloreme, being a part of a space enveloped by surfaces/frontiers, always possesses a density of matter corresponding to its internal volume. This forbids that its perception, as a unit or in agglomeration, would be that of a kind of abstract plane endowed with only two dimensions. Indeed no material reality can have solely two dimensions. Only a logical fiction can conceive of a point without dimension or of a plane in two dimensions, as suggested by Euclidean definitions. But a logical construct cannot be equivalent to the physical matter serving as the semiotic instrumentality of visual language.

Both surfaces and volumes are here defined in terms of the topological properties of the relation of envelopment. It is a relation by which an object is inserted in a whole which becomes in part or in total its immediate environment in a global proximity. This notion opposes the intuitions of Euclidean geometry, as Piaget explains: "Topological space ignores, indeed, any distinction between container and content. It is, in contradistinction, proper to Euclidian space to imply it continuously" (1952; 31).

Topology considers, therefore, the envelopments and the enveloped, the container and the content, as sharing the same properties. The first term is not immobile and the second one mobile, in relation to one another. The two elements maintain the same possibilities of expansion or contraction, typical of all topological quantities.

This phenomenon explains another fundamental characteristic of the coloreme, namely that, while it is delimited by an ocular centration, it remains essentially linked with other regions that surround it. Separation between coloremes does not produce emptinesses or voids, similar to the silences arising when the sounds forming phonemes, morphemes, or propositions in the verbal language are no longer produced.

The coloremes are always bound to other visual regions in an unbroken perceptual contiguity which radically distinguishes them from all other sensorial stimuli, tactile, kinesthetic, etc. This characteristic distinguishes them from the verbal linguistic phenomenon where, as Prieto (1964; 16) observes "the speech acts present themselves in the form of blocks or cross-sections, of different lengths, separated by silences, that is, those moments when one does not speak."

The elements of visual language are presented in a fundamental physical continuity which is at the same time the characteristic of the visible world itself: *for the eye, everything touches everything,* as Piaget's young interlocutors had already observed. Within perception, there are no chromatic silences between coloremes in a visual text. The notion of a possible void between two groups of coloremes is not one revealed by perception, but is the introduction of an abstract, nonvisual point of view foreign to the visual field itself.

The set of relations that are established between different juxtaposed coloremes influences in an essential way the structure of each. In other words, the coloreme, which is always situated in a diversified context, can be known only through those interrelations it establishes with the elements of that context. These interrelations, arising from the multiplicity of centrations effected on regions of the visual field, constantly modify those established previously by virtue of the dynamisms of both the visual variables and the perceptual process.

While having its own distinct internal structure, the coloreme is, at the same time, a region which acts on and transforms its environment, only to be in turn transformed by it. This fundamental relational function affects its perceptual appearance in a manner unknown to the linguistic verbal unit, even if we agree on the definition given to the latter by Prieto (1964; 154), as an object which "does not precede, as such, the relations of which it is recognizably the terminal point."

The consequence of this situation is that the visual variables which constitute a coloreme cannot be "described" as identical to some previously established repertoire, but are completely new events born through their interrelations with other perceived coloremes in the visual field. They always appear in a specific constellation which transforms their quality/ quantity through a process of dynamic interaction by which they diverge and converge, or are integrated one into another, producing complex models of continuous topological spaces.

In the past, certain researchers, conscious of the dependence of visual semiotics on perceptual processes, have alluded to the necessity to establish the first elements of visual language on topological notions. However, they have not taken any decisive action in this regard. We refer particularly to the interesting research undertaken by R. Lindekens (1971) into the semiotics of photography.

He recognized that "perception depends on the previous learning of the parts of an object, a process encompassing a series of visual fixations and depending on the visualization of an amorphous mass containing certain foci, to then succeed in seeing a distinct figure" (53). According to him, a verbal or iconic identification of this "amorphous mass" is not at all required in order for perception to be effectuated. He quotes numerous experiences which "attempts to prove that, effectively, the unit resting on separate physiological basis, and independent psychologically, can be perfectly perceived without identification" (51).

It seems that the ideological refusal to admit as perceived objects the zones of a visual field which remain unnamed influenced nevertheless Lindekens. He did not develop the results of his demonstration of the fact that a slight modification of distinctive traits (or in our terminology, visual variables) for instance, in typographical variations of the alphabet, involves an important modification in the "meaning" ascribed to each letter by a group of perceivers. This meaning was expressed in terms of diversified aesthetic and emotive connotations, such as "nice," "elegant," "delicate," "aristocratic," "strong," and so on. But Lindekens also defined a correlation with another level of meaning, qualified as "infra-verbal" or more "intralived" than either thought or verbalized experience (198). The pursuit of the ever evasive function of meaning has prevented this researcher from exploring further the notion of contrast in the functional mechanisms of visual signifiers.

This last step seems to us essential in the study of visual language because the visual variables constitute the material sine qua non of reality as visible. The analysis of interconnected visual variables within the coloreme affords access to the first semiotic structures of this mode of representation. As such, it permits the description of dynamic units which are the very "building-blocks" of various visual texts. In effect, the energetic intensities and interactions of coloremes sampled in the works of Cezanne, Matisse or Pollock, present entirely different dynamisms which already give information on each artist's basic manipulation of visual language. This diversified structure of coloremes betrays organizing mechanisms at play in smaller areas, susceptible to repetition or contradiction on larger syntactic levels.

Still more important, given that ocular fixation allows for continued recourse to foveal/macular liaisons in the visual field, experimentation with coloremes will play a continuous role in the perceptual relations to a visual text, interfering at the end with reactions provoked by larger agglomerates of visual regions.

As the observation and description of coloremes require a very particular attention, we feel that it is necessary to provide additional information on the very nature of the visual variables that constitute them.

Chapter Two

The Visual Variables

The semiotic material which transmits visual language is to be analyzed in relation to its components, the visual variables. As stated earlier, the term 'coloreme', given to the basic unit of visual language, corresponds to the percept that limits a regrouping of visual variables in the momentary unit of an ocular fixation.

This definition of semiotic material contrasts with earlier semiotic approaches on two main grounds. A comparison with some definitions offered by J. Mukarovsky in his essay on "The Essence of the Visual Arts" (1976: 241) shows this clearly. Stating that "each art has something different that distinctly separates it from others, and this is its *material*," Mukarovsky goes on to say that, in visual arts, "their material, and only theirs, is organic, immobile and relatively unchangeable matter."

This insight into the nature of matter may seem outdated in the post-Einsteinian era when matter could be better described as mobile, energetic, and under constant change. Furthermore, visual semiotics should be more concerned with the "visual" aspects of matter than with its physio-biological ones. Problems of "visibility" are essentially dependent upon perceptual processes that seem as mobile and changing as their target, the phenomenon of light reflection on opaque matter.

Mukarovsky ignored the importance of the perceiver's standpoint in the constitution of the semiotics of visual arts as opposed to the "unique" position of the producer of the representation. We submit that the perceptive function is as much at work in the case of both, since the producer is not only the first perceiver of his work but also perception is inherent in the production process. Both producer and perceiver are equally dependent on their perceptual relations with the functional elements of this language, the visual variables.

These variables can be described as belonging to six distinct categories: color/tonality, boundaries (which produce form), texture, dimension, vectoriality, and position in the plane. As we mentioned earlier, none of these visual variables can be considered independently as a basic unit of visual language, because at the same time that one is present, the others are manifested. All variables are always globally present, in every point of the visual field. The term 'coloreme' is given to the percept that determines the regrouping of visual variables in the unity of an ocular fixation on the field.

The perceptual nature of the relation to the visual field calls for a distinction between two categories of visual variables. The first group, formed by color and texture, is more directly linked to the objective characteristics of colored matter constituting the visual field: they are called plastic variables. The second group of visual variables, the product of a larger implication of subjective, mental processes in the synthesis effected on this material, are called perceptual variables: dimension, boundaries, vectoriality and implantation or position in the plane. No visual perception exists which can be produced outside of the conjunction of these two categories of variables.

The list of visual variables here established, with some modifications, draws on the landmark work of Jacques Bertin entitled *Sémiologie Graphique* (1973), which has become a seminal text for the semiological approach. With these modifications dictated by our fundamentally different fields of study, we will use the set of variables that Bertin has designated as "retinal variables"; namely, texture, tonality, color, size, orientation, form, and position in the plane. Bertin's definitions were confined to the proper field of his investigation, graphic semiology, and do not concern the visual language as such (Saint-Martin, 1989). Like the alphabetic printed language of the Gutenberg era that McLuhan (1962) qualified as a supposedly visual environment, graphism constitutes only one form of transcription of the auditory verbal speech, the latter predefining the organization, meaning and functions of utilized visual signs. In this context, the message of graphic signs is not linked to the particular dynamic of a spatializing language, but to the illustration of previously fixed sequences of verbal concepts.

In graphism, through a kind of semantic parenthesis, these signs can receive a quasi-monosemic denotation, provided that one does not use more than two or three semantic variables. By definition, graphic signs do not serve to form a continuous space, because the graphic representation postulates nonsignifying regions on the bidimensional surface of the plane. In contradistinction to this, the visual language used in what one designates as an artwork, for example, cannot possess regions which do not present significant variables and it always regroups them in three dimensions.

Thus, in the case of visual language, it is not in those predefined concepts which one tends to associate with visible signs that one will find the constituents of the plane of expression, but in the structure of the colored material itself. By virtue of its variations, the material produces the differential qualities capable of being wed to their own referents. Like sounds in auditory language, visual variables are quantities/qualities that are offered to sensory perception and are not abstract or synthetic products through which one would seek, simply at a logical level, to organize or regroup heterogeneous data. The visual variables are the source of those data, set apart by an ocular centration in the external field amid the relational mobility that determines the coloreme as a dynamic function.

This particular situation requires that visual semiotics develop the study of these complex variables which have not until now been very well verified by a demonstration. While we attempt to define these visual variables verbally, we must emphasize that their full meaning is better understood by an "ostensive" definition. The words used, according to Wittgenstein (1958; no. 65), serve only "truly to indicate how the meaning could unfold . . . in pointing a finger at the visual field."

2.1. Plastic Variables

2.1.1. Universe of color

Color is the product of a perceptual phenomenon localized at the interfaces of matter which are in contact with air. Any work of visual language achieves existence essentially through color organizations, as does visible reality itself. But, strictly speaking, color cannot be considered as a 'property' of matter itself. It consists rather of the spectral composition of the light reflected from an object, according to its specific structure of absorption and reflection of light rays.

From the scientific point of view, color is defined, at the macroscopic level, as the reactive capacity of materials to rays of light. It is by no means redundant to recall that, at the microscopic level, color terms no longer designate a color referent in itself. They are applicable only through an artificial injection of lighting and colorants in order to become the basis of a system of description, where the references to color are purely arbitrary and conventional. Indeed, colors injected in the microscopic milieu do not correspond to colored characteristics of elements, but rather constitute only an artificial instrumentality for the differentiation of heterogeneities and trajectories that do not have color. However the addition of color to these microscopic units allows the perception of internal morphological and functional structures through groups, textures, and so forth which derive from deep structures. Similarly, in outer space, as W. O. Quine noted, color does not have more significant existence: "Color is king in our innate quality space, but undistinguished in cosmic circles. Cosmically, colors would not qualify as species" (1969; 127).

In the macroscopic environment, color terms derive their capacity to designate objects from an accumulation of chromatic mass in diverse expanses great enough to correspond to an optical perception. Within the limits of macroscopic space, the preeminent existence of the coloristic phenomenon has not contributed, however, in any fruitful way to the understanding of the natural world. Even if we live, at the anthropomorphic level, in a space of qualities manifestly "chromatically biased," this sine qua non character of human experience could never serve as a correlative by which to understand or to describe the surrounding reality with cogent basic hypotheses.

Thus, the fact of color, the most obvious of all facts in sensory experience, cannot serve as a reference in the recognition or the description of constant or regular events. It cannot constitute a concomitant factor sufficiently reliable to help in the understanding of the development of phenomena in space-time. Modern science was constituted, perhaps, by the definitive giving up of the attempt to derive from the color of natural elements, as alchemy tried to, pertinent data concerning their nature and their behavior: "Credit is due man's inveterate ingenuity, or human sapience, for having worked around the blinding dazzle of color vision and found the more significant regularities elsewhere" (Quine, 1969; 128).

Certainly, at the pragmatic level, as Quine further comments, colors have played a role in the primary definition of the surrounding world, providing provisional identification of useful or dangerous objects for survival; "Color is helpful at the food-gathering" (127). An observation of a colored phenomenon can, at this level, serve to support some inductive generalizations of character, however highly relative. A researcher, H. Yilmaz, has nevertheless shown "how some structural traits of color perception could have been predicted from their survival value" (Yilmaz, 1969; 90), but it remains a rare occurrence.

But even in this restricted domain, still very little explored, the characteristic of color does not serve to distinguish, in any continuous and rational way, those elements essential for nourishment or protection from their opposites. Numerous variations in colors, which would be so important in other sectors of qualitative perception, are not significant and should be neglected to the benefit of other categories, if one looks to establish a science of edible resources for man or animals. Whereas, among other generally observable traits in natural objects, a large number serve to identify species or categories, color, omnipresent as it is, does not constitute most frequently an essential trait from which the universe can be described in any experimental or scientific way.

Color can only be described with some precision outside of

difference

spontaneous sensory experience by physics and optical instrumentation. At the level of human perception, it can only be apprehended through the intermediary of ideas of similarity or difference, notions indeed familiar and often used but which science cannot use because they cannot be quantified. As Quine puts the case: "Similarity being a matter of degree, one has to learn by trial and error how reddish or brownish or greenish a thing can be and still be counted yellow" (1969; 121).

This problem has already been recognized in visual arts theory, as evident in J. Veltrusky's assessment of art historian E. H. Gombrich's endeavors in this respect: "Gombrich has probably contributed more than any other scholar to the necessary critique of the loose and naïve way in which the concept of resemblance has been used in art history" (1976; 257).

In the 19th century, Chevreul had already classified 20,000 natural tints perceivable by the eye, and there are millions perceptible through scientific instrumentation, depending on the variations of wavelengths, luminosity, degrees of refraction or reflection, and so on (Birren, 1969; 50). Not only is it difficult to quantify that area where a given color would be correlative to a certain definition or to a certain concept of this color, but its necessary position between other colors will modify the initial data that one would have wanted to establish with precision.

This fundamentally elusive character of color, its difficulty in being described in objective and systematic terms, explains why, from such an immediate and common sort of experience, men have taken such a long time in elucidating certain of its foundations and properties. This has led Birren to quote the physicist Maxwell who said: "The science of color must be regarded essentially as a mental science" (1969; 53). The Ancient Greeks themselves could only conceive of a theory of color by borrowing more or less pertinent philosophical conceptualizations. One wonders, for example, about the fact that simple and primary colors were designated by Aristotle as the manifestly complex and unstable colors of natural elements, that is, of fire, of air, of water and of earth. And circa 1666, Newton defined primary colors in relation to the seven spheres or primordial planets.

A long process of abstraction in human thought was necessary to the establishment in the 18th century of a theory of primary colors which appears to the contemporary sensibility as almost evident, that is, the system of colors defined from the generative spectrum point of view. It was only circa 1730 that J. C. LeBlon identified the three primary colors—red, yellow and blue—which, by the mixing of their luminous rays, produced other colors. This proposition was modified at the end of the 18th century, and red, green and blue were posited as the source of composition of others in the ray of light.

At the beginning of the 19th century, Goethe himself, despite his familiarity with the analysis of the spectrum, established in a still more restrictive way the primary colored elements (1976). He only recognized as such yellow and blue, by virtue of an analogy with the phenomena of night and day, thus still treating colors by associations that Wassily Kandinsky was later to qualify as purely literary.

Physical optics proceeded, in the 20th century, with the study of the phenomena of radiation of light, or the composition of spectral light, across diverse types of prisms, which produce approximately 134 to 207 colors, according to researchers. The physiology of vision began, for its part, to elucidate the structure and functioning of the organ of sight and its links with the visual cortex. But these data did not prove to be very fertile for the analysis of the phenomenon of color in human experience, since physiological variations are not parallel to physical variations (Boll; 1962; 23). This phenomenon can therefore only be apprehended through a better understanding of the process of human perception.

However, regardless of the volume and the minutiae of systems of descriptions and of nomenclature of colors, defining their parameters of frequencies, wavelengths and energy, one could never be assured that an identity existed between this physical reality and the color which an observer perceived. The colored aspect of a section of material perceived visually depends on the organization of the perceptive field in which it is situated and not on its own chromatic constitution. As Crosmann had already established in 1953, there exists an indefinite number of rays, of different spectral compositions capable of presenting, for a given observer, an identical aspect at the level of color (Boll, 69).

Furthermore, the two human eyes do not see colors in the same way, in a spontaneous way, before being subjected to a gestaltian type of adaptation (Legrand, 1957; 75). These differences are accentuated with age and are sometimes greater from one individual to the next, because of the coloration of crystalline as well as individual variations of the yellow pigment of the *macula lutea*, in which the capacities of absorption of short waves vary in the different groups (77).

Not only do the perceptual context and the individual and endogenous mechanisms of perception modify perceived color, but also a given pigment can modify its color in an objective and measurable way, according to the technique of display, dilution and superimposition which is used: "The way of displaying the pigment and mixing it with other colors considerably influences the optic properties of the color obtained, and this in a 'objective and real' way and not only as a fact of perception" (Guillot, 1957a; 174).

As soon as a color is expanded on a particular surface, it takes on a certain textural aspect which modifies its chroma in its very structure and perceptual appreciation. While certain colors change when the density of the pigment carrying them is modified, others do not change at all. Moreover, any modification of visual variables, beside that of texture, will involve a modification in the chroma of the color.

Contemporary chemical colorometry has identified more than 50,000 nuances and tonalities of color which it distinguishes through a numeri-cally-based system. Visual semiotics does not choose to follow in this course since any abstract identification of a nuance cannot be referred as such to a region of the visual field where it would be modified by the context.

It is important also not to overestimate the contribution brought to semiotics by various systems of color which more or less schematize both the colored reality of the spectrum and the opaque colored pigments, in order to produce a repertoire based on a generative system of color. The various classifications of color, those of Goethe (1976), Ostwald, Munsell (1969), Itten (1970), Birren (1969), Küppers (1975), have indeed been de-veloped according to certain needs or pragmatic hypotheses. They do not teach us about the dynamic properties of color, their behavior and in-teractions. This will remain the task that visual semiotics will have to undertake from its own specific point of view.

2.1.2. Dynamism of color

The continuous movements and changes which affect color in the process of perception, observed and recognized for many centuries, have certainly discouraged any early attempt at a systematization or a categorization of colors. In fact, to identify a color within a previously established scale of nuances, tones and tints and to give it a verbal equivalent cannot be of any real assistance in the description of a perceived color, even if possible. As J. Albers has emphasized: "In its visual perception, a color is almost never seen just as it physically is" (1963; 5). In other words, to see a color is to properly perceive modifications that a pseudocolor (that which is defined objectively and a priori) undergoes as soon as it is perceived in a real environmental context. Seeing a color, as Albers explains, is to "see the action of this color, as well as to feel the effects of relations between colors."

The research of Albers has served to demonstrate not only that one color summons up innumerable different readings, but also that different colors can be perceived as quasi-similar in certain kinds of environments. One could even go so far as to say that a given color does not exist, since an isolated color does not exist and will, in fact, never exist. In all perceptual experience of reality, it is impossible to see one color that is not juxtaposed with or surrounded by another color.

It is also necessary to be aware of the fact that each time one thinks of a specific color, when one speaks, for example, of red or blue in a theory of colors, one is speaking of an abstraction in the same sense that one speaks of roundness. The terms which designate color refer to a concept of mass, that is, to all that participates in the redness or the blueness itself. But this color that we are supposed to see in our mental universe, isolated and equal to itself, never existed and will never exist in external reality. All the reds or blues that we perceive in the world will always be different one from another and also from any abstract visual concept/percept which takes shape in our mind.

To perceive a color or experience a chromatic sensation is a phenomenon of a psychological order born of cerebral activity, from the moment when the process of sight is set in motion by the light stimulus reaching the eye. The fundamental characteristic of this process is first to be uninterrupted, with the consequence that any colors perceived in succession are modified by the preceding ones. It is not indifferent also, when the eye encounters a tone or a precise tint, if it was previously adjusted to a neutral or sombre vision or if, "to the contrary, it had already undergone a color adaptation" (Küppers, 1975; 37).

Indeed, the first ocular fixation on a colored area affords a chromatic impression whose internal dynamism can easily be felt. In terms of fractions of seconds, adaptation to the color is effectuated so that it does not appear the same at the first glance of the eye, at the second, or the third moment. In particular, during a prolonged stare, a nuance will lose its saturation, little by little, as a result of simultaneous contrasts or other interferences. This explains how, for example, the larger the dimension of a red area in a work is, the less there is of red in that work as perception is prolonged.

These movements and transformations in the observed color, which seemingly preclude any attempts at the measurement and quantification to which external reality yields, have caused certain theoreticians of color, such as Itten, to confer on it a somewhat ambiguous status between matter and psyche: "The effects of color belong to the eye of the spectator. However, the most profound and truest secrets of color are, I know, invisible even to the eye and are only perceived by the heart alone. The essential eludes any conceptual formulation" (1970; 21). Similarly, this dynamic character of color does not lend itself well to a phenomenological approach of an always evanescent colored essence. One can believe, with Wittgenstein, that "there is no such thing as *the* pure color concept" (1978; 1, 73, par. 26e), inasmuch as a pure concept has to be equivalent to a stable identity.

More simply, one must recognize that the strict dependence of a colored phenomenon on the endogenous activity of a perceiver, added to its status of vibratory energy, does not render the percept of color so very much different from other percepts. The color perceived is perhaps only one among the best examples illustrating the structure of any percept. By nature, percepts, as Köhler has pointed out, are totally subjected to the law of change: "In the nervous system, the excitation produced by a continuous stimulus does not remain constant, in general, in time" (1967; 21). This continuous internal transformation, which is amplified by the addition of chromatic interactions issuing from the visual field itself, would explain, undoubtedly, the fact that the memory of colors is one of the most difficult to achieve within the whole family of percepts.

Linked to all the other visual variables and only appearing in unison with them, color depends, in its very structure, on the wave-like and particle-like material which transports it, on light itself, and on the perceptual processes which causes it to surge up from opaque matter. Matter in itself is not colored, but rather colorless, but the double action of luminous rays and perception always presents it otherwise. This therefore is the paradoxical existence of color, a unique construction of human perceptual system, which will be utilized to represent: (1) in a mimetic function, a very superficially colored material reality; and (2) in an expressive function, a human experience which possesses nothing properly colored, produced by the sensory-motor, affective, or intellectual channels which link a man or woman to that reality.

In order to understand and describe this elusive phenomenon, visual semiotics has to use a verbal terminology little adapted to the expression of movement and of change. Linguistics has also developed a relatively inadequate vocabulary for the abundance of chromatic events in reality. Until more knowledge is gained into the structures of auditory and visual percepts, the attribution of certain colors to corresponding concepts of verbal phonematics seems to us hazardous, as does the belief that verbal phonematics can serve to arbitrate in the conflicting problematics concerning the specificity of a chromatic phenomenon (Vallier, 1979).

2.1.3. Nomenclature of colors

The marked incapacity of verbal language to establish the nomenclature of colors is a notorious and distressing fact. Among the many statements to this effect, we may cite that of Harald Küppers: "While man can in general distinguish approximately 10,000 nuances of color, his vocabulary furnishes him with only about a dozen different terms: black, white, grey, blue, yellow, red, green and brown are the essential designations which form the basis of this vocabulary" (1975; 15).

If one considers the general difficulty that human beings have in perceiving unnamed objects and placing them in a system of knowledge or a systematization of their experience, one can understand the reasons for the delay in humankind's becoming aware of the structure and the referents of visual language. The advances in knowledge in the 20th century do not lead toward any solution to this problem. The magnitude of the needed nomenclature forces scientists to establish more or less universally accepted identifications, through a series of numbers and not verbal terms. Moreover, when scientists use more familiar words, these differ as to the "referential wavelengths" to which they apply them, rendering hopeless any attempt to correlate them to perceptual referents.

The limits of the familiar vocabulary of nomenclature are aggravated by the imprecise and variable character of its modes of application in different cultures and societies. While using the modern guidepost offered by the spectral division of light, linguistics has observed a large number of ambiguities in the reference of morphemes applied to colors in different languages: "Behind the paradigms that are furnished in the various languages by the designations of color, we can, by subtracting the differences, disclose such an amorphous continuum, the color spectrum, on which each language arbitrarily sets its boundaries" (Hjelmslev, 1963; 52).

But similar referents in the perceived object do not correspond to identical morphemes. Thus, the boundary which the English language recognizes between green and blue does not exist in Welsh, and the boundary between blue and gray is equally lacking, as well as that which distinguishes gray and brown in English. In turn, the domain represented in English by gray is, in Welsh, cut in half in such a way that one half is included in the English zone of blue, and the other half in that of brown, according to Hjemslev.

The ancient languages are also distinct from modern languages in the application of morphemes relative to color:

> Similarly Latin and Greek show incongruence with the chief modern European languages in this sphere.—The progression from 'light' to 'dark', which is divided into three areas in English and many languages (*white, gray, black*) is divided in other languages into a different number of areas, through abolition or, on the other hand, elaboration of the middle area. (Hjelmslev, 1963; 53)

Thus, the field of morphemes related to colors is articulated differently in different languages, undoubtedly through analytic hypotheses retaining inclusive/exclusive divisions which do not derive directly from empirical observations. One could not presume that the Welsh did not perceive, by a different form of colorblindness, optical impressions producing a distinction between green and blue. A similar phenomenon occurs regarding the interpretation of time. Certain languages, such as Danish, offer only a distinction between the preterite and the present, and use the present for the domain that is covered in other languages by the future tense. Other languages, such as Latin, ancient Greek and French, will distinguish several kinds of preterite (Hjelmslev; 54).

It would seem illusory, if not absurd, to try to offer an adequate schema of the field of color which would stem only from the terminological variation of one language, whether French or English. One must establish on grounds other than terminological the fundamental notions which can clarify the chromatic phenomenon in visual language.

Is it necessary to observe that the phonomatic field of vowels would no better provide grounds for a morphological or semantic differentiation of colors. The number and the definition of vowels vary from one language to another and their boundaries are established differently in different linguistic contexts: "Eskimo distinguishes only between an i-area, a u-area, and an a-area. In most familiar languages the first is split into a narrower i-area and an e-area, the second into a narrower u-area and an o-area" (Hjelmslev; 55).

Similarly, in Arthur Rimbaud's Sonnet of Vowels, we observe an individual experience of projection of a chromatic content associated with phonemes. It depends totally, moreover, on a unique linguistic/cultural context which cannot serve as a viable basis for the development of visual semiology.

2.1.4. Systems of production of colors

The epistemological organization of the field of color has been made difficult because of the confusion which obtains among: (1) the system of color defined by optical science by means of the diffraction of luminous rays through a prism, namely the spectral analysis of color; (2) colors seen as the results of the reflection of natural light on material objects; and (3) colors as they reveal themselves and behave in perceptual experiences. The classical disputes concerning the number and identity of primary or complementary colors followed from a confusion among these three levels, particularly with respect to the nature of "objective" or perceptual colors.

2.1.4.1. PRISMATIC COLORS

In 1796, using a triangular prism, Newton achieved a division of an uncolored luminous ray, producing the group of spectral colors. They represent eight chromaticities: red, orange, yellow, green, blue, indigo, violet and magenta. These colors, constituted of luminous waves, present a particular form of electromagnetic energy. The light waves are not colored in themselves but produce, by a refractive process through a prism, sensations which are perceived by the eye as colors. Among the great number of luminous radiations, the human eye can perceive only those waves whose frequency varies between 400 and 800 millimicrons, but these are not all present in the prismatic division.

Among the prismatic colors, six appear as fundamental and are called monochrome, in that they can be defined by a relatively precise and distinct wavelength. These are: blue, violet, green, yellow, red and orange. Magenta is not monochrome since it results from the superimposition of two zones of the spectrum, the red-orange and the blue-violet. The monochrome or primary colors cannot be seen directly in the natural environment, nor as colored light, nor as colored bodies, because these tints would then be transformed or sullied by other nuances. Outside of the spectrum "only developed technical means permit us to obtain monochromatic colors sufficiently saturated and to render them visible" (Küppers; 66).

This explains the complexity of using as a chromatic model the system of prismatic color and of applying it to colors produced in a totally different fashion. Even here, one must also take into account the fact that no precise nomenclature exists to identify the most important nuances of the spectrum and to apply them to other sectors. Rudolf Arnheim (1954; 348) recalled that in Hiler's compilation the following series of names was given by different observers to a light frequency of 600 millicrons: Orange Chrome, Golden Poppy, Spectrum Orange, Bitter Sweet Orange, Oriental Red, Saturn Red, Cadmium Red Orange, Red Orange. The same was true of other color frequencies.

If reference to the system of colors produced by the spectrum is reinforced today by the division of light used in television, other media are structured in a different way. Thus, in printing, magenta, yellow and cyan blue which cannot be obtained by mixture, are defined as primary. In other areas, like painting and sculpture, the question is still more complex as it is related to the so-called 'reflected' color, allowing a nonluminous matter to be perceived as colored.

2.1.4.2. REFLECTED COLORS

The colors which the eye perceives in the surrounding world are not produced in the same way as those which stem from the refraction of luminous rays through a prism. Colors are, however, always conceived as emanating from luminous rays and considered as radiant energies, vibrations, of which the particulars are apprehended by the eye.

The most recent research on the physiology of the eye has shown the existence of three types of cones or color-receptors in the eye which react to three of the zones of the spectrum: blue-violet, green and red-orange (Küppers; 348). In this way, one could speak of these three colors as being primary at the level of the eye function. But the perceptual origin of color vision has not yet overtaken or modified the prevalent theory, mixing elements from the spectrum theories with those of the reflected color theory.

The theory of "reflected color" proposes that physical, opaque matter (of which pigments/mediums of the artistic practice are a part) is composed of a variety of materials possessing different capacities of absorption and reflection of the luminous wavelengths reaching them, thus constituting visible colors. When all the wavelengths of luminous rays are reflected by an opaque material, one describes the surface as being white; when all are absorbed by the material, it is then perceived as black. When the material absorbs only long waves (those we call red) and medium waves (those we call yellow or green) and sends back or reflects only short waves, these produce the sensation in the brain of what we know as blue.

In the same way as spectral analysis does, the theory of reflected color offers the hypothesis that a luminous ray can reflect simple noncomposed waves, called primary colors and diversely composed waves, called secondary or tertiary colors. The primary colors are conceived as simple, pure and well-saturated. In both the prism and an opaque base, a group of four fundamental colors is said to exist: blue, yellow, red and green (Jacobson; 1948). Through mixing, these primary colors would produce secondary and tertiary colors. Although composed, these can still be considered pure tints if they do not contain any black or white.

This hypothesis created a problem concerning the definition and status of primary colors, since this sequence of production is highly theoretical. As noted earlier, one cannot encounter these primary colors in the natural environment (as reflected by objects or by material constituents of visual language), because they would be largely modified by surrounding light, the effect of shadows, the interaction of colors, the variations of atmospheric strata, and so on.

More important, as Chevreul has already explained in the introduction to his "Principles of Harmony and Contrast of Colors," the emergence of primary colors is impossible in empirical reality. When light is reflected by an opaque body, there is always the reflection of white light and a reflection of colored light, as Chevreul explains:

> It must not be supposed that a red or yellow body reflects only *red* and *yellow* rays besides white light; they each reflect *all kinds* of colored rays; only those rays which lead us to judge that the bodies to be *red* or *yellow*, being more numerous than the other rays reflected, produce a greater effect. Nevertheless, those other rays have a certain influence in modifying the action of red or yellow rays upon the organ of sight; and this will explain the innumerable varieties of *hue* which may be remarked among different red and yellow substances. (43)

In other words, ordinary perception can never in practice see these pseudo primary colors in their pure state, unless one agrees to designate as a primary color the ensemble of nuances, tints and tones which red, for example, can undergo when it is reflected within a real environment.

Historically speaking, this has been the ruling decision. One assumes that an object always possesses a constant, precise and often primary color, irrespective of its reflective behavior or the effects of its environment and illumination. Under the name of "local color," it has been long assumed that reality presents itself to perception in terms of fundamental and simple colors, which were more real, so to speak, than the actual transformations that they undergo in their environment. Artists produced ideally chromatic objects, as defined by an a priori theory of color. The denial of this constancy of local color, through the works of Constable and the Impressionists, changed the modes of visual representation toward a greater fidelity to perceptual experience (Ehrenzweig; 1967). But even if the perceiving public has finally admitted that a tree can be blue or red and not only brown, depending on the effects of the surrounding light or the interaction of colors, the notion of primary color continues to play a major role in the theoretical dimension of the visual discourse.

In spite of the fact that primary colors are not observable in external reality, they continue to be considered in the sector of reflected colors as the alphabet from which colors are constituted.

In this alphabet each element is considered as remaining identical to itself, like a concept, as long as a definite term designates it. If its conceptual meaning is difficult to produce, anyone can recall its image by the use of its label. It was presumed that human beings could form the same visual/mental image of a color, whether primary, secondary or tertiary, at its point of maximal chromaticity and saturation, and that this "pure" image served as a common point of reference for any citation of a chromatic phenomenon. Characteristics of a concept were bestowed not only on mental images, but also on the memory recall of what would be better described as a percept (Saint-Martin; 1985a).

As pointed out earlier, the mental visual image of a color possesses only a very fragile and ephemeral status in the mind and is different for each person, since this image is constructed of fragments of perceptual experiences disengaged from their context. The mental images, as will be explained later, are subject as well to specific chromatic transformations along the laws of complementarity. Given this perceptual context, it is difficult to imagine what nuance is evoked as a 'true red' or a 'true blue' by the individual as a response to the hypothetical essence of redness or blueness.

Even when it is a question not of a nuance of color to be remembered in an always identical way but rather of a color to be recognized, a color familiar and often perceived in reality, perceivers encounter great difficulty in fixing characteristics. The pedagogical experiences of Albers (1963; 3) demonstrated how different observers fail to identify, among a certain finite set of nuances of red, that particular red that they know well, for instance, that used in the popular Coca-Cola advertisement.

We conclude that the primary colors play the same role as "good forms" in our individual perceptual systems, inasmuch as they are few and simpler than other colors. Other colors are referred to them in order to accentuate similarities or differences, with a view to simplifying the chromatic organization of the whole visual field. This implicit reference to the primary 'good' colors, even if they vary with respect to each individual, serves at the same time to point out the dynamic qualities specific to each.

2.1.5. The hierarchical system of Arnheim

This hypothesis was already partially adopted by Rudolf Arnheim, in his 1954 attempt to elaborate a theory of conjunction and of disjunction between colors. This hypothesis was grounded, as most classical and contemporary harmonic theories, in reference to modes of production of colors. But instead of making assumptions as to an a priori theoretical system, Arnheim strove for a perceptual consensus on the "recognition" of a few saturated colors, mutually exclusive, namely blue, yellow, red. Green could be added, for the sake of those who refuse to recognize its composite character. These chromas, argued Arnheim, are each easily distinguishable from the others because each one, when pure, excludes the others, and none can serve as a transition to another (1954; 342).

The experience of these chromaticities would form the stable "perceptual" basis from which other tints would be measured, their reciprocal relations forming reference points for chromatic movement. Even if Arnheim does not make this comparison, these fundamental colors would be situated at a stable, conceptually absolute level, corresponding to a 'good color', with which the usual chromatic deviations would be compared. This good color would serve as a 'good gestalt' of the chromatic pole in relation to which variations and chromatic transformations would be experienced and evaluated. With respect to mixed tints which are less saturated, sombre or bright, perception would evaluate their relative proximity, deviation, and distance from the fundamental good colors, which would stand for more stable, substantial, and satisfying ones. Thus, the family of reds (cinnabar, cadmium, vermilion, etc.) would be animated in the perceptual process through their comparison, reconciliation, and the sensation of their deviation in relation to a fundamental red which each perceiver establishes as that which reflects, for him, what is the most red in the red. This good color, which always remains a perceptual pole, is based in part on a subjective requirement and in part on an objective fact, as this color is rarely encountered in the chromatic field.

In contrast with the fundamental colors, all other colors present themselves as a melange, to varying degrees, of two or three among them, by the inclusion of certain of these tints and the exclusion of others. These combinations present, therefore, mixtures of quantities/qualities of chromas, from which Arnheim elaborates the notion of the "dominant" tint for the color which is found preponderant in the mix and that of "subordinated" for the other, reserving the qualification "separated" for the one(s) excluded. The differences between primary colors are seen as producing separations and distances between them, leading in mixed colors to possible discordances or disharmonies.

On the one hand, the less the mixed colors possess common elements, the more readily they appear as separate. However, colors which contain some common elements, like green and orange which share yellow, would always retain the possibility of an internal dissociative movement, given the heterogeneity of blue and of red that they contain as well.

The relations between mixed tints would offer the structural possibility of being perceived as near or far, or in conflict, depending on the particular quantities that combine with each of the fundamental colors. Between two mixed colors, harmony would be established, Arnheim proposes, according to the common fundamental color that they contain, which plays a structurally isomorphic role as dominant or subordinate. If in one the fundamental tint plays a dominant role and in the other serves as subordinate, the asymmetry of functions would create for the spectator a discord which would be seen as unharmonizing. This absence of harmony would constitute an imbalance which stimulates perception to produce other centrations in the visual field, in view of attaining a desired equilibrium.

Arnheim (1954; 342–343) gives the example of the following chromatic mixtures of two colors, where the priority position of a term in the pair indicates its dominant role:

blue	violet	blue/red	purple	*red*
red	yellow/orange	orange	red/yellow	*yellow*
yellow	green/yellow	green	green/blue	*blue*

Thus, in the blue/red mixture and the red/yellow mixture, the relation of dominance is inverted while in the central column, for example, the fundamental colors would be positioned, ideally, as equal in the constitution of mixtures; this could be a model of an "ideal" secondary color.

Unfortunately, as we will develop later, the human eye does not seem to possess the capacity to recognize either the specific components of a mixed color, or their chroma, or their respective quantities. But the most significant gap in this harmonic system stems from its failure to take into account the fact that color is always modified by the visual variables through which it appears. It fails also to consider the impact of other characteristics of color beyond that of chroma, such as luminosity, saturation and complementarity.

In general, the theories of harmony which seek to provide a rationale, however unsuccessful, of characteristics of prominent works in visual representations are based on the existence of some common characteristics between the colors used. Thus, Itten (1970) foresaw the possible accords between dyads and triads and Ostwald, as Arnheim explains (1954; 335) proposed that harmony would exist between two colors if there is an equality in their essential elements. However, Ostwald only considered as essential chromatic identity and saturation, and not luminosity, and ignored the influence of chromatic complementarity as well as that of other visual variables. Only the colors which face one another in the circle of colors that he has established would be truly harmonious. This proposition does simplify but also considerably restricts the problem of harmony of color in visual works. For his part, Munsell (1969) bases harmony on the principle of an element common to two colors, but one which is realized on the principle of compensation, since the greatest luminosity of a color balances to the weakest luminosity of another.

We believe that these chromatic theories cannot be experimentally verified. Not only do they extract the variable of color from other variables which transform it such as dimension, texture, and so on, but they do not relate it to the other influences always subjectively attached to the process of perception. Thus the chromatic component of saturation is not apprehended in the visual field according only to the norms of a system of production of colors. In the domain of figurative art, in particular, it is obvious that saturation is not apprehended in itself but in relation to external objects that are represented. As Arnheim pointed out: "a red can seem lighter as the color of blood but very dark when it refers to a blushing complexion" (1954; 337).

Indeed, the figurative representation continuously puts in play the concepts of norms or of good color, which is foreign to the dynamism specific to visual variables or to any harmonic theory which seeks a foundation for chromatic organization. We know that, from the beginning of the 19th century, Chevreul (1981; 145) claimed that, in the art of tapestry, which was at the time devoted to figurative representations, "the harmonies of contrast of colour must generally predominate over those of analogy"—that is, of resemblance with the colors attached to the natural objects serving as referents.

The plastic variable of color is therefore subjected not only to the composition of rays reflected by matter but also to the interactions between a colored area and surrounding colors and also between human visual experience and the field of color.

The difficulty in relating a perceived color to an ideal scale is so great that one could better substitute for the term of 'color' the expression 'effects of color', since a color perceived or remembered changes with its support, its environment, and its function. It is also fitting to observe that the chromatic division into six terms (primary and secondary) is obviously sketchy and far too abstract to support any theory of chromatic correlatives to human vision. Other categories must be added, mainly the tertiary colors obtained by mixtures of primary and secondary colors. But instead of considering these as labels of identification, it is necessary to see them rather as limiting notions, poles with difficult-to-assign boundaries, or as terms of mass, relative to a color in which, in varying degrees, observable phenomena of visible reality participate.

Accordingly we believe it important to substitute for the notion of primary/secondary colors the notion of chromatic poles which we feel can more readily account for the chromatic phenomenon.

2.2. Chromatic Poles

The prevailing state of affairs in the perception of chromatic phenomena prohibits the establishment of a system of colors and of relations between colors on qualities defined as absolute, constant, and precisely isolated. Rather than attempting an impossible synthesis of already-existing systems of colors (which respond, indeed, to other needs), or establishing a repertoire from the variations of nomenclatures in various languages, or even inventing a different vocabulary to designate colors (of which the referents would vary according to the experience of each), visual semiotics will propose a system of description of chromatic phenomena which will rest on two basic postulates. The first is inspired by the most recent hypotheses of the neurophysiology of vision which define the receptor-cones of color as reserved not for the activation of one color alone, but rather for a whole range of colors, a cluster of nuances relating to a colored pole and presenting common characteristics: for example, red receptors react, for that matter, to vermilion, carmine, minium, etc. Thus, we will speak in this case about the red chromatic pole.

The second postulate rests on the research of Berlin and Kay (1969) into various primitive and advanced societies, which established that a dozen chromas (of Greek, Xpomos, color) are recognized and named in a universal manner everywhere in the world. This list is perhaps not complete since the authors have refused to recognize as colors those terms which were linked to a concrete object existing in the world. Moreover, while recognizing the difficulty of defining a society as primitive or sophisticated in terms of technological development, these authors point out that the more developed societies recognize and differentiate verbally a greater number of colors. Visual semiotics will propose that these colors, recognized and named by all human beings, constitute specific chromatic poles, each different from the other, rather than entities defined and named according to one hypothetical and unique chromaticity. In this sense, each of the names of the primary, secondary, or tertiary colors must be considered as having a plural referent. When, for instance, the interlocutors of Berlin and Kay classified a color under the rubric of red, it cannot be presumed that they thought of "this" specific red when they heard the term "red"—but rather of one of the multiple reds which lean toward this chromatic pole.

Considering, moreover, the chromatic practice employed in the visual arts, visual semiotics will recognize thirteen chromatic poles, two more than Berlin and Kay proffered, and consequently a greater number than the eight colors specified by Bertin for graphic semiology (1973; 20).

These chromatic poles are red, blue, yellow, green, orange, violet, ochre, purple, brown, rose, white, black, and gray. This basic list regroups those colors called primary, secondary, and tertiary, defined not by additive or subtractive processes of natural light or by processes of electronic production or printing, but rather by the empirical experience confirmed by observation of artistic *praxis* dealing with the light reflected by an opaque body.

These chromatic poles regroup, therefore, the earlier established primary and secondary colors: red, blue, and yellow and green, orange, and violet, and incorporate the tertiary colors as composites of a 'simple' color and a secondary color. Thus, purple is the result of a mixture of red and violet, and ochre, of yellow with orange. Brown also constitutes a specific pole with the combinatory variations in its composition: orange/blue, yellow/violet, and so on.

Further, this list affirms the chromatic character of white and of black which thus become chromatic poles independently of their tonality value, that is, of their capacity when incorporated within another color to render it lighter or darker. We believe that from the refraction of luminous rays, as well as normal perceptual experience, one cannot maintain the hypothesis of Mondrian (1967b) which would make black and white non-colors. In luminous rays, white represents the sum total of colors and black, their total absence, because they represent the presence or absence of illumination. But white reflected by an opaque material is never an absolute brightness or, in other words, a total absorption of luminous rays. As Goethe observed justly, white can only be seen as "the first, opaque occupation of space" (1976; 61). Even if white represents the lightest of colors, it cannot be identified with uncolored light, because it offers variations which permit the distinction of graduated scales of whites, more or less clear, or more or less refractions of other chromas: lead white, eggshell white, and so on.

Similarly, black is always a colored mixture and not a total absence of reflected light. Artistic practice has always understood this fact, as attested to by Largilierre's teaching to his pupils, at the end of the 17th century, of the modes of fabrication of at least a dozen different types of blacks (1981). Even a philosopher like Wittgenstein (1978; par. 152, 36e) perceived that at least two different color names would be necessary to designate a shiny black and a matte black.

Just like other colors, white and black require, for their perception, an illumination/lighting of a material by luminous rays. Without lighting, they, like any other chroma, cannot be perceived; their perception is linked, even if it is in different proportions, to quantities of luminous rays that their carrying material absorbs and those which they themselves reflect. This does not imply in any way that the chromatic nature of white does not in itself exist and that it is only the result of illumination. This has been shown by research into the constancy of color: "If, for example, the degree of whiteness were a simple function of the intensity of reflected light on a surface, then a white paper in a reduced light would appear darker than a black paper illuminated in an intense way" (Gelb; 197). And this is precisely what is not produced. It is necessary, therefore, to conclude that white and black each possess, for perception, a color aspect which makes them real chromatic poles.

Certainly, the status of black and white remains special since, besides offering a particular chromaticity, they can in a systematic way, when mixed with other colors, make those very colors lighter or darker, thus modifying most of the other dynamic characteristics of those colors. We will discuss this at length in the later chapter on the phenomenon of tonality and its repercussions for the law of successive and simultaneous contrasts.

It should be pointed out that all the colors belonging to regroupings of chromatic poles can also be called clear or dark, according to their own register and independent of any intervention of white or black in their constitution. This characteristic of light or dark in chromaticity is not easily expressed in words but involves highly important kinesthetic and tactile effects which influence visual organization. Albers noted the double status of this notion: "the darkest color is visually that which seems heavier or that which contains more black, or less white" (1963; 13).

We include, moreover, among the chromatic poles, following the observations of Berlin and Kay, the chroma known as pink, which has been denied this status until now, since it seemed the result of a tonal modification of red. We also include gray as a specific pole, though a certain technical vocabulary applied up until now to a large number of secondary and tertiary colors, even if they contained neither white nor black. This chromaticity represents, for us, the passageway between white and black.

The notion of chromatic poles is heuristic because it avoids the substantialist concepts that are often associated with a vocabulary which uses the notion of primary colors in the sense of pure colors without mixtures. The chromatic poles can be analyzed and described according to the most significant characteristics of colors: namely, chromaticity, saturation, tonality, luminosity and complementarity.

2.2.1. Chromaticity

Chromaticity designates the specific sensory characteristic which distinguishes a color and differentiates it or opposes it to another color. It is maximal when one gives the maximum density to the application, for example, of a given pigment. Thus, a first layer establishes a chromaticity but may leave zones more or less laden with pigment; another layer provides an area, in a compact way, with zones more and more dense with this particular color. However, a point of optimal saturation exists, after which any addition of the same color will set in motion a tendency toward blackening; the effect is inverted if too small a quantity of pigment is used within a color. In the same way, the smaller a colored region is, the less it is saturated with its own chroma (Galifret, 1957; 43).

The chromaticity of a color diminishes also when one incorporates white or black, or when it is under the influence of too much or too little illumination.

2.2.2. Saturation

Saturation is the maximum level of chromatic intensity that a color can reach without being transformed into another color or without diminishing radically its particular quotient of vibrations.

Saturation results not only through the mode of application of a color but also through interrelations established between a given color and those which surround it. These interactions between regions of a polychromatic field can diminish or augment the saturation of a color at the same time as they transform its chroma. Chromatic saturation must, therefore, appear as a limit which, if it cannot be measured by scientific instruments—since it is transformed in the perceptual relation—does play a considerable role in the organization of the visual field.

2.2.3. Tonality

Tonality appears to us as a proper characteristic of color, inasmuch as it is defined as a quantity of light and darkness brought to a given color by its admixture with black or white. In using the vocabulary of Chevreul (1981; 78, par. 5) and not the more recent and quite varied usages, we will call a color mixed with black a tone and a color mixed with white a tint.

Altogether distinct vibratory phenomena exist between dark colors at their point of saturation and colors which become darker by the intervention of the color black, that is, by a different family of reflected rays. This holds true as well for white and the admixture of white chroma with reflected waves of another chroma. The phenomena of tonality have played a major role in the traditional teaching of drawing because of their functional role in the production of volumetric illusion. They have sometimes been identified with the notion of "values," in the description of a visual work, although they have always only been complements to the efficacy of chromatic values.

2.2.4. Luminosity

Luminosity designates the intensity of the vibration of luminous rays which perception detects in every chromatic region. On the subjective level, it is linked to the particularity of the nervous influx which connects the retina to the visual cortex (Monnier, 1957; 17). On the objective plane, it is derived from the interaction between reflected waves of white light and of colored light of variable wavelengths and frequences in a perceived region. It is also the result of interactions among reflected waves of one region and those of surrounding regions in the visual field. These interrelations among varied wavelengths at the heart of reflected rays are perceived, in color, as a vibration or in other words, as a dynamic activation which modifies the characteristics of this color in its relation to others.

A color will be all the more vibratory, expansive and radiant as it has more luminosity. This luminosity does not depend only on its physical structure and relations with surrounding colors but also on the type of dispersion that a color has undergone. Particular vibrations can be obtained by what has been called among artists the "touch," or the synthesis of the speed, length, tension, matter, and composition present in a brushstroke. More sophisticated means will play on the superimposition of one tint on an analogous tint, and so on.

Carried to its maximum, luminosity becomes a sort of radiance which does not seem to be attached or restricted to the dimension of the region where it appears. As Rudolf Arnheim expressed it, "We associate radiation with an absence of surface texture. Objects appear opaque and solid by their texture, which establishes the boundaries of their surface. But a radiant object does not stop the gaze in fixing it at this external threshold" (1954; 315). Its limits are not defined by the eye. The object seems to be overlaid by a film of color rather than to present a surface of color. Light seems to take origin in the object and at a distance removed from the perceiver. "All luminosity which appears strong in relation with its environment tends to eliminate surface texture; and an absence of texture will favor the effect of radiance."

A more luminous color recedes in depth, and colors of the same luminosity regroup in perception. The contrast between two colored regions depends more on their different luminosities than on their chromatic diversity: a red figure on a green ground becomes indistinct, if the two regions have an equal luminous intensity. The luminous equality then dissolves their boundaries (Monnier; 17).

This points to the important role played by luminosity in relations established between coloremes through the dynamism of their boundaries and chromaticity. Dark colors, in effect, which contain or do not contain black, all reflect a variable luminous intensity which modifies the interaction between these and surrounding colors.

One must not confuse the luminosity of a color, which is the effect of the luminous vibration constituting it in relation with vibrations of colors which surround it, with the illumination which results from a particular lighting emanating from the exterior of a visual work and which renders it visible.

The constancy of chromaticity and luminosity under the influence of varied illumination has long been an object of study in the psychology of perception. David Katz (1935) in particular, not only established clear correlations between the color of an object and that which the lighting creates, but also developed a dual gradation of characteristics (insistence and accentuation) for white and black regions subject to different sources of lighting: ". . . that which is the most illuminated of the two colors is always the most insistent but not always the most pronounced . . . One can therefore affirm that there are not two surfaces of the object which can be perceived according to the same color when they are differently oriented in relation to the light source" (Gelb, 1967; 198).

The different lightings or illuminations transform the chroma of a color because they interfere with the ensemble of reflected waves. As Hans Wallach (1961) specified: "The quantity of light reflected by an opaque object and which stimulates the eye depends not only on the color of the object but as well on the quantity of light which falls upon the object, on its 'illumination'."

This led to the recognition of a constancy of luminosity, as when an object will seem to have the same color under different lightings, that is, when the colors seen will be similar to those which are perceived under the illumination of white light.

A too-bright illumination originating from the exterior and shining on a visual field can dissolve and destroy the chromaticity of regions on which it falls. In all cases, changes in lighting sources modify the color of a region. The case is the same with what is called "natural lighting," paradoxically considered constant, when the spectral composition of daylight coming from the sun is subjected to constant variations. The position of the sun at its zenith, at high noon, offers an elevated proportion of short waves which lend a bluish reflection, while the movement that it makes in an oblique position will give a more reddish and warmer lighting. In a house, a studio or a museum interior, the luminous sources always represent a range of extremely wide variations which are capable of transforming, with luminosities and chromaticities, all the internal organization of a visual work.

One must not confuse luminosity—nor the effects of lighting emanating from a source external to the visual work—with the effects of the mimetic fiction of a source of internal or external lighting in the visual representation itself. Both freeze represented objects in an immobility opposite to the very dynamism of the visual field. At its most simplistic level, this effect of external lighting can be produced by the direct use of white and black which mimics the brightest points of a volume or zones of shadow. At other times, the introduction of white and black in colors, producing a tonal gradation in relation to a source of light, may simultaneously destroy chromaticity, saturation, and luminosity.

These effects of lighting, added to the dynamism of colors, have as a principal function the hollowing out of spatial volume, according to alternations of shadow and light. Lighting also produces an illusion of external Euclidean volumes, according to points of view determined by the position and distance between the object and a supposed source of lighting. The adjoining to a pictorial mass of a projected shadow will have the same effect of constitution of volumetrics, while the distinctive contrasts between dark and light regions will produce effects of superimposition between regions.

The developments in pictorial art, since the beginning of the 20th century, have been based on a rejection of the simulation, in the visual representation, of sources of lighting foreign to the internal luminosity of color, which would mimic scenes of external reality. There has also occurred a rejection of tonal contrasts which reduce the intensity of colors themselves. This has been explained by Hans Hofmann: "Since light is best expressed through differences in color quality, color should not be handled as a tonal gradation to produce the effect of light" (1948; 68).

2.3. Complementarity

Complementarity is, like luminosity, an "immanent" characteristic of the phenomenology of color. Chevreul explained it thus: "To put color on a canvas is not simply to color the surface where the paintbrush has been applied with this special tint, but it is equally to color the adjacent space with the complementary of this color" (In Blanc, 1880; 563). This subjective perceptual phenomenon means that any perception of a color necessarily involves the projection by the eye, in the visual field, of another color, called its complementary.

This physiological phenomenon is constant and even children, in their drawings, respond to each color or group of colors by using the complementary color.

This visual movement has been explained by various hypotheses, some seeing it dependent on "retinal fatigue" or the wearing out of the chemical quantities which constitute the diverse receptor-cones of colors, thereby provoking the surrounding cones to a greater activity. Goethe added to this explanation the "law of completeness," according to which the eye, aspiring to see the totality of color, fills up the registers of luminous waves absorbed by bodies and not presented in a colored reflection. He wrote:

> When the eye sees a color it is immediately excited and it is its nature, spontaneously and of necessity, at once to produce another, which with the original color comprehends the whole chromatic scale. A single color excites, by a specific sensation, the tendency to totality . . . To experience this completeness and to satisfy itself, the eye seeks for a colorless space next to every hue in order to produce the complemental hue upon it. (317, par. 805)

Goethe called this need for a chromatic totality felt by the organism the "law of *completeness*." When the eye realizes through perception one of the fundamental chromatic possibilities, it immediately searches to see or to produce in the visual field the emergence of other colors reunited in the complementary, in order to recreate the chromatic totality:

> We stated before that the eye could be in some degree pathologically affected by being long confined to a single color . . ., the demand for completeness which is inherent in the organ, frees us from this restraint; the eye relieves itself by producing the opposite of the single color forced upon it, and thus attains the entire impression which is so satisfactory to it. (Goethe; 319, par. 812)

Similarly, the artist will be essentially engaged in strategies to provoke, distinguish, and satisfy this demand for totality that man cannot gratify in the contemplation of nature: "Nature perhaps exhibits no general phenomenon where the scale is in complete combination. By artificial experiments such an appearance may be produced in its perfect splendour" (Goethe; 320, par. 814). The rainbow itself does not offer an example of the totality of colors, "for the chief color, pure red, is deficient in it, and cannot be produced, since in this phenomenon, as well as in the ordinary prismatic series, the yellow-red and blue-red cannot attain to a union" (Goethe; 320, par. 814).

Through these links with the psycho-physiological process of perception known as successive and simultaneous contrasts, Goethe established a coherent theory of aesthetics, based upon a specificity of visual language and its capacity to structure a dynamic space in three dimensions. The production of complementaries, in creating new junctions between regions and modifying their reciprocal positions, institutes a topological mass possessing a differentiated and shifting interior volume.

The theory of complementary colors, having been constructed on a hypothesis of primary colors, will vary according to the historic variations of the definition of these primary colors. Newton spoke of seven colors, Goethe and Schopenhauer of six, Ostwald of eight, Munsell of ten. Goethe defines the principal complementary colors as being: red-orange and blue and vice-versa, red and aquamarine green, violet and leaf green. Munsell (1969) defined complementary colors as being the pairs yellow and purple, blue and orange, red and blue/green, purple and green, and so on. Newton mentioned, on one occasion, the complementary relation of gold and indigo. These variations do not question the reality of the phenomenon of simultaneous or successive contrast. They only reveal the diversity of the experiential phenomenona of color in a visual field. Albers neatly summarized this complexity in saying: "The complementary of a specific color, when it plays into different systems, will appear different" (1963; 41).

These divergences also reflect the difficulty encountered in obtaining the necessary material pigments to reconstruct the phenomenon of total color reflection, as exemplified in the ray of light. Optical theory defined complementary colors at the level of luminous rays as those which, superimposed or added, yield an effect of white, that is, the totality of wavelengths composing the colorless luminous ray. This definition was adopted by several aesthetic theorists, from Charles Blanc (1880; 561), who evoked in his *Grammaire des Arts du Dessin* this totality of white light, to Munsell, who spoke of the production, within systems of color, of an equivalent to that white light in the realm of reflected colors: perfect gray (1969; 28).

Borrowing the model of optical colors was predominant in the field of visual arts. Theoretically, as Charles Blanc wrote, "we have therefore called 'complementary' each of the three primitive colors in relation with the binary color which corresponds to it" and "reciprocally, each of the mixed colors, orange, green and violet (produced by the mixture of two primitive colors) is the complement of the primitive color not used in the mixture; thus orange is the complement of blue, because blue has not been used in the mixture which formed orange" (1880; 561). This widely disseminated formulation, based on the additive properties of lightwaves, has remained prevalent, even though the electronic composition of color imposes another opposition, being that of yellow as the complement of blue. We are more aware today that there exist hundreds of identified shades of reflected red, blue, and yellow, which contain other chromatic components and will produce correlatively varied types of complementaries.

The law of complementarity is very easily observable when a colored surface is positioned on a white or grey field, producing a clear chromatic aureole or the strong emergence of the complementary color. The complementarity will be manifested, also, in relation to the phenomenon of tonality, that is, a dark region involves the projection of a luminous zone to its boundary and a clear one accentuates the darkness of its immediate surroundings.

It is widely recognized that two complementary colors, when placed side by side, will each heighten the other, will vibrate or shine all the more, and will reach the maximum of their chromatic intensity. The complements will also play a major role in the organization of the spatial field, because the eye, seeing a certain color, will spontaneously search for and be drawn to that color's complementary which might be found in another place in the field. This remarkable phenomenon implies an attraction between colors which is no longer based on the gestaltian law of similarity, but rather on heterogeneity. On the visual plane, complementary colors will spontaneously regroup for the eye in a particular succession or binding group. This effect is so strong that, when complementary colors are juxtaposed in a smaller region, they tend to regroup in an autonomous fashion and isolate themselves from the ensemble, thus creating a disjunction in the spatial fabric.

However, when the complementary of a given color is not found in the same visual field, an extremely strong tension is immediately created for the perceiving eye and ineluctably results in the production of simultaneous and successive contrasts of color and tonality.

Nevertheless, despite this changeable multiplicity, constants of transformation have been defined which, when applied to circumscribed elements, modify the chromatic regions in a regular manner.

2.3.1. Laws of interaction of colors

The regularity of the process of interaction between colors, arising from both chromatic materials and the mechanisms of visual perception, has resulted in the formulation of various laws which articulate syntactic rules defining the relations between the elements of visual language.

2.3.2. Laws of equalization

The most general law regarding colors, movements, or transformations follows the parameters of gestaltian observations which posit a universal tendency of stimuli to be transformed in order to attain a similarity or a homogeneity, or to recover a predefined totality/completeness. In the first case, the phenomenon of equalization refers to changes happening among several different surfaces, so that an attenuation of their differences is produced. This visual movement has been particularly studied by C. Musatti (1957; 94): "The surface which undergoes the equalization on the part of another surface is enriched by a chromatic or brightness component which corresponds to the color or the brightness of the other surface."

This phenomenon of equalization is facilitated for surfaces seen as parts of a unique figure, that is, in a gestaltian or formal totality. The effect of chromatic equalization has been commented on only marginally in texts on color because this visual movement seems to contradict the laws of simultaneous contrast. It is not the case, however, since one and the other are produced in specific states of the visual field and a passage from one to the other is a frequent phenomenon. The emergence of works of the Op Art movement in the 60s have made this effect familiar to us.

It is produced especially, in fact, when short or long linear masses of different colors emerge on a homogenous chromatic surface. Thus, a red surface crisscrossed with blue lines becomes violet-like, or orangeish when crisscrossed by yellow lines. But this effect is also produced between several differently colored surfaces; if these colors are contrasted, a neutralizing effect will be felt by the heightening of tints which are common to them.

Musatti determined that this effect is constant but that it can be stronger when; "the relation between the general extension of a surface and the development of its contour is very small, the action that this surface exercises upon another contiguous surface is an action of equalization instead of being an action of contrast" (95). But occasionally a lengthier observation can produce the inversion of the equalization in contrast. In the same way, "there exist situations where a colored surface exercises on a contiguous surface an action of equalization, while undergoing on the part of this same surface an action of contrast" (Musatti; 99).

It so happens in a bichromatic square, where a red field is crossed by prolonged yellow strokes up to the periphery, that reds become more violet and yellows more orange.

The phenomenon of equalization does not transform only the chromatism of the neighboring region and, by that, all the plastic variables which are dependent upon it; it acts also on the global perceptual field and spatially transforms it, in the same way that blurred contours do: "The phenomenal aspect of yellow and of blue brought upon a grey is very particular; it is a little as if there were a yellow and blue powder on the grey" (Musatti; 95). Inversely, a gray powder will appear on the blue and the yellow.

As is the case with all visual movements, the effect of equalization is not produced if the percept is interpreted in relation to a concept of an objective, external object, the notion of "real" objects not permitting the development of syntactic interactions between elements of visual language: "This equalization is not produced for colors seen as colors of objects, but for the chromatic components which produce the impression of luminosity, or the general chromatic level of the visual field" (Musatti, 1957; 99).

This chromatic equalization produced in a field seen as unitary, "would represent only a particular case of this law of perceptive homogeneity" (Musatti; 100) which, on a more general level, would furnish the foundation of simultaneous contrasts themselves in spite of their apparent contradiction.

2.3.3. Chromatic simultaneous contrasts

The chromatic simultaneous contrast, also known as "antagonistic induction," is the phenomenon which results when a chromatic surface contiguous to another surface of a different color is enriched by a component antagonistic to the color of the second surface. As mentioned before, these antagonistic components have been called complementaries, since their juxtaposition in a luminous or opaque milieu reconstructs white light or neutral grey respectively.

The existence of two types of simultaneous contrasts, tonal and chromatic, extensively treated by Goethe in his *Theory of Colors* of 1810 and explained under the form of laws by Chevreul in 1839, seems a permanent and indisputable acquisition in the field of visual perception. Considerations about these simultaneous visual movements between two regions are an indispensable element in the thinking of all 20th century theoreticians of color (Itten, Birren, Ostwald, Küppers etc.). But a few among them, perhaps because they found these laws too obvious, have dedicated to this phenomenon the type of exhaustive examination undertaken by Chevreul, to which we must again refer the reader in order to complete our brief observations on chromatic phenomena. In fact, most modern theoreticians, given their didactic and pedagogic concerns, or their desire to rationalize and simplify an elusive subject, have a tendency to schematize the essentials of these laws, so as to be able to disregard their troubling consequences. Inspired undoubtedly by his artistic practice, Albers, who was also an eminent teacher, even if not entirely explicit on the theoretical level, has greatly deepened our understanding of this subject through continued empirical investigations that qualify as truly presemiotic. Above all, he has demonstrated the changing and pluralistic character of chromatic phenomena and of the simultaneous and successive contrasts that color continuously produces.

Gestaltian scientists established some decades ago that simultaneous contrasts of color and of tonality are part of any experience of the visual field. In Köhler's words:

> Take color vision: when a gray object surrounded by a white surface is
> compared with a second object that, physically, has the same gray color but is
> surrounded by a black surface, the gray-on-white object looks darker than the
> gray-on-black object. Similar effects of the color of the environment on a local

color can also be demonstrated when the surrounding colors in question are so-called hues, that is, red or yellow or green or blue. In a red environment, for instance, a gray object tends to look greenish, and so forth. (1969; 41)

The basic phenomenon which supports this theory refers to the fluidity of visual percepts and more specifically, to the fact that any colored region sees its color modified by the continuous effect of an ocular fixation. The gestaltian laws clarify the nature and direction of these chromatic changes, through which any simple color, if such ever existed, which is an object of perception is modified so as to become a composed or mixed color.

According to the traditional law of simultaneous and successive contrasts, when the eye perceives a given color, a reaction is immediately produced by which it projects on this very color, and more so on a neighboring region, its complementary color. If the eye perceives blue, it projects its complement, orange; if it sees red, it projects green; if it perceives yellow, it projects violet. Or, if the eye sees a red region, situated in the visual field beside green, this latter green will become much more intense and saturated, acquiring new dynamic properties. If the first region is blue, and the neighboring one yellow, this one will seem to be overlaid by an orange "film," undulating, penetrating and moving finally over both regions.

The projection of the complementary color approximates the status of a transparent color because it does not appear as being quite connected to the underlying surface. The term "film" tries to indicate the way in which it is spread out upon other surfaces, analogous to the manner in which Katz (1935) made the distinction between surface and film colors. The surface color appears to ordinary perception as hard and easy to localize on any plane, coinciding with the contours and the position in depth of the region. But the film of color most often presents itself on a frontal parallel plane, often in contrast to underlying regions, and seems to hover above it as a moving, indecisive plane, somewhat penetrable to the eye (Itten, 1970; 15).

Chevreul had already demonstrated that, when two planes of primary color are seen in juxtaposition, each of these planes is subjected to the addition to its own chromaticism of a movement toward the complementary color. Thus the perception of two regions, one red and the other yellow, will produce a tendency for the red to become violet and for the yellow to become green; or, again, the perception of two regions, one yellow and the other blue, will make them change respectively toward orange and indigo.

When two juxtaposed colors are a primary and secondary color possessing a common color, the modification brought about by the projection of the complementary color will act to subtract that common color in the two regions. Thus, when two regions offer blue and violet, the modification will involve the blue towards green and violet towards red, with a weakening of the blue which is their common color. This explains why two colors which are part of a range or gamut of colors belonging to a certain pole, like blue/violet or red/orange, will be more differentiated in a juxtaposition. Furthermore, in juxtaposed red and yellow, the simultaneous contrast will remove any yellow that might be contained in the red, pushing it toward violet, and diminish any red in the yellow, to push it more toward green. Thus, when two mixed colors having a common color are juxtaposed, they lose their common color so as to appear even more differentiated.

When complementary colors are juxtaposed, each becomes more intense and saturated, but also more stable or inert because they are less susceptible to chromatic modifications, since complementarity has already been achieved in perception.

The juxtaposition of a color to a white region makes the complementary immediately appear clearly; thus when an artist puts a color on a white paper or primed canvas, he has colored the adjacent field with the complementary color. In the same way, the juxtaposition of a color to a black region produces a complementary in the black region, that is, a coloration by the complementary of the light still reflected in small quantity in this region even if few colored rays pass through.

When a gray region is put on a colored ground, it is immediately tinted by a film corresponding to the complement of the colored region. In this case, a region of medium size is more affected by this transformation than a very large region.

The effect of simultaneous contrast is felt starting from the zone where the colors are differentiated, that is, from their common boundary. However, simultaneous contrast can also be experienced more or less between two regions which are separated and at a distance from one another in the visual field, since the visual centration can pass rapidly from one to the other. In a general way, the more that regions offer clear and neat contours, the more the simultaneous contrast will be effectuated. If the boundaries are blurred and toned down, the effect is dissolved for both tonal and chromatic contrasts. In diminishing the neatness of contours and in substituting a gradual transition of intensity, "we can expect that between the two zones is established a process of reciprocal interaction and phenomenally the respective clarities tend to be equalized" (Kanizsa, 1957; 113).

It is impossible to deduce a priori, outside the experience of perception of a given visual field, the chromatic transformations produced by simultaneous contrasts of colors, following a simple verbal labelling of colors which are present there. This is a result of the fact that projected complementary colors are modified according to the real composition of colors and not according to their dominant chroma. The eye, as has been noted by all authors since Chevreul, is incapable of consciously recognizing the nuances which compose a color offered to perception, that is, the real components of a so-called primary color or of a composed color. As expressed by Itten, "we cannot perceive the nuances in a composed color. The eye does not resemble the musical ear, which can distinguish each of the individual tones in a chord" (Itten, 315). But the eye does respond perceptually to those components.

2.3.4. Simultaneous contrasts of tonality

The law of chromatic contrasts posits that, under constant conditions of illumination, all colors undergo considerable variations as a consequence of perceptual centrations and action of neighboring colors. Similar phenomena are produced in the domain of tonality. But it is not always easy to distinguish, in the changes which black and white produce or which they undergo, that which depends on their chromatic quality from that which depends on their quantity of dark or light.

The visual movement provoked by the inscription, for example, of a black form in a white environment, or the inverse, produces the effect of a figure on a ground, that is, a separation in depth between these two elements. This depth is less pronounced, but is always present, when these two elements tend toward a gray of the same value or tonality. But, at the same time, the mechanisms of tonal contrast will be deployed, accentuating or diminishing the quantities of clear or of dark on affected regions and modifying their apparent dimension, density, or saturation, and their distances in depth.

The most important effect created by the tonal contrast is the accentuation of the clarity in the region which surrounds a black form, and the accentuation of the darkness in the region which surrounds a clear form. As expressed by Goethe: ". . . If we look at a black disk on a light gray surface, we shall presently, by changing the direction of the eyes in the slightest degree, see a bright halo floating round the dark circle" (11, par. 30). This phenomenon is produced around all possible forms and not only circular forms and with all colors which are darker than their environment.

When two grays are placed side by side and perceived as such by the eye, an accentuation of the difference between the two grays is produced; in other words, the darker gray will appear even darker, the light gray lighter.

Köhler observed this modification of tonalities when different tones are juxtaposed, notably in the case of a gray object set in a light or dark environment. The two levels of gray are perceived as different functions by the rods of the eye which assure the perception of differences of luminous intensity or tonality, while the cones react to colors. These rods, tinted with a red ingredient, are decolored, little by little, under the effect of light, changing to orange, yellow and white. This process of decoloration corresponds to an energy-generating process and sets in motion physiological excitation. When a luminous stimulus ceases to act, the pigment of the rod is regenerated, thus recovering its proper perceptive properties.

One of the most well-known effects of tonal contrast is the flickering flashes of light or of shadow which appear at points of interface when a white grid is placed upon a black ground or a black grid upon a white ground. One has often observed this effect in certain works of Mondrian. As detailed by Wilhelm Fuchs, this sort of effect becomes prominent when the eye stares at the grid itself and is erased when the eye stares at the ground (1967; 101). Furthermore, when white areas are juxtaposed with black areas, but in a progressive succession of grays, they create a vectorial movement which evokes the rotundity of volume.

Another important visual movement apropos black and white is the production of colored after-effects, stemming from the phenomenon of retinal fatigue at the time of the perception of numerous black and white elements contrasted on one and the same surface.

The simultaneous tonal contrast which enriches white, gray and black to a degree of clarity or shadow antagonistic to that of the adjacent region will tend in the same way to render the different regions of color lighter or darker; and this effect can be felt throughout the ground of a spatial field if the field is homogenous.

Moreover, the juxtaposition of white or black to colored regions produces a variety of different effects. White applied in close proximity to another color heightens its intensity, in removing from this color all the white that it can contain in a latent manner. Similarly, in receiving the complementary of this color, it will reinforce the chromaticity of this film of color. However, the tonal contrast existing between the color of contrast and the white, necessarily less dark, will overlay this color with a darker film which can diminish its quality of saturation.

In a similar way, a black area neighboring another color also diminishes its dark tonality and strengthens its chromatic intensity. It will also recover the film of the complementary with a greater luminosity and a lesser quantity of black in its composition. All these interactions vary according to the dimension of regions, their reciprocal positions, the quality of their boundaries, the intensity of their colors and of blacks/whites, and the nature of the surrounding chromatic milieu.

2.3.5. Successive chromatic and tonal contrasts

One must not confuse simultaneous contrasts of tonality and of color which are effected even on separate and distant regions in the visual field with the successive contrasts of tonality and of color. The first only transform the tonal degree or the quality/quantity of color in the two regions considered. The successive contrasts cause more than a tonal and chromatic modification; they result in a configuration/contour of a dimension analogous to that of the initial region, thus producing a 'virtual form'.

Thus, when the eye, having looked at one or several colored regions over a certain length of time and produced numerous simultaneous contrasts, turns its gaze toward another region of the field, it will project on this region an image or configuration having the contour of the first region, but endowed with a complementary color or a tonal antagonism. It produces, therefore, a complementary successive image, an after-image, possessing a shape and a dimension analogous to the first percept but endowed with a chromatic and tonal contrast. This image, circumscribed in a given shape which is superimposed on a new region possessing its own contours, introduces a very considerable degree of complexity in this new region by virtue of the disparity between the dimensions, color, tonality, texture, of the region focused on and the superimposed film.

Similarly, when dark forms are vividly disclosed on a light ground, an after-effect will project an analogous light-form on a neighboring ground and vice versa.

The successive tonal contrasts will also change the dimension of forms or of regions, since a dark object, or a darker one, will appear smaller than a light object of the same size. As for chromatic successive contrasts, these will institute continuous transformations in the chroma, the saturation, the luminosity, the dimension, and the position-in-depth of perceived elements, multiplying the interrelations among elements already perceived and elements newly perceived, and changing the structures of organization of the visual field that they progressively constitute. Successive images have a dimension which varies with the distance taken in relation to the visual field. They disappear with time, like simultaneous contrasts, but can, like these, be summoned again or reanimated after a blinking of the eyes, a slight movement of the eye, or by the new percept caused by a change of luminosity in the visual field.

The interaction between the successive image and the new region viewed is called a mixed contrast. It is produced when the eye perceives in the new region of focus a mixture between the new color and the complementary of the first region, carried by the successive image.

There still exists a very large number of other tonal and chromatic transformations which are carried out in the perceptual process. Although their effects are constant, and a point of consensus among numerous observers, these transformations are still set under the rubric of "accidental images," as called by Buffon, who was the first to observe them. These include, for instance, chromatic modifications and projections resulting from a too-strong vibration, or luminous bursts in the visual field, characterized sometimes as "aggressions" of the eye, although the recurrence of these soon render them normal and innocuous, if not banal. They have been the object of particular preoccupation at the center of the Op Art movement, producing tonal and chromatic simultaneous superimpositions in the 'moiré' effect, the emergence of chromaticisms from white and black regions, and so on.

The expression 'colors of memory' designates those colors "perceived" by reference to a known and remembered tint, foreign to or nonexistent in the actual context. Any prolonged observation of an enlarged visual field may produce these colors of memory, since each color perceived can be transformed by the memory of colors previously perceived. We do not class them in terms of plastic variables since they do not correspond to a material correlative of a specific perceptual activity in a present situation, but rather in terms of perceptual variables. When projected on the visual field, these colors derived from memory are subjected to the law of successive and simultaneous contrasts.

The law of simultaneous or successive contrasts explains those transformations undergone by the field of visual representation, when a given epoch or certain artists break with the habitual use of certain colors, enlarging or restricting the number of colors actually used. These artists disrupt the visual field, not only by incorporating a new tint, but also by modifying all the dynamics of complementary transformations to which the eyes of spectators were accustomed. When Titian uses only four colors, Rubens seven and Mondrian three, the whole system of chromatic mobility is radically transformed, in as sure a manner as when El Greco uses purple as the complementary of yellow or the impressionists and neoimpressionists eliminate black from shadows.

Already the presentation of the law of contrasts as based on a relation of two terms, instead of on a real interrelation of one term with all those which surround it, has appeared as a lacuna to Gestalt psychology. As early as 1925, Max Wertheimer explained: ". . . the experiences show, for example, that when I see two colors, the sensations that I have are determined by the global conditions of all the situation of the stimulus," and not by two limited regions in the visual field. He was led to conclude that the experience required, among other things, "that traditional theory of visual contrast be replaced by a theory which took into account the conditions of the whole and its parts" (1925; 5).

The research of Albers added numerous elements to the law of simultaneous and successive contrasts by connecting the modifications of color to the form which they circumscribe, to their quantity and position, to the number of times they appear, and to saturation and luminosity. He emphasized the importance of the articulation of frontiers, that is, the nature of the boundaries which separate or connect different regions of colors. Similarly, he linked this phenomenon to the quality of the ground in which a color appears: "Any background subtracts its own nuance from the colors it bears" (1963; 41), modifying, therefore, with the chromatic and tonal intensity of the two regions, the nature of their complementaries. Albers also described the presence of inverted simultaneous contrasts where, in the place of the complement, in certain circumstances, it is the first color itself which is projected on a neighboring surface.

2.3.6. Optical mixture

Chromatic perception is modified still further by the phenomenon of an optical mixture which occurs when two juxtaposed tints, perceived at a certain distance, produce in the eye a third color, called the resultant color. In a certain way, the specific action of these two first colors is annulled, rendered imperceptible or even invisible, to the benefit of the third color. As opposed to the color which results from a mixture of colored pigments themselves, this third color—obtained by way of an optical mixture— retains all its luminosity. These resultant colors are produced even more when the first contrasting tints are present in equally small quantities.

Another source of chromatic movement stems from the phenomenon of adaptation of colors among themselves. Thus, a blot of intense red will bring out the red components in the surrounding colors. This adaptation is a consequence of simultaneous contrast, because the projection of the green complementary in a neighboring region reactivates, at the same time, the anticomplement red which is contained in this same region.

Another type of transformation occurs in the case of the color conveyed in a watery medium or transparent fluid. Instead of offering color a stable color surface like, say, oil, gouache or pastel would, it presents a volumetric color. In other words, the color undergoes transformations pertaining to its very position in the volume or the type of envelopment presented by the fluid volume. As Albers said: "In practice, the majority of watercolors have volumetric colors: several layers superimposed augment their dark character, their weight and chromatic intensity" (1963; 13).

2.4. Texture

Texture is a property of material bodies primarily apprehended by the sense of touch, evaluating what is hard or soft, rugged or smooth, penetrable or not penetrable, continued or discontinued, and so on. All tactile percepts are gathered, compared and contrasted, and interrelated in an organic space capable of unifying their extreme diversity.

But the intimate connections established by experience between what is touched and what is seen at the same moment tend to blur for common knowledge many distinctive traits of these two universes of perception.

In visual semiotics, we understand by the term 'texture' a plastic variable designating a property of colored matter in its innermost depths as well as on its surface, whereby it presents various inclinations and disjunctions which modulate in different ways the absorption and refraction of luminous rays on opaque bodies, thus modifying their chromatic effects. As interpreted in terms of vision, texture will also be instrumental in the construction of distance appreciation and depth effects.

Like the term 'color', the term 'texture' is a plural term, since the diversities of texture are countless, constructed as they are at several levels of the visual work. In the first place, the microstructure, or the grain of the surface on which the perception of the color is realized, always corresponds to a particular type of discontinuity in the retinal stimulation whether it concerns wood, canvas, glass, or paper: "Because a color has been spread out on a certain surface, it is going to take on a particular aspect" (Guillot, 1957a; 81). This determinism is not uniquely psychophysiological, but is based on an objective property of the support of the visual work. This particularity can be masked, accentuated, or transformed by the composition of pigments and the manner in which they are physically spread out. But it will always produce ways in which color appears that modify the chroma of the pigment and consequently change the spatial organization of the global perceptual field.

Because the texture of the support can be masked superficially by a certain way in which the pigment is spread out, Chevreul failed to recognize its crucial importance in painting, whereas he pointed out the major role played by the cruciform pattern in the woven threads with which tapestry is always faced (192, par. 874). But more recent studies have pointed out that, when the colored surface is not anchored in an underlying level of cyclical or alternating variations, it has the tendency to become more mobile and unstable in its localization, taking what has been called "the diaphanous aspect of color in expansion" (Kanizsa, 1957; 108).

The effect of texture is also produced by both the internal structure of a pigment and by the manner in which it is spread. The study of materials which visual artists use in the course of creating artworks is relatively recent. In fact, as explained by Rabati: "it is only from the end of the 18th century that progress in chemistry has allowed us to pursue a rational study of the principal constituents (suspension mediums and pigments) of preparations, of which the processes of elaboration were, up until then, jealously guarded" (1957; 155).

The same pigment can, in effect, modify its chroma in space and time, according to its stability and the nature of its internal pulverization. This, moreover, defines its proper texture.

> Following the pulverization of a pigment, in a more-or-less fine way, its color *will change* . . . at first in proportion to the product becoming more refined, the surface is augmented. When the grains are large, we have the impression of a very colored object; when the grains are small, there are many reflecting surfaces, the powder reflects a lot of white light and it appears clearer. (Guillot, 1957a; 169)

Similarly, the technique of spreading out, of dilution, of superimposition of layers of pigment, can make the same color vary: "The way of spreading the pigment and of mixing it with other colors considerably influences the optic properties of the color 'really' obtained" (Guillot; 174).

Marcel Guillot pointed out also that the pigments used by painters, "even finely pulverized . . . remain very strongly colored" (169). In other words, they participate, through and through, in the chromatic property that they convey.

The effects of glazes, which have been sought by traditional painting, present particular chromatic effects, because of the specific superimpositions of diluted pigments in different mediums of suspension, acting therefore at varying levels of texture: "A glaze formed by a white pigment diluted in turpentine, spread in a thin layer on a black ground, gives a bluish grey because the black panel does not reflect light diffused laterally" (172). However, on a white ground it will produce an orangish grey.

The differences in texture produced by different brushstrokes, or the manner in which pigment is spread, from discontinuous stippling to greasy and smooth beaches more or less marked out in relief, are better known today because of the American Action Painting or the Quebec Automatism artistic movements. Let us recall, in this regard, the impact of the types of boundaries of a mass on certain effects of texture. As expressed by G. Kanizsa, when the contour of a mass is neat following a sudden change in type of stimulation, its color appears as dense and intense, but when the contour or boundary is more indefinite, following a gradual change in the type of stimulation, the chromatic mass becomes diffuse, dusty, and as though covered with a veil of smoke (Kanizsa, 1957; 110–111). This purely optical textural effect is far from being unique, since any modification in the continuity of a given texture will produce, at the same time, different colors, forms, vectorialities, dimensions, and positions in depth.

Produced by a variety of techniques, such as thickening or thinning of the layers of pigment, the seedlings of blots in variable reliefs and the introduction of materials underneath or into the pigment, the variations in texture seem to directly indicate a privileged contact with matter. But texture, like color, does not adequately inform us of the nature of the material of which an object is made. In the general experience of reality, as well as in the domain of visual language, it is through repeated and accumulated experiences of concrete manipulations of objects that we learn to link certain textures to certain materials. It was on the basis of many common misapprehensions that Duchamp, who opposed the notion of visual perception as a purely retinal reading, with a grand sense of irony filled an iron cage with small blocks of marble resembling cubes of sugar. Indeed, a similar texture can refer to different materials: sugar is lighter than marble, melts in water, possesses another flavor, and so on.

The general reference to an illusion of matter, so commonly attributed to texture in visual works, can mask one of its most important properties, which is the fact that it is an essential component of visual language. Whatever its reference to tactile space, texture can only be recognized in visual representations by way of the organ of sight. In painting and most often in sculpture or architecture, texture is perceived not by the hands or the cutaneous surfaces of the body, but by the eye. Moreover, the research of J. J. Gibson (1966) has shown the unique contribution that variations in texture make to the visual apprehension of distances in depth. This visual variable thus affirms the potentiality of visual language to make reference to nonvisual spaces, that may be in fact not only tactile but also postural, kinesthetic, etc. In other words, visual semiotics has to be concerned with any further information that cognitive sciences may offer about the many sensory spaces which are elaborated through experiences of reality. Though they do not have their point of origin in visibility, they may be represented and organized by the spatial quality of visual representation.

The definite distinction between textures belonging to the very structure of visual components and those which are only referred to should help us to be aware of the specific interrelations between tactile and visual spaces. The figurative type of painting has widely developed the fictional possibilities of the representation of tactile experiences by the production of pictorial textures dissociated from those of their reference. Often, a relatively smooth surface will afford, by a play of tonalities, illuminations, and a sliding effect between forms and colors, the illusion of uneven, chaotic, and shaggy textures. These could refer to briars and shrubbery, velvets or sequins, rocky grounds, tempestuous seas, etc.

A type of treatment of pictorial pigment which creates these illusions of texture is not any more "concrete" than another which presents its proper texture as an object of perception. A wood table, represented in a pictorial work, is not made of wood; and the leaves of trees do not incorporate the components of leaves in external reality. Any material body possesses a texture as well as a color, and both, put into visual language, are capable of connoting an object or an experience stored in our memory. This is what made Noël Mouloud say, in his *La Peinture et l'espace:* "An 'informal' art knows very well, by the processes which speak directly to vision, to evoke this contact with matter" (1964; 94).

Instead of referring to verbalized objects which belong to the external world and which as referents are often ambiguous or polysemic, numerous contemporary artistic movements have been led to use the textural characteristics of the matter itself, which are the very components of visual language. Far from being nonreferential, this form of representation refers precisely to experiences of reality where the dynamisms of hardness, softness, penetrability, elasticity, smoothness, glossiness, pastiness, sharpness, and so on, have been known and experimented with widely. Instead of abstractly referring to illusory 'objects' by mimetic suggestions, these forms of representation solicit concrete experiences pertaining to the materiality itself of the organized elements in the visual field. The dynamics of concrete experience, based on memorized experiences, become an organized part of an awareness, instead of remaining isolated elements, dispersed in the heterogeneous sensory-affective spaces.

2.5. Perceptual Variables

In addition to the plastic visual variables, color and texture, there exists another group of constant stimuli which form part of the coloreme, that is, this correlative region of a centration in the visual field. If plastic variables are perceived almost directly, the variables called 'perceptual' are the more complex products of endogenous mechanisms of perception acting on external stimuli. These are: dimension, position in the plane, vectoriality, and the boundaries/contours which will produce the regroupings called 'forms'.

2.6. Dimension or Quantity

Quantity corresponds to an essential characteristic of any expanse of matter reflecting luminous rays. The quantity (or dimensions, or size) of material observed in a centration presents itself as a mass or an elastic solid possessing three dimensions (thickness, height and width) even if they cannot be metrically measured.

In this context, the notion of mass refers to the 'quantum' of material energies distributed in an expanse of matter forming various aggregates in the visual field. If one would make an analogy with the notion of mass as used in physics, one would say that, in the visual field, mass is defined as the quotient of resistance of its own energies in their interaction with the energies of the ambient field which act upon it, imposing a certain number of tensions, changes and visual movements. This quantity or topological mass is always endowed with an internal volume, as explained above, characterized by an axiality, a vectoriality, and a given expansion.

The dimension or quantity of a given aggregate is a major factor in the transformations which elements undergo in the visual field. As we have seen, a color of too-small dimension cannot be assured of its chromaticity and is transformed according to an optical mixture. On the other hand, a much more extended color is transformed differently by way of the chromatic effects of the complementarity which plays upon it and adjacent colors.

Each of the other visual variables at the heart of a coloreme is subjected to a variation, according to its quantity, which transforms the equilibrium of internal energies and "brings closer" the region to the perceptor. Albers has already commented on this in the case of color: "An augmentation in the quantity of a color—independently of the dimension of the format— will reduce visually the distance" (1963; 13) between this color plane and the spectator, thus producing an effect of proximity and intimacy. This same movement toward the front can be produced as much in a partial region as in the global visual field. This expanding in the dimension can be achieved within a continuous element, or by the regrouping of several discontinuous elements, under a certain form of neighboring.

In a coloreme, the evaluation of the dimension of its various components can be made by a comparison with its internal elements or in relation to the components of neighboring coloremes. However, the determination of the dimension, at this level, depends upon measuring instruments used, as well as upon the dimension of other objects, large or small, with which an object is compared. Also, the scale of appreciation of the dimensions of a coloreme will differ from that used in a larger region or in a global work. However, it must remain proportional in these diverse regions using an internal system of gradients of dimension based on the coloreme being multiplied a certain number of times.

This proportional scale evaluates the number of times that a coloreme can enter into the surface/volume of another region. This scale is topological and nonmetric, since it takes into account the effect of expansion which an element undergoes, through chromatic or tonal simultaneous/successive contrasts.

2.7. Implantation or Position in the Plane

This perceptual variable corresponds to the relative position of groups of coloremes in relation to the three dimensions (height, width and depth) in the specific field under consideration. This position is determined by two series of parameters. The first concerns the relations of distances with regard to the external peripheral sides, defining the visual field, and the second, the internal relations of these elements accentuated or not by the energies of the infrastructure of the Basic Plane. This system, which constitutes a syntactic structure of visual language, will be described more fully at a later point. We will devote ourselves here to describing the characteristics of the third dimension, depth. It is necessary to specify at the outset that this notion of depth does not refer to simple relief or that physical condition, resulting from textures and corresponding to the effects of elevation or of lowering of pigment in relation to a level surface, which represents the support of the visual work. It is rather a third dimension constructed as an inherent element of space by the perceptual processes themselves.

There exist two modes of spatial depth in the syntax of visual language: optical depth and illusory depth. Any positioning of visual stimuli, at one point or another of these different categories of depths, modifies some of the visual variables which compose them: chroma, dimension, tonality, texture, and so on. This is why, even if it is a product of the perceptual synthesis, the position in depth in the plane constitutes an essential characteristic of the basic visual unit, that is, an actual visual variable.

2.7.1. Optical depth

Optical depth is that which is produced by the proper interrelation between colored elements, to which are added the influence of textures or of degrees of distinctiveness of contours, which will cause a given zone to move forward or to recede in relation to another in the visual field. But it is primarily by their very chromatic quality that coloremes and groups of coloremes will acquire different positions in spatial depth.

In a general way, the tradition has stated that red zones were to advance, blue zones recede, and yellows be situated between the two. However, as we have already pointed out, hundreds of nuances of primary colors exist. Those which are truly put in action in a visual field, being transformed by other variables, such as tonality, vectoriality, dimension, or texture, may behave quite differently without contradicting the law of universal movement of visual elements toward the front or rear.

This optical depth has often been commented on by producing artists. Thus, the constructivist artist El Lissitsky wrote: "New optic discoveries have taught us that two regions of different intensities, even when they rest on a plane, are seized by the mind as being at different distances from the eye . . . In this space, distances are uniquely measured by the intensity and the position of strictly defined regions of colors" (1968; 354).

The French artist A. Herbin described the same phenomenon differently:

> Painting has no need for a third dimension, neither in reality nor by whatever artifice, because color manifested in an expanse of two dimensions, possesses in itself a spatial power. Certain colors express space in depth (blues), others space in front (reds). Certain colors express radiance from within to outside (yellows), others from the outside, within (blues). (1949; 94)

The positions of colors in depth vary not only with the structure of the other visual variables that they convey, but also with the environment in which they are inserted and which acts, in its turn, on the visual variables constituting the chromatic element. As expressed by J. Itten:

> When six tints, yellow, orange, red, violet, blue and green, are juxtaposed, without intervals, on a black ground, the luminous yellow appears to advance distinctly into the foreground while the violet recedes in depth in the dark ground. The other tints take an intermediary position between the yellow and the violet. A white background will modify the effect of depth. Violet seems to advance far from the white ground which retains the yellow with its close luminosity. (1970; 77)

When orange is interposed in the distance in depth separating yellow and red, the distance between yellow and orange is proportionally inferior to that which separates yellow from red. The same happens with the distance which extends from yellow to red/orange and from red/orange to blue, whereas the intervals between yellow and green and green and blue are proportionately larger.

A more luminous tint on a dark ground will advance in proportion to its luminous intensity and will recede in the same way on a clear ground. When tints of equal luminosity seem lighter or darker, the light tint seems to advance and the dark one to recede.

Contrasts of saturation between two shades produce another effect of depth. The more saturated tint advances, the less saturated one recedes. But if they are of the same saturation and luminosity, the contrast of the clear and the dark will produce a contrary effect.

Certain intervals in depth between two colors can be so distant that they produce an effect of rupture between two regions, as if separated by a void or a nonenergized space. When a single element seems to be at a too-distant interval in the forefront in relation to an ensemble, it is said that it "floats" in front of the pictorial plane. Similarly, an element which recedes too suddenly and too far into the rear produces a hole, a void, a spatial discontinuity that perception cannot compensate for to maintain a pictorial unity.

Albers studied the production of depth that he called the illusion of space, created by the qualities of neater frontiers/contours which lend to various crisscrossing stripes nearer the periphery of the canvas an over-under effect. In other regions of the work this effect would be reversed or annulled. Albers confirmed the findings of Gestalt psychology to the effect that, when two similar forms are situated one above the other, they will assume a different position in the depth of the field. In a general way, moreover, Albers proposed that any quantitative increases in saturation and dimension of a color cause it to appear closer to an observer. The majority of his experiments were devoted, however, to the topological relations of neighboring/proximity, or separation/distancing, produced by distinct or indistinct frontiers. He experimented with the possibility of obtaining changes in the luminous intensities of adjacent colors, and the resulting disappearance of frontiers, which in themselves accentuate the interpenetration of one color upon another, at the same level of depth.

Albers reappropriated the fundamental notions of the "push and pull" proposed by Hofmann and its undulatory movement within the pictorial mass as well as the variations in the harmonics when changes are introduced in illumination, direction, and the sequence of the reading of a series of regions.

The theoretical teaching of Hofmann had pointed out, in the movement of 'push and pull', the fact that the pictorial plane reacts "automatically" in a direction opposite to and with an equal force to any visual stimulus which it receives. Thus, any plastic element which, by its own dynamism, positions itself at the front of the pictorial plane, pushes neighboring elements toward the back and vice versa. Specifically, Hofmann defined color as the plastic means of creating "intervals," that is, energetic regions interrelating quite distant areas through the harmonics of color. This harmonics, therefore, designates those tensions existing between colors that are situated at various distances in the three dimensions of the visual field: "Swinging and pulsating form and its counterpart, resonating space, originate in color intervals. In a color interval, the finest differentiations of color function as powerful contrasts. A color interval is comparable to the tension created by a form relation" (Hofmann, 1948; 67).

Several hypotheses have been offered for the movement of colors in depth in the visual field, linked most often to the structure of the visual apparatus. In *Vision in Motion* (1947), L. Moholy-Nagy wrote: "The lens of the eye does not stare at various colors in the same way. Red thickens the lens and renders the eye farsighted; this transformation gives red a closer position than blue which flattens the lens and renders the eye myopic."

A decade later, a scholar, Marcel Guillot, made a case for the variation in the degree of contraction which the crystalline lens of the eye must effectuate to establish focal distance, that is, a point where luminous rays gather together:

> We know that this distance is not the same for different colors. The result is that it must be accommodated in a different manner if it concerns blue or red. When the distance is of ten meters, you must make an effort, when it is three you must make another. If two objects are at the same distance, one blue, the other red, you feel, in an instinctive way, that you have accommodated in passing from one to the other, as if one of the objects was close and the other far, whereas the distance is the same in the two cases and that it is the color which is not the same . . . There is an effort of accommodation for the various colors and because of this there must exist a space of colors. (1957b; 151)

But he also noted that if, in general, reds advance and blues recede, artists may wish to impress them with different positions and do this by other procedures, such as playing on values and contours.

We can place among the phenomena deriving from the perceptual variable of position in depth the effects of transparency. These result from the perceptual estimation of a superimposition of two colors or two tonalities, whereas one of the tints appears as situated below, that is, behind the other color. An analagous effect of transparency is produced in the perception of a composed color or of a color subjected to the effect of equalization or complementarity. The different energetic vibrations of these various wavelengths produce stimuli which are estimated as more behind and more in front in relation to others in the same colored mass.

In the same way that it is not possible to fix in immutable definitions the characteristics of such and such a color, it is impossible to define a priori the position in depth that a color can occupy. Not only do these characteristics change according to the field or the perceptual context, but the trajectories of perception can modify already perceived characteristics, thereby producing particular visual movements and transformations in the interrelations between regions. We will call 'optical perspective' the ensemble of the network of depths defined in the visual field by the unique dynamisms of colors and tonalities and the spatial organizations so derived.

2.7.2. Illusory depth

Illusory depth is a perceptual phenomenon which does not result from the dynamics of the visual variables as such. But it is realized through the adoption of a system of conventions, adding to perceptual mechanisms the impact of logical and conceptual knowledge, in order to produce the illusion of very great depths in the visual field of representation.

This illusory depth is the product of a combination of often quite imaginary points of view, in that they are not often realizable in concrete experience. They are codified, in various cultures, according to almost two dozen perspectivist systems. The complexity and the diversity of these systems and of the norms of representation they require qualify them as syntactic modes of approach to experience which are the object of a description below, as parts of the syntax of visual language. We note only that any illusory mode of hollowing far distances in the visual representation remains dependent on the dynamics of the optical perspective which creates a topological shallow depth. These two types of perspectives can enter easily into conflict within the dialectics of visual propositions.

2.8. Thermal Values

The vocabulary of the artist's studio has often linked the positioning or effect of movement in depth of chromatic elements to their thermal value: warmth and coldness. Warm colors advance, cold colors recede. Clear tones are interpreted as warm and neighboring colors of blue as cold. But the thermal estimations vary most often with the perceivers and the producing artists, as a result of associations stemming from the mnemonic repertory of each, in connection with nature or cultural facts. These thermal evaluations do not correspond to any reality of the spectrum's luminous rays. The energy of the photons, for example, which produce a wavelength corresponding to red, is much less than that of the photons which produce blue. (Boll, 1962; 25).

The perceptual estimation of a given color as warm or cold refers undoubtedly to the experience of organic thermic space as well as to an aspect of tactile space, both closely linked in this matter, but conditioned more by external causalities than by properties of chromas. Lived experience teaches that material surfaces are literally heated, to variable degrees, by radiant energies of natural light. In this regard, a black surface which absorbs the majority of rays of light can, when it is exposed to light, become literally warmer than a white surface. But this effect is less notable with other surfaces of color, opening the door to a wide variety of estimations. By association, visual perception may connect contradictory characteristics to colors if observed in different contexts. Indeed, green-blues and blacks are, at times, considered as cold colors, and yellows, reds and whites as warm colors, when associated with the sun's radiance.

Kandinsky, who believed it necessary to use, in large measure, the thermal properties of chromas in his theory of color, did not fail to recognize that "any color, without a doubt, can be at once warm and cold" (1977; 70, note 1). Albers corroborated this ambiguous status of color in his own teaching. Although blue seems cold and the yellow/orange/red group seems warm in occidental tradition, "there also exist warm blues and cold reds at the interior of their own nuances." He also added that "if we mix white, black or grey with these colors, personal interpretations of temperatures risk rapid divergence" (1963; 59).

All these contradictory testimonials have persuaded us not to retain the notions of warm and cold as actually operative among the characteristics of colors, although assuredly such associations on the part of a perceiver will determine many dynamic qualities and movements of the chromatic region to which they are attached. But it is only a question here of a connotation and not of a constant and internal character attached to perceptual mechanisms.

2.8.1. *Gravitational values*

It is a similar case for the notion of weight which various tints seem to possess, the darker appearing heavier, or more subjected to a gravitational attraction. This movement toward the bottom or the top in the pictorial field, in our view, is not linked to color itself but rather to the position of plastic elements in the field of autonomous forces which construct the Basic Plane. This is exemplified by the various forms mentioned by Kandinsky which, while remaining the same, do not have the same weight when they are placed in the top left corner or in the lower right corner of the canvas. Whereas it has been traditionally recognized that the darkest color in the pictorial field, the one containing the most black and the least white, was the heaviest visually, an experiment of Albers demonstrated that the perception of the quantity of black or white that a color contains, a relatively simple operation it would seem, could not be made by more than two thirds of his advanced students (1963; 33).

There has also been a belief in the ability to reach an objectivity in this respect by recourse to photography, but this position ignores the fact that the recording of lightness or darkness on the retina differs from the sensitivity of photographic film. In white and black, this film yields a lighter white and darker blacks than the eye perceives. In the same way, color photography cannot provide us with information about the perception by the eye, because it deviates even more than does black and white photography, overestimating the luminosity and intensity of blues and reds (1963; 34–35).

In the domain of sculpture or architecture, the perception of relative weight and of the resulting equilibria between elements cannot normally be formed directly. Most often, it requires the resort to prior verbal information which would state that a mass is made of bronze, steel, wood, for example. The weight is not perceived by the eye but deduced solely from acquired verbal knowledge. While this perception is a characteristic of tactile and kinesthesic experience, it is not a property, as such, of visual language.

In conclusion, it appears that the antinomies of warm/cold and light/

heavy, which have played so important a role in the presemiotic theory of Kandinsky, are not intrinsic properties of visual variables, but constitute an active source of indirect connotations. In order to take into account the effects of movement and positioning which are sometimes linked in visual representations to these nonvisual aspects of reality, we have kept as a distinctive trait the notions of light and dark about which there seems to be ready consensus.

2.9. Vectoriality

Vectoriality or orientation designates the perceptual variable that indicates the direction in the three dimensions taken by the energetic movement of a coloreme, or a group of coloremes. It is perceived as a directional tension of the visual variables, capable of acquiring a virtual prolongation in the field or of establishing relations with close or distant regions in the visual field.

In contrast to the position in the plane which accounts for the transformation which the visual variables undergo, for the fact of their localization in the visual field, vectoriality corresponds to the inscription of a moving tension in these variables. It is related to Kandinsky's conception of movement which he defined "as a tension plus a direction" (1975; 91), the term "tension" implying specific forces or energies. The groups of movements or vectorialities at the core of coloremes are interlinked and reverberate, generating virtual movements as well as virtual visual variables. The energetic intensity of vectors depends, in large part, on their mode of insertion in the Basic Plane.

Our substitution of the notion of vectoriality for Bertin's variable of orientation is quite significant in stressing the difference between graphism constructs and visual language. As well as carrying the topographical components of direction (up, down, oblique, sideward), vectoriality stresses the more important energetic level of behavior of purely visual components. Vectoriality is direction plus force, tension, and energy.

2.10. Boundary or Contour

The boundary variable, also called frontier or contour, corresponds to a qualitative change between two neighboring regions in the visual field, likely to produce open or closed forms. The traditional plastic analysis never considered boundary in itself, but only as a secondary effect in the situation where a synthetic grouping of numerous coloremes could determine what has been called a 'shape', that is usually a closed form. The dynamics of the boundary/contour results from the sort of liaison or passage existing between two visually differentiated zones. Boundaries may appear as distinct or diffuse; they are marked by a contour/line or by a graduated change, by an autonomous plane or by a simple juxtaposition of contrasting planes. An extremely graduated transition between two zones does not lead to the presence of a contour/line, but rather to a zone of color or tonality more or less homogeneous in relation to its neighboring regions.

The contours or frontiers do not merely play a primordial role in the ease/difficulty of passages, or the type of communications possible between regions. Like textures, frontiers have a direct effect on the chromatic quality of the region they encompass or on the organizational structure of the surrounding spatial field. When a contour is neat, the internal color presents a solid and dense aspect; as the degree of transition (also called marginal gradient) becomes softer, the color becomes powdered and airy, passing gradually from the aspect of a solid to that of a penetrable volume. With respect to diffuse boundaries or borders: "The most remarkable effect concerns the tissue of the chromatic substance which from being compact, smooth and solid becomes soft, velvety, pasty. It acquires, in addition, a certain density and seems localized in front of the surface which serves as its ground, like a layer of powder or a film of smoke spread over" (Kanizsa, 1957; 110).

Thus, two grey or colored circles, identical except for the distinctiveness of their contour, will be perceived as entirely different from the point of view of color, density, texture, position, and so forth. This transformation in the plastic variables of a region, attributable to the state of its boundaries, is echoed in all of the surrounding spatial field which takes on the same qualities of softness and impreciseness as the zone of blurred contours. Kanizsa explains this phenomenon: "When the contour is distinct (following a sudden change in the type of stimulation), a stable and precise organization is produced; when indefinite (following a gradual change in the type of stimulation), the structure of the field is unstable and these characteristics of spatial organization are related also to the color [of this spatial field]" (Kanizsa; 110).

The "Musatti effect" is the name given to this phenomenon by which the transformation of contours has as its results not only a considerable increase in the equalization among neighboring regions but also a modification of the spatial organization which depends on chromatic qualities: "Grounds lose, in large part, their compact aspect, they become more dissolved, more airy, as if a tenuous layer of mist or a shadow was spread out before them" (Kanizsa; 112). In blurred frontiers, it is very difficult to perceive varied chromatic zones, but when there is a sudden transition between two regions, the chromatic differentiations which accompany it are easily perceptible.

2.10.1. Forms

The variable of boundary/frontiers plays a dominant role in the perceptual constitution of differentiated ensembles known as 'forms' or shapes. But it should be remembered that other visual variables, such as color or texture, are just as important causal factors of "forms" as boundary is.

Any form is produced by an intensification or regrouping of visual variables according to topological and gestaltian relations. Resulting from a convergence and an interaction of several visual forces, all forms possess a determinate orientation or vectoriality, that is, a tension oriented toward an angular variation in the three dimensions. Moreover, as figures, they can be defined only by their relation with the environment from which they are differentiated.

2.10.2. Open or closed forms

Considered as a subcategory of the boundary/frontier variable, forms can be divided into two general groups: open forms and closed forms, demarcated or not by a line/contour. Any form whose frontier is constituted by a linear element, demarcated or not, which, after a hypothetical point of departure, returns to itself, is called a 'closed' form. This linear element, when it is marked, is called line/contour or, by way of abbreviation, simply contour. When the line/contour cannot be reunited with its point of departure, or when the boundaries of a mass seem almost indistinguishable from its environment, the form is qualified as 'open'. Linear, textural, chromatic quantifications of masses which reach the peripheral sides which delimit the format of the work (which we call, further on, the Basic Plane) are called 'open' forms, provided that the end of the pictorial system is not underscored by an added line/contour. A linear form of contour can also envelop a group of closed or open forms, constituting the ensemble as a closed form.

In the closed form, the movements of the forces which constitute it (or vectors) are more accentuated as the gradient of the curves varies. By contrast, in the open form the movement of the oblique creates the strongest tension, because of the continued reference to the horizontal or vertical axes. In the case of many oblique forms, similarly oriented, their particular tension is accompanied by an oscillation toward the virtually closed good form which can envelop them.

Like a figure on more open ground, a closed form will see its internal volume amplified by associations with known external objects describable by both closure of forms and tridimensionality.

A form called linear or unidirectional, which is somewhat extended in the two dimensions of width and height, acquires at the same time a characteristic of surface and of mass, endowed with a three-dimensional internal volume.

2.10.3. Actual and virtual forms

From their vectorialities, both those of their components and those which characterize their global gestalt, forms constructed by visual variables actually materialized in the visual field produce nonmaterialized 'virtual' forms expanding their own energies. In the same way, the masses, as open or closed volumes, can be virtual or actual, and any virtual prolongation of opened, linear and bidirectional elements produces an open virtual mass. Virtual forms, like actual forms, are proportionately more dynamic as they are better integrated in the axial energies of the Basic Plane or its formative sides.

In closed forms, which are always closed volumes, vectorialities can produce actual or virtual movements. Thus, symmetrical polygons (squares, circles, regular stars, and so on) possess a tendency toward peripheral rotations around their central axis. However, most frequently, perceptual mechanisms accentuate to a greater extent their movement along the horizontal axis. This horizontal, lateral movement will go toward the right or the left depending on whether one or the other of the frontiers is more or less 'rigid' or closed. Rectangles or triangles in which the height is greater than the width will undergo a movement along the vertical axis (Arnheim, 1954; 402).

Inversely, any closed forms which can make a rotation along a central axis, whether horizontal, vertical or diagonal, possess a quality of symmetry. In the same way, any form of which a section of the frontier is a right line is capable of making a rotation on this element-hinge and of producing a virtual, symmetric volumetric form.

Any symmetrical form produces a particular visual movement which subdivides it into two parts, thus producing an oscillation between its gestaltian unity and the vectorialities of its parts.

Furthermore, any asymmetry is interpreted in its energetic relation to a potential symmetry. One of the most common pictorial themes, the representation of the human face, is made dynamic by the tension established between the two sides of the face, which are always asymmetric, in contrast to the two 'good forms' produced by the symmetric rotation of the right side on the left or the left side on the right.

All open, unidirectional or polydirectional forms are prolonged in the neighboring visual field according to their vectorial orientation. By their regrouping, open forms produce actual internal volumes; by their prolongation, virtual internal volumes. Similarly, the regrouping of closed forms produces virtual internal volumes.

2.11. Repertory of Forms

The semiotic description must, at the level of the basic element as at the syntactic level, be able to account for movements and interactions which dynamically intervene in the forms or in the superregions produced by visual discourse.

Given the deficiencies of existing repertoires of forms (Barrett, 1983), which exclude open as well as virtual forms, both of which are fundamental components of visual language, we have developed a system of classification of forms which is presented in Appendix II.

Chapter Three

Syntax of Visual Language

3.1. Syntactic Rules

One of the prime objectives of a grammar is to describe the greatest number of possible enunciations of a language with a limited number of syntactic rules established at a generative level of its structure.

The syntactic rules of the visual language are constituted by the set of operations and functions through which perceptual mechanisms establish interrelations among the basic elements in diverse visual fields. Their application results in the construction of specific spatial totalities.

The visual field is defined as a force-field where given energies produce particular effects leading to different types of spaces. These energies are provided by the aggregates of reflected light first differentiated in the perceptual units of the coloremes. These are the locales of incessant transformations activated by the subjective processes of perception as well as by interactions generated by the coloremes themselves in a visual field.

In other words, the syntactic rules of visual language are regulators of energy and visual transformations, and not merely a description of relations between some sort of substantial and stable elements. The coloremes themselves, as mentioned above, are not units that predate the emergence of visual variables, but they are produced by and transformed coextensively with them.

Coloremes could be compared to corpuscles only if these were defined, as Bachelard (1951) did for the basic units of physical matter, as particles having neither assignable form nor dimension, that are flexible and penetrable and that can exist, as nuclei of energy, even under a very little quality of individualization.

Coloremes are defined as nuclei of energy since they are made up of matter. As Bachelard has pointed out, Einstein has "attributed an energy level to the resting mass of an inert body" (1951; 110). Coloremes are even more so since they are, as percepts, made up of vibrations of reflected light.

To define the syntax of the visual language as the ensemble of regular modes of production of visual movements that constitute dynamic invariances is to imply a conception of movement different from that of classical mechanics which only considers the sort of movement produced by the collision between two bodies. Bachelard has reminded us that even Nietzsche still carried over this limited intuition of the dynamics of movement in his philosophy:

> In truth, Nietzsche only lived for the will to strike. The shock and the stimulus, the attraction and repulsion, constituted for him dynamic, fundamental images. He did not understand those trembling movements, those hesitant movements, this whole phenomenology of vibrations, oscillations, rhythms; a phenomenology which gives a unity to complexity, which institutes the notion of frequency at the level of a primitive concept, of a simple concept . . . Nietzsche did not either have access to this enormous problematic of a movement which, born in a center, sets in motion the whole of a milieu, dynamizes the whole of a space, calls on multiple hypotheses to explain the reactivity of space. (1951; 52)

While geometric concepts are necessary to describe any visual spaces, the geometry which is needed should incorporate dynamism and movement. Again, as Bachelard recommended to physicists, semioticians should reject "the ultra-realist intuition of the movement as systematically attached to a defined mobile at a physical point . . . Instead of a determined mobile it is a *dynamic environment* that one must study" (1951; 184).

The energetic character of basic units and of syntactic laws between elements is also increased by the mobility inherent in the processes of perception which alone can constitute the visual *text* as such. Indeed one can analyze a visual statement only after having actively constructed it according to syntactic structures proper to this type of language.

If N. Chomsky (1980) could contend that competence in verbal grammar belongs to the order of unconscious knowledge, the intuitive use of visual syntax by producers belongs to the same category, the more so since no overt, conscious theory about it has ever been evolved.

Analysis of visual language has been so much more difficult to achieve since no external criteria could establish that a proposition about its structure was adequate, or that one given visual statement corresponded to a valid enunciation more than another. As we have mentioned earlier, the visual speaker, that is, an artist or a producer of a visual representation, does not enjoy a theoretical authority as to what belongs or does not belong to this language. On a great many occasions, visual representations produced by other groups (or of one school compared to another, like the Academicists vis-à-vis the impressionists) have been denied the property of belonging to "visual language." But these deviant forms of representation were duly recognized as legitimate by cultural collectivities at a later date.

Paradoxically, the semioticians who study visual language are not generally "users" of this language and thus would not possess a linguistic competence acquired from practice, analogous to that of the grammarian of verbal language who is himself a user.

Visual semiotics will therefore be able to invoke for its validation mainly internal criteria of deductibility and coherence, as well as the fact that its propositions on the grammatical structure of visual language allow for the actual functioning of visual language in its diversified forms. It should not exclude any of them, past or present, without the consequence of offering an inadequate description of the foundations of that language. In addition, it must be able to describe the modes of production of future types of visual statements, which will result from transformational rules applied to the same basic units.

The syntactic rules that allow the formation of particular spatial fields will necessarily contribute to later semantic interpretations of these forms of representation, since they determine the linguistic functions and preside over the interrelation of elements in the global text. But their semantic function may be even more important, as suggested by R. Jakobson: "All languages are founded on a system of grammatical categories and the meanings of these categories are characterized by being binding for the speakers" (1980; 119). It follows that "grammatical meanings play a fundamental role in the linguistic thought and verbal communication" (110). We suggest that the case is similar for visual language, making the elucidation of the nature of its syntactic structures more urgent.

By definition, visual grammar is required to describe the operations by which basic elements are determined and interlinked through basic rules so as to form more complex ensembles. These rules are interrelated in an orderly fashion and in such a way that the first level operations are necessarily accomplished before the second level ones, and constitute their indispensable foundation. The first level rules provide a basis for the higher level operations which regroup a greater number of elements in more and more complex perceptual schemas.

The grouping of basic elements in visual language is carried out according to certain laws and with the aid of perceptive operations which in turn are influenced by the structure and organization of each particular visual field. Thus the syntactic interrelations between the first correlatives of perception and subsequent percepts constitute agglomerates or subassemblies generated by certain operators. Regroupings of regions or superregions result from other operations, up to the elaboration of systems of regions, of subregions and of superregions, that will be in turn organized in "systems of systems" by higher level dialectical operators.

The syntactic rules that regulate the joining of coloremes and transform their internal/external functions call into play a variety of operators and may be regrouped on three principal levels as follows:

A. The rules of regrouping of coloremes among themselves that depend on:

(a) topological relations,
(b) gestaltian relations,
(c) the laws of interaction of colors.

B. The rules generated by the insertions of coloremes within the energetic infrastructure proper to each visual medium; that is, the Basic Plane for the pictorial, the Virtual Cube for the sculptural and its environmental extension for the architectural.

C. The modal rules that preside over effects of distance and which are inscribed in various codes or systems of perspectives. We will comment presently on the first group of syntactic rules (A), while full chapters will be devoted to the second and third groups.

3.1.1. Topological relations

The first group of syntactic rules that govern the relations and functions of the coloremes is based on the topological relationships that have been recognized as primordial in the "construction of the real." In the 1940s, the genetic epistemology of Piaget established that the first geometrical model of space used by human beings is not Euclidian geometry but topology. This spatial model of the organization of perceptual experience remains throughout human life the basic means by which one constructs his notions of reality. As we have devoted an earlier work to the study of topological functions in pictorial representation (Saint-Martin, 1980), we will summarize the essential features of the more important of these notions.

Acting as a qualitative intuition in advanced mathematics, topology relates in common experience to a "pure perception" of spatial relations as forming a homogeneous, continuous, syncretic totality. This continuum of space is based on the sensation of the proximity of stimuli in the visual field and leads to the intuition of a space without holes, ruptures, or voids. This spatial continuum is not a given, but is the result of an organization of the perceptual field into a number of fundamental relations.

Topological relations are established in the visual field on the basis of the tensions animating the visual variables themselves, activated and expanded by the perceptive activity of the observer. The interrelations established between diverse points in the visual field, called 'paths', can be of two types: a) locomotions, resulting from a de-centration or changes in the points of viewing, or in the position taken by the perceiver in relation to the visual field; b) communications, which are occurring as a result of the interrelations arising from the various dynamisms proper to the material energies constituting this field. Both are fundamentally subjected to and describable by notions belonging to topology.

K. Lewin (1935; 80) has defined topology as "a non-quantitative discipline which deals with the possible modes of connexions between various spaces and their elements." Any other modes of structuring or modelling spaces have to be built on such topological stratas, to which are added other perceptual mechanisms or conceptual and logical organizations. Properly speaking, many of the latter are not spatial as they lack the quality of continuity.

The relationship of *neighboring* is the most important topological notion by which the function of continuity is constructed in any spatial field, whether physical or perceptual. Its importance to physical sciences was underlined by Bachelard (1951; 6) when he stated that any force in the continuity of a field "presents itself as determined by the condition of *neighboring*. This term, vague in the everyday language, acquires all of the desirable conciseness in mathematical expressions" (1951; 6).

This intuitive relation is produced in the perceptual field through a subjective mechanism operating on external data. It establishes a proximity or a most immediate connection among elements that could otherwise be described as existing independently from one another. It may stem from a homogeneous contiguity, from an attraction, a fusion, an assimilation, or a similarity sufficiently dynamic to force a binding between elements. The strong continuity it produces is basic to the constitution of topological masses as well as in the production of a space conceived as a plenum.

The antagonistic relation of *separation* is mostly brought into being by an external causality or the estimation of a difference, and consequently of a disjunction, between groups of coloremes in terms of some visual variables. By definition, in this context, the notions of contiguity or juxtaposition between diverse aggregates of coloremes imply that they have been perceived as separate.

The fundamental relationships of neighboring or separation are not assigned to visual regions because of the consideration of a single characteristic among visual variables, since none as such can determine the level of energetic intensity of a region. They are the result of a perceptual estimate and a synthesis integrating all visual variables in a region, along with their interaction with the ambient field. Both notions are the source of the emergence of the topological notion of *limits*, boundaries or frontiers, where the nature of the connections or passages between separate regions can be recognized.

The *order of succession* is the type of relationship set up among coloremes when some of the visual variables are repeated in the three dimensions. It implies a similarity between one or more visual variables forming the coloremes or in their dynamic interrelations within the field. It occurs under a variety of organizations, such as:

Repetition : AAA – BBB
Reiteration : ABC – ABC
Recurrence : ABC – DEF – ABC
Symmetry : ABC – CBA
Asymmetry : ABC – ABCD
Alternation : AB – CD – AB – CD
Inversion   : ABC – ACB

A regular alternance in depth produces a type of "woven" space, while a "folded" space results from the superimposition of interrelated layers of groups of coloremes in the third dimension.

By definition, groups of coloremes made part of a succession differ among themselves, given their different points of implantation in the plane. They will be further modified by their structural function in a succession.

Properly speaking, a serialization is an order of succession imposed upon a limited number of separate elements through a similarity between very few of the visual variables. The term also applies to a repetition of these elements, but in changed positions in the two dimensional plane and consequently in the third dimension, offering endless variations of internal structures:

A – B – C – D – E
E – D – C – B – A
E – C – D – B – A
B – E – C – A – D
E – B – D – C – A
E – A – B – D – C
A – C – D – B – E

And so on.

The orders of succession, established by perception between distant regions, constitute the basic function of rhythm, specific to any individual space of representation.

The notion of *envelopment* corresponds to the interrelation among several coloremes when some totally surround others. A semi-envelopment partially regroups some coloremes around others. In a topological context, this relationship occurs only within the notion of continuity, creating the strongest bonds of connection and dependence between regions and adding to them a new range of dynamisms, such as:

A A
A B A
A A

Topological envelopment is realized only when the differences among visual variables pertaining to the enveloping and the enveloped are neutralized by the establishment of a neighborhood relation, producing continuity in depth. It is also felt as an asymmetrical group given the contrasts between the vectorial energies defining the container and the content.

Encasing or emboxing is the phenomenon by which some regions are perceived as if they were "inserted" between other regions, similar or dissimilar, such as the position of B in ABA or ABC. It can be a global or a partial characteristic as in the case of envelopment, from which it differs by virtue of the stronger separations caused by contrasts between their respective constitutents, as well as by the firmness of their boundaries. As the region encased is estimated as a part of a particular system, this relation isolates both elements inside the global field.

The topological relations are to be understood in their potentiality for the constitution of *continuity*. This seminal notion is a function that results from the state of the basic elements being perceived as sufficiently similar, close, dense, and compact, so that no disjunction can separate them to the point where a breach, or a void of energy disrupts them.

Spatial continuity must not be confused with temporal continuity, or the duration continuity, which may or may not accompany the consciousness of any experience, perception included. The feeling of duration put forward by Bergson cannot establish a spatial continuity, as Bachelard already observed: "For Bergson, continuity is an immediate given of consciousness. It is this *intimate continuity* that we jilt in discontinuous grasps of external experience" (1951; 55).

According to Bachelard, should a new ontology today be based not on common sense but rather on more objective information about the nature of reality, the idea of continuity would become very problematic, since "the most compact matter is taken by common sense as an assembly of very dispersed corpuscles" (1951; 107), that is, a discontinuity.

For semiotics of the visual language, discontinuity is a primal occurrence arising from perception itself, given the multiplicity of heterogeneous stimuli encountered; it also arises from the logical levels where semiotics is assumed to operate as a science explaining effects by causes: "Any causal phenomenology is necessarily discontinuous because one speaks of an effect that follows a cause only for an effect that *differs* from the cause" (Bachelard, 1951; 206).

But this logical type of discontinuity does not affect the continuous/discontinuous spatial relationship which perceptive activity establishes at the level of topological relationship. Continuity appears here as a constructed intuition reorganizing the discontinuous aspects of material events. In the same way, a spatial continuum is not a given datum but a construction of perception itself.

We will finally consider the notion of *vectoriality*, which is differently interpreted in various geometrical contexts. Many systems of geometry afford a progressive transition between a non-Euclidian geometry, such as topology, and the Euclidian model, and they differ greatly among themselves.

Projective geometry reorganizes the spatial and topological field by introducing the vectorial point of view of a straight line extended to infinity. It thus offers a system of generation of forms from peripheral rather than focal forces. This non-Euclidean geometry has been a major factor in the elaboration of Suprematist and Constructivist forms of representation, as well as in Mondrian's Neoplasticism, in the first decades of this century. The terms "a-logical" or "irrational" were used to describe this intuition of a space as infinite. Not only could the objects inserted in that space be interpreted as infinitely close or distant, but they would be described from various simultaneous points of views (El Lissitzky, 1968).

The notion of vectoriality is fundamental in projective geometry, where it is defined as a linear oriented progression. In topology, it corresponds more to a planar or mass thrust animating internal volumes. It characterizes in particular the centripetal-centrifugal energy animating the central and peripheral layers of a topological region, as well as its capacity to react to the vectorial forces of the ambient field.

The vectorial elements of projective geometry lead to the construction of Euclidean space. This spatial model restricts its constitutive coordinates to the perpendicular meetings of straight lines in three dimensions. The first two coordinates, meeting at 90 degrees, form the so-called bidimensional plane, while the third axis, also perpendicular to the vertical/horizontal lines, represents the dimension of depth. This constant mathematical grid determines the position of any point in space, as well as a nonvarying distance between two points. Useful at the macroscopic level of experience, this Euclidean grid cannot be used to map more proximate perceptual spaces (tactile, thermal, and so on). Nor can it be used to map or represent internal, psychological or emotional relations which are unquantifiable dynamic phenomena.

3.1.2. Gestaltian relationships

At the level of aggregates of coloremes, the visual variables are governed by the Gestaltian "laws of perception." While the findings on visual perception achieved by the experimental psychologists regrouped under the name of the Gestalt school are recognized as constituting laws, analogous to Newton's laws of motion in physics (Rock, 1975; 281), they have not been systematically applied as structural means to describe the organization of the visual field.

We have already tried to establish that, both in a restricted and in a larger part of the visual field, movements among visual variables are achieved in conformity with the laws of visual movements proposed by the Gestalt theory (Saint-Martin; 1990).

From the summary offered by Köhler (1940; 134–135), we recall briefly the more important of these perceptual structural processes:

(a) The visual field is first organized by the constitution of the *figure-ground* relationship. When a denser agglomerate of visual variables is present, it is endowed by perception with the characteristics of a figure and the surrounding areas acquire those of a background.

As it establishes among others a superimposition of the figure in front of the ground, this process is instrumental in creating fictional space, that is, the percept of a distance in depth between the two regions.

(b) The visual variables are above all regrouped according to the factor of their *proximity* in the three dimensions.

(c) Visual variables are perceptually regrouped so as to present an approximation of a more regular, simpler, relatively closed and symmetrical totality, called a *gestalt*. The visual movements involved in this process are said to respond to the pressure of the *good form*, that is a perceptual tendency to actually "misinterpret" more or less the actual data so that they would correspond more to geometric patterns possessing a strong internal structure.

We assimilate to this process the tendency to associate familiar remembered schemas to aggregates of visual variables, so as to achieve a rapid recognition of "objects" in the visual field. The pressure of the "already known" in the interpretation of visual aggregates is the basis of the iconic recognitive function.

(d) Similarly regions, lines, or vectors, that can be joined in a virtual *good curve* will do so, that is, a continuous and simple arabesque.

The same happens with elements that lend themselves to the making of a good angle, that is, a right, acute or obtuse angle.

(e) Strong regroupings are produced under the influence of the factor of *similarity* between some or most of the visual variables, the most effective being the similarity in color. It may be of importance to point out that in the two dimensional expanse, there cannot be total similarity between two elements given their differences of position in the plane. Besides bringing regions closer together, the factor of similarity tends to establish a homogeneity of the field.

(f) As most Gestaltian researchers have acknowledged the influence of acquired habits, of knowledge, and of experience on perceptual processes (Gabar, 1968; 55), one may rightly add as common factors in perception the affective and conceptual structures of the individuals, their needs and abilities, which affect the nature and extent of their involvement in perceptual activities. As shown by Rorschach's conclusions to his renowned test on perception (1947), emotional factors play a major role in an individual's aptitude to apply to the entire visual text the gestaltian factors of groupings (Saint-Martin, 1968). While these appear basic and universal, they are not necessarily made use of by every viewer confronted with a visual representation.

As much as a verbal text would not be adequately apprehended if some grammatical categories, be they pronouns, genders, or tense of verbs, were not recognized, visual semiotics proposes that a description of any visual representation is not adequate without a recognition of how the various syntactic categories are applied.

Both topological and gestaltian operators are at work in any viewing of a visual representation. While gestaltian processes are applied when separations are recognized, topological intuitions still act upon the internal constituents of these regions and can contribute to minimalize the contrasts between some visual variables in view of attaining some measure of neighboring.

The regroupings produced by both topological and gestaltian operators are perceived as more or less stable totalities, dependent on larger regroupings. Any grouping can thus become a subgestalt for a potentially larger gestalt. Under the effect of prolonged and multiplied centrations, these very regroupings may dissolve and their constituents appear as isolated or regrouped differently with other regions of the field.

3.1.3. The laws of interaction of color

The principal laws of interaction of color are those of equalization, simultaneous and successive chromatic and tonal contrasts, the optical mixture, and other regular effects not yet adequately categorized. While submitted to gestaltian factors of junction/disjunction, they produce phenomena that cannot be entirely explained by them.

These interactions between colors can produce intimate junctions between contrasting elements, dissolve boundaries, produce new virtual forms, modify the dimensions, positions and vectorialities of regions, and so on.

Given the complexity of behavior of the various chromatic events and to avoid repetition, we refer the reader to our previous chapter dealing with the specific mechanisms of the interaction of colors.

3.2. Specificity of Visual Linguistic Fields

The various types of visual language (painting/photography, sculpture, architecture, etc.) do not differ by their use of visual variables that are common to all, but rather they are differentiated in their syntactic and semantic structure by analytical hypotheses that have given them birth. These provide permanent and different infrastructures that we call the Basic Plane, in the case of painting or photography; the Virtual Cube, in the case of sculpture; and the environmental Cube, in architecture.

The concept of the Basic Plane was developed by the artist Wassily Kandinsky in his efforts to produce a grammar of pictorial creation. This expression can be used in a general way to refer to those grammatical structures that establish the specificity of visual linguistic fields. In this respect, the proposition of Kandinsky is as fundamental to the development of visual semiotics as was Troubetskoy's phonology to the development of verbal linguistics. It is indeed only by the structure of the Basic Plane that the visual variables used in various forms of visual language cease being pure material data in order to acquire linguistic functions.

It is important to distinguish sharply between the Basic Plane of painting, of sculpture, of architecture, and the pictorial plane or the sculptural plane, at the level of effective creation of an artwork in these sectors.

The Basic Plane is an infrastructure antecedent to any production of visual discourse. It presents a potential spatial energy allowing visual variables, which are physical quantities common to any visual reality to be inserted in a context where they can be given linguistic functions.

By contrast, the pictorial plane or the sculptural plane designates a level of energy resulting from the use by the artist of a group of visual variables that possess the potentiality of self-organization according to the topological and gestaltian syntactic rules. But they can be defined spatially only through their interactions with the structural energies of the Basic Plane.

The pictorial Basic Plane or the sculptural Virtual Cube correspond to the dynamic functions linked to the support/format that carries the pictural or sculptural message. It necessarily antedates production of any pictural plane and conditions the movement of plastic energies produced by the artist. The infrastructure of the Basic Plane, independent of all strategies of artistic production, organizes a level of constant energetic constraints that impose specific grammatical linkages/transformations to coloremes that are incorporated within.

Thus, in addition to specific syntactic operations that result from the perceptive recognition of visual variables in coloremes and the functions that are acquired by regroupings of coloremes, these linkages are determined and transformed by their insertion into the infrastructure of the Basic Plane. These operations are regrouped in an ensemble of specific energetic trajectories that we will describe with respect to the pictorial and sculptural Basic Plane. Grammar of visual language will be completed by the study of particular syntactic modes corresponding to the various systems of perspectives.

Chapter Four

The Pictorial Basic Plane

Whether the visual representation is defined as a 'space of life' in which the perceiver must engage himself for an indeterminate period of time or as a space of free movement demanding his perceptual attention, or as a particular environment in relation to which he must situate himself in a global sense, it still remains true that it presents itself in a specific way in the surrounding space. In contrast to many natural objects, pictorial representation (painting, drawing, photography, and even video) presents itself to vision as a *limited frontal plane;* namely, as a "surface" of minimal thickness, on which material elements are deposited or embedded.

This frontal surface is usually presented vertically, in such a way as to allow for an equivalent or relatively equilibrated refraction of luminous rays. Even when presented occasionally in a horizontal or oblique mode, on floor or ceiling, its structure still refers to the dynamics of the frontal plane, one whose first characteristic is to appear to general perception as alternately concave or convex.

This material frontal plane is the physical support of all pictorial representation, in the sense that information theory gives to the notion of channel in message transmission. Its internal and material structure is determinant as far as organizational potentialities of its element are concerned. The first studies on the visual representation support were made by the artist Wassily Kandinsky, a pioneer in the semiotical analysis of painting. Developing Signac's analysis of postimpressionism, Kandinsky was further inspired by the Saussurian revolution and the preliminary discoveries of Gestalt psychology, in the project of constructing a grammar of creation which would have as its goal the explicitation of the first elements and syntactic laws of pictorial language. This research was the fulcrum of his teachings at the Bauhaus, which involved, as he wrote: "a study of the primary elements . . . and a utilization of the tensions present in these elements as a language" (Kandinsky, 1975; 8). It is on the basis of this definition of the plastic work as a field of differentiated forces and conflicting tensions that he developed his grammar of the pictorial work. But his more lasting and substantial contribution undoubtedly lay in his intuition of an even more fundamental field of forces than the pictorial one, one which conditions the function and meaning of even the most primary elements. This underlying physical support for any visual representation was called by Kandinsky, in 1926, the *Basic Plane*. While we are offering a different description of the internal structure of this field, we have kept the same name as an homage to the artist's seminal intuition.

This primary structure-field possesses an undeniably objective character in that it exists outside the human organism; this material structure gives rise to specific constraints in the external relation between human perception and representational objects. Indeed, the Basic Plane cannot exist independently of the artist's and viewer's subjective spatial processes of perception, yet it maintains an irreducible objectivity by reason of the "resistance of matter," as Piaget noted, to our attempt to structure reality.

It is a material plane which preexists any attempt at visual representation and it is necessary to stress the primal autonomy of this objective field upon which artistic projection is inscribed. It is offered as an organized, underlying and permanent gestaltian structure which is continuously transforming the discursive paths used by the artist. It appears also as a semantic field, having a proper organizational density which is confronted by the "impulse to signify" of the human visual speaker.

Thus, in addition to syntactic operations that result from the perceptive recognition of the visual variables in coloremes or groups of coloremes and the functions of junctions/disjunctions they produce, syntactic relations are determined and transformed by their specific insertion into the infrastructure of the Basic Plane. These result in particular modalities of perspectives which, as syntagmatic coded organizations, carry additional semantic connotations.

Kandinsky defined this Basic Plane as the "deliberate limitation of a portion of the universe on which the composition is to be executed" (1975; 75) or "the material plane which is called upon to receive the content of the work of art" (1976; 115). The first definition can be misleading since it does not specify that this portion of the universe must present itself as a certain type of surface, whose particulars would depend on the elements which produce it. The deliberate limitation by which this portion of the universe is selected is much more than simply the placing in a frame of some part of the universe along with the undifferentiated aggregate of its properties. It also establishes specific structures by which the pictorial field will be engendered. On the other hand, the second definition is also ambiguous since it tends to identify this underlying structure as an abstract two dimensional plane, a notion familiar to geometry but not an entity in the concrete world.

The Basic Plane is by no means synonymous with the so-called iconic image-field which, as Meyer Schapiro has astutely pointed out, is subject to various constraints arising from the expressive function of its nonmimetic elements: margins, framing, orientation, and so forth. Rather, it is that material field itself which exists prior to the inscription of any mimetic or nonmimetic sign. In effect, it is the primordial field that Schapiro evoked as constant:

> Where there are no frontiers to the field, like the paintings in prehistoric grottoes, unframed images, on rocks or vast walls, we center the image in our own view; in a defined field the center is predetermined by the frontiers or the format and the isolated figure is characterized in part by its position in this field. (Schapiro, 1969; 223–224)

In the first case, the visual movement which establishes a frame in which to center the image results from gestaltian pressure; the second case demonstrates the interaction between the figure and the field formed by the Basic Plane.

By virtue of its objective materiality, and whatever its shape, material composition, or dimensions may be, the Basic Plane has a particular structure which presents—prior to any human intervention—a series of specific "tensions" which interact with the gestures produced by the artist and the material elements that he uses.

The structures of this Basic Plane establish a group of coordinates which generate a particular relation of signifier/signified, analogous to those syntactic structures with which one must compose when attempting to represent and convey meaning in any existing natural language. However, these characteristics of the Basic Plane which are the first 'signifiers' of the pictorial object must not be confused with the global metaphors or interpretations which have been ascribed to it, and which vary, irrespective of the nature of its specific constitution, according to different epochs or forms of sensibility.

For Alberti, for example, the Basic Plane was a planar cross section made at a certain distance in the path of the visual cone, in relation to which the laws of foreshortening and linear position had to be developed in order to suggest depth in front of and behind this limiting panel, despite the inherent flatness of the surface (White, 1972).

Braque saw the Basic Plane more as the synthetic symbol of a concealed reality, awaiting the creative act to bring it to the surface of the visible: "When I begin I feel as if my painting were on the other side, merely covered with white dust—the canvas. I only have to dust it off. With one paint brush I sweep the dust off the blue parts, and I have other brushes for the greens or the yellows. When it is all clean the painting is finished" (Braque, 1969; 28)

At times Kandinsky himself celebrated the "empty canvas," calling it a "pure, chaste virgin," or a "pure canvas which itself is as *beautiful* as a painting" (1964; 35). Such analogies, by virtue of their overly synthetic nature and the diversity as great as the sensitivities of the artists themselves, cannot serve as a basis for semiotic research deliberately grounded in the properties of the signs themselves, which offer a common structure which all artists must confront in the objective materiality of the Basic Plane itself.

4.1. Plastic Elements According to Kandinsky

Kandinsky's contribution to the study of the Basic Plane continues to be a seminal one today. But while it has contributed in an absolutely radical way to the transformation of the notion of pictorial field as well as to its perception, it has to this day never been seriously questioned by artists or art theoreticians.

Kandinsky was the first to consciously recognize the importance of this "organism" with which the artist is constantly in dialogue, and to try to describe its characteristics. However, on the basis of his approach to the analytical elements of the pictorial discourse, namely point, line, then color, the subsequent description of the Basic Plane is entirely dependent on the intuitions by which these elements are defined. But as Gestaltian psychology has shown, a gestalt is more than the addition of its parts. In the Kandinskyan approach, the material plane that exists as a whole is not permitted to be apprehended in its proper characteristics.

The principal difficulty in Kandinsky's analysis lies in his use, when defining the basic elements of the pictorial discourse, of a geometrical or "logical" intuition, rather than a consideration of them in terms of their material, spatializing, and dynamic reality. His analytical approach can be readily discerned in the sort of qualitative leap indicated by the title of his major work which, as it has been already noted, should be read as: "Point and Line Related to Plane" (Sers, 1970; 33). With no accompanying explanations, Kandinsky effects a leap from the geometric domain to the material and sensorial field of space.

Euclidean geometry defines its basic elements as ideal concepts which do not have the same characteristics as material objects existing in space-time and which are not subject to the same laws. Kandinsky readily admits that his basic definitions are borrowed from Euclid's geometry. His analysis begins as follows:

> The geometric point is an invisible thing. Therefore, it must be defined as an incorporeal thing. Considered in terms of substance, it equals zero.

Hidden in this zero, however, are various attributes which are "human" in nature. We think of this zero—the geometric point—in relation to the greatest possible brevity, i.e., to the highest degree of restraint which, nevertheless, speaks. . . .

The geometric point has, therefore, been given its material form, in the first instance, in writing. It belongs to language and signifies silence (1976; 25).

And Kandinsky develops an admirable meditation on the interior "walled-in by the exterior."

Despite the poetic richness of the associations he makes between writing and plastic presentation, Kandinsky never explains the means by which this "incarnation" or materialization of the nonvisible geometric point came about, nor does he account for the essential transformations undergone by this notion, from the incorporeal to the verbal and then to the plastic context in which it is now postulated. In particular, its "im-mobility" becomes highly questionable by virtue of the continuous in-teractions which animate any matter in real space-time dimensions.

Kandinsky continues as follows to define the line: "The geometric line is an invisible thing. It is the track made by the moving point; that is, its product. It is created by movement—specifically through the destruction of the intense self-contained repose of the point. Here, the leap out of the static into the dynamic occurs" (1976; 57). In this context, only an "exterior force" can make this point move, creating the so-called absolute contrasts between 'passivity' and 'activity', as the primordial tensions between the plastic elements themselves. The generative link between the point and the line thus established on a geometric level will not be applied to the line and the plane by Kandinsky, despite the Euclidean precedent.

To begin with, the Basic Plane is set forth as "the material surface called upon to receive the work." However, this "material surface" will not be considered concerning its possible three-dimensional aspect. It will be solely defined by the relation that it maintains with already-observed characteristics of the fundamental elements themselves; namely, the point and the line. Even the further description of colored elements will be entirely attributed characteristics of the point and the line, as well as the forms that these produce.

Moreover, from this point of departure in the field of Euclidean geometry, one could expatiate at some length on the multiple con-sequences of Kandinsky's decision to consider the point and the line as the basic constitutive components of the pictorial discourse, at the expense of color which was only added later as a harmonious, but less structural, extension. This is surprising if one considers the enormous place that the color phenomenon appropriates in his landmark text *The Spiritual in Art*, published in 1911.

We may recall in this regard that, as early as 1918, Mondrian had suggested that color was the main element in the production of plastic phenomena through the principle of "determination," since line was only an element derived from the affirmation of color. Determination, he wrote:

. . . is achieved in painting by determining *the color itself* as well as *the color planes*, this process consists of counterbalancing the fusion of the colors by establishing a given type of border—either by a plane having an antithetical value or by line. *Line* must in fact be seen as *the determination of the planes* (of color), and for this reason it is important in painting. Nevertheless, plastic art is created by planes, and Cézanne could say that painting consisted solely of contrasting colors with others. But plastic art can also be seen from the viewpoint of line: strongly contrasting planes produce lines" (1967a; 105).

This concept of the line, resulting from a consideration of visual reality itself, is structurally distinct from that which is based on the geometric universe, which is only a logical or mental universe.

Later, Russian formalism, as explained by Nikolai Taraboukine in 1923, presented simultaneously these two concepts of line, while emphasizing that the line as an autonomous arabesque was not an essential element of painting itself, but rather of the language of drawing: "Although line is not part of the series of fundamental elements of which painting consists, it does play an important role. Moreover, line is an essential element of drawing," because it creates the spatial illusion of volume and because it serves as a "border between two contiguous colored surface-planes" (1972; 117–118).

This special emphasis placed on the elements of drawing as opposed to those of painting, the result of a long cultural tradition which influenced Kandinsky as he himself recognizes in his autobiographical texts (1970; 274), contributed to the complexity of the evolution of his work which cannot be explained in "pictorial" terms only. And despite Mondrian's early declarations in the texts of the journal *De Stijl*, this tradition also influenced the evolution of his work, as he acknowledged in a letter to James J. Sweeney: "Only now (1943) have I become conscious that my work in black and little colored planes has been merely 'drawing' in oil color. In drawing, the lines are the principal means of expression, in painting, the color planes" (Sweeney, 1961; 62).

But the chief drawback to Kandinsky's approach lies in the conceptual gap it opens between a logico-geometrical definition of the pictorial elements and a spatial conception of these same elements, corresponding to the infra-logical intuitions basic to the construction of the sensorial space-field, as Piaget (1956) has demonstrated. These concrete spatializing processes do not, in effect, obey the same principles of organization and do not behave in the same way as those governing the elements of Euclidean geometry, which Kandinsky used. Other geometries, based mainly on topological intuitions, are better suited to account for their reciprocal modes of interrelation.

4.2. Plastic Elements and the Basic Plane

With respect to the Basic Plane, instead of describing the material energies contributing to its structure, Kandinsky ascribed to it various characteristics of its so-called constitutive elements (the point and the line), to which he added organizational principles based on the spatializing activity of the perceiver himself, such as concepts of left/right, cold/warm, and so on, which are not actually part of the Basic Plane itself but are transferred to it by a mechanism of projection.

Nevertheless, Kandinsky emphasized the importance of making a clear distinction between both these force-fields, the Basic Plane and the more commonly known Pictorial Plane: "a fact which is of immeasurable importance and which must be viewed as something independent of the powers of the artist is . . . the *nature of the Basic Plane* itself" (1976; 116). By virtue of their permanence and objectivity, the actual structures of the Basic Plane are constraints that exist prior to the beginning of any work of visual representation. They must be compared to those basic verbal and grammatical structures which determine the semantic function according to relatively fixed coordinates, such as linear sequences and positions of nominal and verbal syntagms, temporal forms, subordinate propositions, and so on (Chomsky, 1957). The expressive impulse of the individual must combine with these structures, even for description of nonlinear experience involved in duration, multiplicity, simultaneity, juxtaposition of levels of abstractions which verbal language seems remarkably unsuited to transmit within its own structures.

The Basic Plane is constituted by the meeting of two pairs of vertical and horizontal parallel lines, determining and limiting a portion of the real so that a planar material surface emerges. At once, the perceiver is confronted with a sensorial fact distinct from the spatial reality that surrounds him or her. Kandinsky noted this difference but reduced it to that which exists between a space which is in front of and a space which surrounds the individual: "It can only be briefly remarked here that these organic characteristics of the plane carry over into the realm of space. Here the concept of the space before the individual and the space around the individual—in spite of the inner relationship of the two—would, nevertheless, reveal some differences" (1976; 122).

Obviously the "space" which emerges from the Basic Plane cannot be said to be the same as that which the individual perceives and experiences normally in front of him. Because of the specific limitation imposed upon the visual field, creating a particular plane having a certain shape, this new object will organize a specific flow of its material energies toward an interior center as against the energy generated by the joining of the limits. This specific determination of an area in the surrounding reality is undoubtedly the result of a decision to constitute in a material place a different level of spatial representation. But this is not purely an illusory or imaginary game; the structuring of various modes of visual representations must make use of material elements and energetic, quantified, sensory energies.

It might be suggested that Kandinsky, in fact, has undertaken the description of those internal dynamisms inherent in the Basic Plane in only an indirect way, when he endows it with the specific energies which animate his discontinuous basic elements (point, line, and the forms engendered by line). These elements are understood as possessing internal tensions which will influence, by analogy and proximity, the plane itself which they produce and on which they are deployed. The term 'tension' refers here to "the more or less active force inherent in elements." According to Kandinsky, the force of the movement which animates the elements results from the added load of "tension and direction." The term 'tension' would designate, therefore, the variations in the energetic charges of elements, producing different qualitative and quantitative effects, but would not include the vectorial charge attached to these elements (1976; 94).

The system of tensions which animates the plastic elements, and by association, the Basic Plane, is described by Kandinsky according to a list of antinomies which refer to various semantic fields such as thermic space (hot/cold), tactile space (heavy/light), kinesthetic space (active/passive), vertical space (horizontal/oblique), visual space (high/low), and psychological space (masculine/feminine). As Kandinsky did not stress the synthetic function of the notion of space, he mentions as a sort of accidental consequence the fact that all these factors produce sometimes an effect of nearness and at other times, that of distance in depth.

These tensions inherent in the plastic elements are transformed when they are integrated in the general context of a Basic Plane sharing analogous tensions, but in a structure of organization which does not vary. Thus the tensions of the elements are modified according to the position they occupy in the Basic Plane (being on top or on bottom, at the periphery or at the center), to the fact that their vectoriality is or is not in harmony with the tensions of the Basic Plane, or by the effect of their dimension in relation to that of the Basic Plane. Another level of tensions is added to those of the elements and of the Basic Plane through the action specific to the production of the primary forms, which is similar or contrasting to that of the Basic Plane. Primary geometric forms: the square, rectangle, circle, triangle, and so on, constituting strong gestalts, as noted earlier, will enter directly into relation with the general format of the Basic Plane, producing specific effects unrelated to the definition of their forming elements.

The principal antagonistic tensions considered by Kandinsky can be summarized as follows:

Right	Left
Vertical	Horizontal
Heavy	Light
Low	High
Warm	Cold
Masculine	Feminine
Active	Passive
Near	Far

When juxtaposed on the Basic Plane, the visual tensions of the elements will either harmonize or produce a disequilibrium. The ultimate pole of equilibrium of tensions is attained by the reiteration of tensions of the Basic Plane in the organization of elements. When this overall harmony is not achieved, the representation is termed as 'dramatic'.

As far as the notions of force, movement, and tensions are concerned, Kandinsky stressed that, if a materialistic approach to the structure of basic elements in the visual discourse is both necessary and fruitful, this did not by any means imply that the pictorial events should all be linked to "elements set in a solid way (material) on a solid Basic Plane, more or less strong and optically palpable." Energy cannot be equated with a static notion of matter. Not only does there exist in visual language "elements without material weight" but the interaction of energies can lead to "a dematerialized surface" (1976; 188). He enumerates specifically three possible states of presentation for both the line and the plane: support plane, plane of accompaniment, and invisible planes (1975; 150). Some elements, planes, and tensions may be said to be invisible, in the sense that they are not made visible locally in signs inscribed on the pictorial plane, but rather result from the interrelations arising among other visible elements. Kandinsky notes that these elements, "invisible" but inferred by perception, do not play any less significant a role in the construction of the work. We have called these perceptual elements, potential or virtual forces according to their origin and their position in the Basic Plane.

Any system of construction or of production of a visual work will consist of injecting new tensions, expressive of human experience, into the energetic systems conveyed by the Basic Plane: "At all events, it may be repeated: each part of the Basic Plane is individual and has its own particular voice and coloration" (1976; 129).

These tensions, which are part of the isolated elements or of the Basic Plane, and which multiply as the relationships among them do, are perceived not only by the eye but also by the totality of a person's perceptual capabilities. The term 'voice' or 'sonority' is used by Kandinsky to designate the resultant synthesis in this process by which a person senses the vibrations emanating from the totality of the diverse tensions of visual elements.

This understandable desire to link visual perception to the totality of the human organism may have prevented Kandinsky from fully addressing the semiotic requisite for a sharp distinction between the plane of expression and that of the content. His description of the Basic Plane still juxtaposes recognition of visual energies with semantic correlations which are no longer of a perceptual order. It seems doubtful, as we will discuss presently, that the notions of high and low, as linked to the concept of weight and gravitation, would be a universal objective phenomenon of the visual field. And if the difference between active and passive forces raises many problems, it is seemingly difficult to accept that characteristics of horizontality, passivity, and coldness have any objective links to the feminine, or their antagonistic traits, to the masculine.

One of the most problematic oppositions, but of the utmost importance according to Kandinsky, is that of tensions which differentiate left and right, in terms of density, lightness and vectoriality. We will examine them in more detail presently, but here note that Kandinsky is ambivalent and uncertain as to how to apply his subjective experience of left and right to the Basic Plane. He describes the problem as follows:

> (. . .) which side of the Basic Plane is to be considered the right and which the left? The right side of the Basic Plane should really be the one which is opposite our left side and vice versa . . . If this were actually so, we could easily project our human characteristics upon the Basic Plane, and we would thereby be in a position to define the two sides of the Basic Plane in question. With the majority of people, the right side is more developed and, thereby, freer, while the left side is more inhibited and bound.

But the contrary is true of the sides of the Basic Plane: "The 'left' of the Basic Plane produces the effect of great looseness, a feeling of lightness, of emancipation and, finally, of freedom" (1976; 119).

Kandinsky's decision is therefore to project upon the Basic Plane, as on a specular image, his own interpretation of the tensions proper to the left and right, disregarding the real plane of existence of the latter.

4.3. Neutral or Disequilibrated Plane

Yet the great paradox in Kandinsky's dynamic intuition of the tensions inherent in the constitutive "lines" in the Basic Plane is to suggest that they can form an equilibrated and neutral Basic Plane, inert in the equilibrium of its contradictions. But he has specifically described them as radically asymmetric and producing a nonequilibrated Basic Plane.

According to Kandinsky, the ideal sort of objective Basic Plane is that of a square. This strongest gestaltian figure is the incarnation of perfect and neutral equilibrium, to which the drive of the artist adjusts in a positive or negative fashion: "The most objective form of the typical Basic Plane is the *square*—both pairs of boundary lines possess an equally strong sound. Coldness and warmth are relatively balanced" (1976; 115).

But it is this "relative" balance which is put into question by the oppositions of tensional resonance attributed to 'lines' (horizontal = cold and passive; vertical = warm and active), or the accumulation of the tensions of left and right and gravitational forces, which structure the Basic Plane along heterogeneous and unequal tensions which will, in fact, violently unbalance it.

Let us consider, in Kandinsky's terms, the tensions linked to the notions of "above" and "below," characterized by a gradual accentuation of the gravitational force: "The closer one approaches the lower border of

the Basic Plane, the denser the atmosphere becomes; the smallest individual areas lie nearer and nearer together and thereby sustain the larger
and heavier forms with ever increasing ease. These forms lose weight and
the note of heaviness decreases in sound" (1976; 117).

Let us stress here that the "denser atmosphere" at the lower limit
belongs to the Basic Plane itself, which thus exercises an action on the
smaller "forms" which are placed there and, by reaction, on the weight of
those "larger and heavier forms" situated toward the upper limit.

Kandinsky says that his "concept of weight" does not correspond to a
material weight, but rather to an expression of an inner force "or, in our
example, an inner tension." He explains it further in a footnote: "Ideas like
'movement,' 'climbing,' 'falling,' etc. are derived from the material world.
On the pictorial Basic Plane, they are to be understood as the tensions
living within the elements, which are modified by the *tensions of the Basic
Plane*" (1976; 117, n.1, *our italics*).

Thus, the lower part of the Basic Plane itself is animated by a specific
internal tension, a density, a weight, a constraint increasing toward the
bottom and resulting from gravitation, whereas the upper half is, by
contrast, light and supple. This primary differentiation, constant at the
tensional level of the Basic Plane, will produce a modulation of its spatial
curve, since denser areas of the visual field appear closer to the spectator.
Thus, the lower region of the Basic Plane will advance toward the front,
while the upper portion, lighter and more mobile, will recede in the
background, as demonstrated in the schematic curve of figures I and II.

Moreover, the opposition of right/left which, according to Kandinsky,
is a property of the Basic Plane, offers a distortion analogous to that of
above/below, and these two distortions furthermore are reinforced by each
other. "The 'left' of the Basic Plane produces the effect of great looseness, a
feeling of lightness, of emancipation and, finally, of freedom" (1976; 119),
to a degree however, slightly less than that which is offered by the quality
of 'above' in relation to 'below': "The 'looseness' of 'above' unquestionably
exhibits a higher degree of loosening up. At the 'left' there are more
elements of density, but the difference from 'below' is, nevertheless, very
great. Furthermore, 'left' stands behind 'above' in lightness, although the
weight of 'left' in comparison with 'below' is much less" (1976; 119).

Figure I: Below/Above Tension

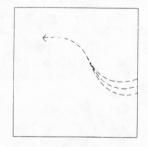

Figure II: Right/Left Tension

The energetic level is reversed for the 'right' side of the Basic Plane, which possesses a stronger density than the above regions, less than the below, but stronger than the 'left'. These variations in density result in the tensional 'rippling effect' of the Basic Plane from right toward left.

Indeed, Kandinsky recognizes the fundamental asymmetry that these various tensions lend to the square format of the Basic Plane when he describes the diversity of forces of resistance met by various lines or forms of the pictorial plane when approaching different limits of the Basic Plane:

> The approach of a form to the border is, therefore, subject to a special influence, which is of critical importance in the composition. The resisting forces of the borders differ from each other only in the degree of resistance and this, for example, can be represented graphically.

Figure III: Displaced Angle of the Basic Plane (According to Kandinsky)

> The forces of resistance can also be translated into tensions and be given graphic expression through displaced angles. (1976; 123)

Thus, the most "objectively" equilibrated format of the Basic Plane, that of the square, is at this point so distorted by the paired tensions of above/below and of right/left, that it gives the effect of possessing "displaced angles." Kandinsky does not elaborate on the consequences of these distorted angles on the plane that they enclose. Nevertheless, this plane is offered thus: a large density or tensional activation of the lower right corner raises it toward the front and make it recede in the background in the direction of the upper left corner. It is an "organic" quality of the plane, which must be transmitted to the space, thus creating in a permanent way a strong "rippling" wave losing itself in the ethereal space of the upper left corner.

It follows logically that Kandinsky postulates a fundamental difference of the tensions between the diagonal which goes from the lower left corner to the upper right corner, which he calls harmonious because it links the corners between which the relatively least difference in density exists and the other diagonal, which ascends from the lower right corner to the upper left corner, which he calls disharmonious or dramatic, since it unites antagonistic regions and produces the maximum difference in internal tensions. The first will be more continuous, less transformed by the tensions which ripple across the plane at the juncture where it seeks passage, whereas the second will undergo more differentiated, dynamic variations along its path. This disharmonious diagonal, however, will undergo another sort of differentiation in that, starting in the "very dense" region and then ending "in the lightest" region, it will have a tendency, according to Kandinsky, to deviate in its direction, that is, to be deflected upwards at its point of arrival, compelled to follow a movement of ascension towards the top and center of the work (1976; 129).

If we attempt to visualize the internal structure of this Basic Plane, not only in terms of resistances of lines and angles, but on its very surface, we obtain an extremely complex sort of surface that is markedly nonplanar and permanently oriented according to its vectorial coordinates. There is a decreasing gravitational density from below to above, and a density of diminishing resistance from the right to left. The Basic Plane shown in figure IV is produced if we reunite these two groups of tensions:

This type of internal structure of the Basic Plane differs appreciably from the fictional pyramidal plane of representation modeled by the classical perspective of naturalist painting. This well known perspective emphasizes the position of maximum distance-in-depth on the upper central axis (or horizon line), whereas Kandinsky shifts it—on the Basic Plane—in the direction of the oblique leading to the upper left corner. But, as is the case with the naturalistic perspective (or Euclidean basic plane), the structure Kandinsky attributes to the Basic Plane has the drawback of establishing, as a permanent matrix of spatial representation, some fixed, asymmetrical and preoriented structures which considerably predirect the artist's projective activity. The artist is constantly forced to struggle against this basic imbalance, developing palliatives, illusory corrections, superficial *trompe-l'oeil*, if he wants to develop different spatial structures, sometimes at odds with those offered by the Basic Plane itself. This changeless, unyielding, and constraining character of the Basic Plane renders the artist's task, in effect, a proverbial Sisyphean task.

We maintain that this situation arises from the fact that Kandinsky

Figure IV: Tensions in Kandinsky's Basic Plane

incorporated into his description of the Basic Plane certain structural tensions which are not inherent in the plane itself, but rather in the connotative structures of projection on the part of the artist, as attested to by the experience of Kandinsky himself. They issue, therefore, from the various structures of interpretation of spatiality made by the subject himself, and not from the external objective characteristics of the Basic Plane. But even if these structural spatial data were universal and constant, acting as a dynamic potentiality of meaning or reference, they are not inherent in perception and do not belong to the material reality of the visual field.

More important, they limit the spatializing representation to a commentary on, a contradiction of, or a confrontation with a fixed, arbitrary and unbalanced "spatial ripple," in order to satisfy its own needs of spatial structuring. But before trying to reestablish more objective foundations for the semiotics of the Basic Plane, let us here briefly examine the notions involved in the question of lateralization, gravity, and active and passive forces, which have played such an important structural role in the formulation of the Basic Plane by Kandinsky.

4.3.1. Laterality and lateralization

Recent developments in neurophysiology have confirmed the existence of a lateralization process in the human organism, stemming from the structure of the cerebral mass which is divided into two hemispheres united by the corpus callosum, the latter itself composed of more than two million neural fibers. Different experiments, notably those of the renowned Dr. Wilder Penfield, have confirmed the presence of a radical asymmetry in the functioning of these two sections which control, in their interaction, the neuromotor activities of the organism (Penfield, 1959).

At the level of psychic functions, three regions essential to the production of verbal language have been localized in the left hemisphere of the brain: 1) the supplementary motor region, at the top, presiding over articulation, 2) Broca's region, behind the forehead, concerned with articulation, storing of vocabulary, grammatical function and voice inflections, and 3) the region of Wernicke, more toward the rear, which, if removed, results in a loss in vocabulary, syntax and semantic function. The centers of language production all seem to be localized in the left part, although, following an accident or sickness, certain regions of the right lobe could "learn" to fulfill analogous functions. But under normal conditions, the removal of these same regions in the right lobe do not impair any of the verbal linguistic functions and would cause only very minimal changes in mental functioning (Jaynes, 1976; 100–106).

On the other hand, when regions of the right hemisphere are electrically stimulated, they produce memories of visual images, voices, smells, spaces, patterns and places. And when these same regions are afflicted with lesions, there is interference in the construction of spatial relations, manipulation of shapes and patterns, recognition of dimensions, textures, solving of intuitive tasks such as orientation in a labyrinth, and so on. The right hemisphere seems able only to find meaning in an element if that element is situated within a context, whereas the left lobe is more oriented to treating discrete particulars outside of any context (Jaynes, 1976; 110, 112, 118). The fact that an individual may be right or left handed has no impact on the separation of tasks in the two hemispheres of the brain. Even frequent interchange between the two hemispheres, which J. Jaynes saw as the origin of consciousness, of mental health, and of "the end of religions," effectively maintains the independent modes of action of each part. Thus there seems to exist a fundamental asymmetry in the functions exercised by each of the two hemispheres at the level of mental operations. This differentiation tends to become more marked from the first years of life until adulthood: "Lateralization—the consolidation of specific functions in one hemisphere or another—progresses gradually from the years of youth, in parallel with the acquisition of verbal skills . . ." (Edwards, 1979; 59).

This phenomenon of lateralization leads to a more radical asymmetry of the two hemispheres and to quasi-antagonistic characteristics between the operations effected by each. As J. Levy said: "The left hemisphere analyzes according to temporality, whereas the right hemisphere synthesizes in a spatial way" (Levy, 1974). One can produce the following table of functional differences between them:

Left Hemisphere	Right Hemisphere
Speech Acts	Basic comprehension of language
Analytic	Synthetic
Attention to details, parts, etc.	Attention to gestalts, totalities
Sequential	Simultaneous, nonlinear
Temporalized	Spatialized
Convergent	Divergent
Digital (numbers)	Analogous (shapes, dimensions, patterns, textures, etc.)
Conventional	Relational

Certain positive moral connotations have been culturally ascribed to the operations of the left hemisphere (good, just, moral, rational) and some less positive connotations to the operations of the right one (anarchic, bad, dangerous, elementary, slow). These connotations are undoubtedly developed and produced by the linguistic core, which is lodged in the left hemisphere. This 'devalorization' of right lobe functions by the left hemisphere is demonstrated as well by the left hemisphere's active propensity to dominate and even to minimize in human behavior the effect of right-hemisphere functions.

It is obvious, according to the above data, that the left hemisphere seems to reflect the structures which have been attributed to verbal language by a host of linguists and semanticists. Conversely, it appears that visual language, or the spatialized and simultaneous representations of experience, would be the product of and essentially depend upon the satisfactory and full functioning of the right hemisphere. Methods of learning to draw and paint have been developed, which are predicated on freeing the individual from the many repressive constraints imposed by the left hemisphere and then dynamically actualizing the repressed right-hemisphere potential, which has been habitually put into check, rejected—if not stifled—since adolescence. This is particularly true in our society, by the prominence given to the left hemisphere (Edwards, 1979; 60). With respect to the art of voice, which depends simultaneously on the two hemispheres, the seminal research of Alfred Tomatis has emphasized a necessity of pushing to its limits the complete lateralization of the organism. Tomatis saw in the achievement of a complete lateralization, that is to say, in the awareness and systematic development of the specialized functions of the left and right, "one of the keys of humanization and there is no language without it" (Tomatis, 1978; 151).

This differentiation has never appeared marked to human beings who, in the course of their development, have difficulty in assimilating the simple concepts of left and right as designating a specific way of identifying what is located at their left or right hand side in the environment. The ever changing referents of these notions have made them problematic. Jean Piaget demonstrated that, far from being an elementary spatial category, the dialectical comprehension of the left of one's own body and the left of other human beings requires a deliberate restraint of one's own primordial egocentric point of view. One must imagine oneself as occupying another position, that of the other, in order to observe the true characteristics and dispositions of objects as seen from the other's perspective.

Kandinsky commented on his own behavior which induced him to negate the other's point of view in deciding, for instance, what is left and what is right: ". . . when, for instance, he [the artist] takes the position of an objective observer in respect to other artists' works. The view that that which lies on my right is the 'right' may, perhaps, explain the real impossibility of maintaining a completely objective attitude towards the work and of entirely eliminating the subjective" (1976; 120, n.l).

Kandinsky's decision to attribute to the canvas in front of him his own determination of what is at right and what is at left corresponds in fact to attributing to it a specular or mirror dimension, which it does not really possess. Contrary to some allegations, one's reflection in a mirror does not inverse the position of objects as being on one's right or left. It would only do so if one takes the paradoxical view that this is not one's reflection but the emergence of another human being endowed with a different point of view from one's own.

The wealth of metaphorical comments on the specular effect and the conspicuous absence of any hard analysis of this phenomenon perhaps result from a confusion with the left/right relation as used in mathematics.

Mathematics does not recognize changes in elements from the simple fact of a change in position, since these elements are defined abstractly outside of any physical context. The similarity, if not the relative identity, postulated between elements in different positions, is the basis of the mathematical concept of symmetry: "An object . . . is symmetric in relation to a given plane E, if it coincides with itself by reflection in E" (Weyl, 1952).

This functional symmetry, which is a perfectly adequate concept in mathematics, does not exist in external reality. Already certain sciences like genetics have observed that a simple lateral difference in disposition for similar biological organizations involves a complete difference in functions (Monod, 1970; 63).

In the case of visual language produced by human concrete gestures, the question of lateralization remains confused because it concerns different levels which have not been sufficiently characterized. Let us take, as an example, the hypothetical case of a painter, draftsman, or lithographer who is working only with one hand, say, the right. Presumably this hand and the arm find themselves under the guiding influence of both hemispheres of the brain, even though the left presides over the right hand motor activity. One cannot conclude that this right hand acts only as an instrument of the organizational structures of the left section. If, in effect, Betty H. Edwards' methodology of teaching art enjoins children to draw for long periods of time using only the left hand, so as to allow the right-hemisphere determinisms to intervene, her real purpose is to lead students to anticipate those spatial organizations already produced by artists who themselves may have used only the right hand. The intent of this exercise is therefore to attempt to free the student from the schemas of spatial representation dictated by the left hemisphere, because of their insufficiency and their links with schemas of verbal apprehension of reality. Eventually the right hand, or, should the case arise, the left hand, may become the sole instrument of production, apportioning the different and antithetical schemas from the two hemispheres of the brain. It is therefore not at the level of the gesture itself that one perceives the signature traces and influences of the left and right hemispheres, but rather in the ultimate equilibrium of the organization of the work.

But what are the parameters of this analysis? And is the Basic Plane itself endowed with a physical lateralization whose characteristics would be differentiated within its material structure? Kandinsky himself asked the question, since the 'left' side of the paper or canvas upon which the artist paints was made to correspond to his own right, and vice versa. Kandinsky answered by privileging the space of representation rather than the physical object. But in thus establishing a specular metaphor in the field of representation, he affirmed a reversal of the usual characteristics that he had assigned to left and right. Thus, the right side, in humans, characterized as "the more developed, therefore, the more free" and the left as "the more handicapped, therefore the less free," reciprocally transform their respective traits in the Basic Plane: "The 'left' of the Basic Plane produces the effect of great looseness, a feeling of lightness, of emancipation and, finally, of freedom" (1976; 119). We would suggest that, instead of keeping to the consequences of a cultural conditioning which does not encourage ambidexterity, Kandinsky attributed to the space of representation the characteristics that neurophysiology ascribed to the right hemisphere as being connected to the "the left side," and vice versa.

The crisscrossing of the modes of functioning of the two hemispheres of the human brain, added to the circumstances of gestural production and perceptual mechanisms, does not clarify this problem. And a supplementary question should be added of a possible lateralization not in the Basic Plane, but in the pictorial plane, that is, in the ensemble of visual variables effectively inserted by the producer at the core of the Basic Plane. One could summarize the main questions as follows:

(a) Given the lateralization of the functions of the cerebral hemispheres, how is this asymmetry reflected in the producer's gestures of one arm?

(b) How can the objective properties of the Basic Plane be identified with the subjective characteristics of human beings?

(c) Is this lateralization an immanent facet of the Basic Plane or is it produced only by perceptual processes, necessarily linked to cerebral hemispheres?

(d) Is this differentiated lateralization a constant characteristic of any pictorial, architectural or sculptural plane?

We are not convinced that the qualitative/asymmetric differences of lateralization belong to the structure of the Basic Plane, which is made up basically of the material energies which enter into its constitution. However, it seems that Kandinsky's observations, applied to the pictorial plane, can be largely confirmed.

Research in this domain undertaken by the contemporary abstract painter Guido Molinari (1980) tends to establish that one can observe a lateral division in a large number of paintings in the classical and contemporary traditions. This division is given in relations of ⅓ to ⅔. Thus, the 'left' of the work, which corresponds to the left of the spectator and may "represent" in some way the right hemisphere which directs this side, tends to occupy a third of the overall dimension of the work. It offers a thematically more synthetic organization, which is less clearly articulated, and is resolved in smaller regions where movements would be those of heavy and slow masses. The right side of the painting, occupying about two thirds of the work, offers a large number of circumscribed or closed regions, which move more rapidly and utilize to a higher degree the coded conventions of perspective at the core of a more circular envelopment. But certain exceptions, in both ancient and contemporary works, hinder us from recognizing this phenomenon as a 'universal' perceptual variable and from including it among the constant visual variables.

4.3.2. *Gravitational push*

We will spend less time on the notions of gravity, of the "push toward the bottom" and "lightness toward the top" that Kandinsky has strongly associated with the characteristics of left and right, in order to make these two categories structural elements of the Basic Plane. If density and 'weight' are linked to certain qualities of color saturation or of textural intensification, as well as to dimensionality and vectoriality, a gravitational push can only be attributed to them through an identification of visual elements with the material bodies in external reality. If material objects are subjected ineluctably to the gravitational attraction discovered by Newton, can the same be said of the visual variables through which eventually fictional objects will be constructed and represented on a linguistic level? And can a perceptual referent, both subjective and objective, such as the Basic Plane, be submitted to the same laws as matter itself? Constituted through the perceptual meeting of four antagonistic and dynamic vectors as the basis of a linguistic, representational context, the Basic Plane can no more be defined as a simple and material "thing," but more appropriately as a psycho-physical structure. It is not a representation of external reality, but an energetic system allowing for different symbolic organizations of spatiality. As such, it possesses neither a left nor a right, nor a top nor a bottom, nor a propensity to fall, qualities which belong to nonlinguistic objects.

Inasmuch as they are constituted by a "sensorial" semiotic material, the pictorial, sculptural, and architectural planes are partially subjected to the law of gravity. Pigments, or other elements affixed to the pictorial Basic Plane, will fall under the effect of their own material weight if they are not adequately restrained by their support, but not the representational "objects" they construct. If this technical constraint is stronger still in sculpture and architecture, thereby limiting their spatializing potentialities, this characteristic does not play a syntactic role in the organization of visual language, but is only produced by semantic connotations, or paraperceptual interpretations. Just as purely optical laws cannot serve as foundations for a linguistic theory of color, neither are the laws of physics any more capable of accounting for the symbolic possibilities which certain materials are endowed with in a linguistic process. As a visual variable, vectoriality (or a movement upward, downward, or to the sides) cannot be arbitrarily predefined, but results from actual interrelations within the visual field.

Without stressing too much the semantically anthropomorphic character of Kandinsky's further interpretations about what constitutes the 'celestial' or the 'terrestrial' in an artwork, we propose that the placement of an element at the 'top' of a given representation does not define it as being 'lighter' than another placed at the 'bottom', just as an element is not any lighter because it is placed at the left rather than at the right. The use of the principle of gravity leads, moreover, to the ambiguous use of notions of 'full/empty' where even the empty has a weight, since "any place in the Basic Plane carries weight" (1975; 139). Many of these ambiguities come from the persistence in Kandinsky's theories of the Euclidean and Newtonian concepts of space, in spite of his intuition, as an artist, of a fully energized and somewhat 'infinite' spatial field.

The fact that a Basic Plane is extremely enlarged, by comparison with an average format, which corresponds to parameters of the human body, is a much more structurally significant question. In this case, the perceiver is seemingly obliged to undertake physical, kinesthetic locomotions in order to see it in all its scope, submitting it to the various points of view and perspectives with which "natural" objects, as well as sculpture and architecture, are apprehended. Similarly, when a pictorial work is very tall or very large, it is immediately subjected in relation to its external globality to the convergences of linear perspective, as is the case with any object apprehended in physical reality. This global apprehension of the Basic Plane, treated as a simple material object, may interfere with the fictional perspectives proffered by the internal visual variables. This characteristic of the very large format pictorial work is also pertinent to the difficulties of perception of sculpture or of architecture, as we will soon discover.

4.3.3. Active and passive forces

In his definition of the forces and tensions which animate the Basic Plane and which are drawn from its formative elements, Kandinsky used the notions of active force (that of the vertical) and of passive force (that of the horizontal) whose actions are propagated in the very plane itself. He did not hesitate, as did Piet Mondrian, to associate the passive forces with the feminine and the active forces with the masculine. Unfortunately, these semantic metaphors constitute the sole basis—of whatever slight value— offered for the use of these categories.

In effect, in a dynamic context—where Kandinsky quite rightly concentrated his efforts—these terms are inadequate and have very little descriptive merit. Passivity there becomes too easily an equivalent of a neutral force, an inert force, leading finally to a contradictory notion of a force-which-is-not-a-force. A passive force, even in Kandinsky's vocabulary, must necessarily be a force of resistance to the action of active forces; it must therefore be provided with an equal and antagonistic energetic intensity. A movement is always active to the extent that it is actualized. Otherwise, it is potentialized. Thus the horizontal movement is an active force of the same order as the vertical movement. If the deployment or the actualization of a movement is halted by an equivalent antagonistic energy, the energy which caused the movement does not disappear; it is contracted and prolonged under the form of potential energy. Also, the meeting-place of two antagonistic forces does not constitute a neutral zone drained of energy but rather a zone where energy is maximized as a result of the interface of these two vectorially divergent forces. Even if it is not actualized, this new energy becomes a potential charge of tension and direction, radiating outward in its proximity and producing a plane of tensions as well as varied vectorial energies.

Given the emphatic role ascribed by Kandinsky to metaphoric, connotative references in the definition of his visual grammar and the description of basic elements producing the Basic Plane, we propose to revise his analysis through a reconsideration of the dynamic sources which produce this Basic Plane. This may help us to understand the syntactic role of this notion in the production of the spatializing, linguistic function of visual language.

4.4. Structure of the Topological Basic Plane

We acknowledge, with Kandinsky, that both the origin and structure of the Basic Plane result from the paired meeting of two parallel vertical and horizontal lines. These paired lines are straight lines, that is the oriented vectors, conveying maximal energy. In Kandinsky's terms, straight lines are "the most concise form of the potentiality for endless movement" (1976; 57). When these paired lines come from maximal antagonistic directions to form a right angle, their energies reverberate in a potentialized form within the internal angles, making possible the emergence of a dynamic field called the Basic Plane.

However, in contrast with Kandinsky, we submit that this Basic Plane is a dynamic field and not an empty plane, simply confined by two paired and parallel lines. Along with his definitions of plastic elements, Kandinsky borrowed the notion of space implicit in Euclidean geometry, that is, of a box the interior of which is empty except for the objects which inhabit it.

By reason of its dynamic origin, this Basic Plane must be defined as an energy-charged portion of space, generated by the radiating energies produced by the angular intersections of the four straight lines. It is through this maximal energizing of right angles that a dynamic structure emerges and is propagated to form a Basic Plane. Irrespective of the physical characteristics of the material support which facilitate its deployment, the Basic Plane is defined as an ensemble of energetic phenomena, taking its point of origin in the peripheral lines and corners that envelop and contain it. This energetic and topological characteristic will remain the essential element which determines the spatial structure of the Basic Plane (see figure V).

The process of energizing produced by the angular meetings which form the corners of the Basic Plane develops in a continuous and diminishing centripetal movement toward the central part of this plane. This energetic structure is derived from the disposition of its vectorial components, producing a strong gestalt. The structural system of distribution of energy in the perceptual gestalts has been described by Köhler through a comparison with the diffusion of electrical energy in an orthogonal sheet:

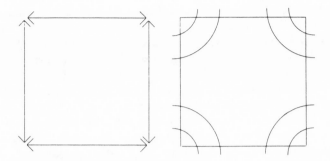

Figure V: Formation of the Basic Plane

> If one charges a thin square plate with electricity, the density of the charge will vary with the points contacted. It will be larger at the periphery than at the center, and will attain its maximum at the angles. But let us imagine that this plate constitutes a part of a relatively very large round cylinder, the charge will be equal at all points (Katz, 1955; 66).

While essentially describable as the interplays of various levels of intensity of energy, perceptual systems are animated by the different categories of actual, potential, and virtual energies offering a decreasing order of forces. The actual and potential levels are established by the contribution of both the visual elements and perceptual processes, the virtual being the unique product of perceptual activity.

Given the significant differences in the energetic densities which reverberate from the corners and formative sides toward the center, this Basic Plane cannot be conceived as an hypothetical bidimensional geometrical plane. Rather, it must be considered as a mass possessing a thickness or interior volume of variable density, forming an undulating curve. This mass is more dense and energetic in the region which borders on the corners and peripheric sides, and less dense and energetic when farther from them. In other words, this energy is proportionately less dense as it nears the central region.

The energy radiating from the corners, which is potentialized as a mass in the region of the Basic Plane where it is spread out, is at the same time both vectorial and decreasing. However, by virtue of its vectoriality, this energetic potentiality flows from the four sides and corners to coalesce in the center. It produces there a subsystem of diagonals, forming the backbone of the Basic Plane as a specific infrastructure in relation to which visual variables will acquire signifying functions in a coherent spatial linguistic system.

The energetic force emanating from opposite corners toward the center, reinforced in pairs, gives rise to potential diagonal lines or vectors which connect opposite corners. The two diagonals so formed constitute the first level of the infrastructure of the Basic Plane, in which the emergence of a structure in the form of an X reinforces the tensions at the center of the plane and serves as a major cohesive and dynamic link for elements in the visual field.

These two diagonal vectors produce two groups of two superimposed triangles whose dissimilar positions and orientations, as demonstrated by Gestaltian observations, involve different energetic characteristics for their various internal regions and for each of their sides, thus transforming the concave and convex pulsions of their surface.

For different reasons, since it depended on high/low and left/right antagonisms, Kandinsky was particularly sensitive to the dissimilar energetic qualities of the diagonals, but failed to point out their fundamental function of dividing the Basic Plane into two triangles. In order to avoid any psychologistic connotation, we will modify Kandinsky's terminology slightly and call the diagonal which connects the lower left corner to the upper right one 'harmonic' and the other diagonal, which connects the lower right corner to the upper left one, 'dysharmonic'. While differently oriented, these two diagonals, born of the same quota of energy, are endowed by the same intensity of vectorial and radiating energy (see figure VI).

By virtue of their structural properties, the four triangles formed by the diagonals of the Basic Plane each give rise to a virtual square plane which will differentiate their internal equilibrium. If one considers the two triangles formed by the diagonals, one is struck by the differences in their gestaltian stability, some resting on their linear basis and orthogonal corners, others on only one point. But they will all give rise to internal virtual squares (cf. figure VII, AEBF and BIHG in the case of the harmonic triangles), freeing from each side of these squares two other smaller triangular regions (ECB, FBD and CBI, DBH). These virtual disjunctions differentiate the Basic Plane into zones possessing very different and mobile energies, as a result of the positions/orientations of their formal gestalt. In the lower harmonic triangle (CDG), the two small triangles resting on their gestaltian base (CBI, DBH) assure this part a stronger stability than that of the two small triangles of the upper part (ECB, FBD).

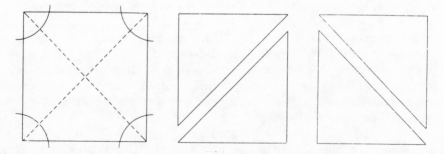

Figure VI: Harmonic and Dysharmonic Diagonals: The Four Triangles of the Basic Plane

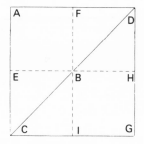

Figure VII: The Two Harmonic Triangles and Their Internal Squares

In their liaison with the square AEBF, these triangles will permit a more flexible and 'informal' spatial synthesis of vibratory interactions in the Basic Plane and, as a consequence, in the pictorial plane articulated by the artist. This is why, perhaps, so many artworks offer in this area connotations such as 'more open' and 'further away', as observed by Kandinsky, although this cumulative dynamism can eventually serve in the articulation of more complex spatialities located at closer proxemic distances.

The second structural armature of the Basic Plane, the cruciform structure, is constituted by the horizontal and vertical axes produced by the decreasing and confluent movement of the energies of the four angles toward the central regions of the plane.

These potential vertical/horizontal energies appear to us as an objective constant of the Basic Plane structure and not, as Kandinsky has claimed, as the product of the very first expression of a deliberate act of pictorial composition. Whether actualized or not by the artist, this central cruciform energy endows the Basic Plane with the capacity to sustain the diagonal thrust of the angular forces, instead of swelling or collapsing in the central region (see figure VIII).

The cruciform energy is reinforced in several ways: first of all, by the strengthening of the focal point at the meeting point of the horizontal and vertical, which had already emerged as a unique and most dynamic region

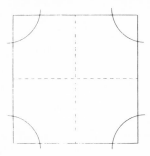

Figure VIII: Vertical/Horizontal Axes

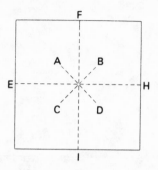

Figure IX: Cruciform Axes and Focal Point

through the crossing of the diagonals; secondly, by the interrelation established between the median points of the peripheral lines, that is, the points where the linear tensions diverge in two opposing directions. From the four median points so linked (see figure IX, points F, H, I, E) emerge potential energetic connections, confirming the tensions and directions of the cruciform axes.

This cruciform axis structures, moreover, the central region of the Basic Plane by way of two distinct energetic phenomena which combine to reinforce the tensions of the focal region. Firstly, the central meeting of the axes produces four right angles (figure X, angles EAF, FBH, ECI, and IDH) which oppose and sustain the pressures of the peripheral angles. Secondly, when the extreme points of the axes situated midway from the peripheral sides (E, F, I, and H) are linked by potentialized straight lines, they give rise to another energetic plane, that of the 'lozenge'.

This lozenge is reinforced by the energies flowing from both the peripheral right angles and the focal right angles. This secondary lozenge plane is extremely stable since its propensity to circularity is held in check by the primordial energy of the four corners. It will be one of the most efficacious instruments for the distribution of angular and cruciform energies in the whole mass of the Basic Plane. It engenders, moreover, a series of triangles, more active and denser near the periphery and potentialized

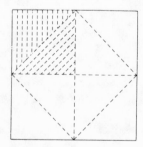

Figure X: Lozenge of the Cruciform

near the center, which are an internal source of energetic diversification of the mass.

The ensemble of energetic forces emanating from the periphery, both from the angles and the antagonistic linear vectors, constitutes the Basic Plane through the form of a mass animated by variable energetic densities in each of its points. The notion of mass refers topologically to a quantity capable of being organized in agglomerations of diverse densities, endowed with indefinite forms and producing variable qualitative effects.

Furthermore, the very dense tissue of this mass is activated by the redoublings, from one point to another, and in a continuous way, of the energy of the peripheral line tensions, establishing the completely generalized infrastructure of a grid, which one will perceive as more or less dense across the entire plane. In the same way, the regular crossing of these horizontals and verticals, ultimately derived from the formative sides and carried out over the entire plane, generates to the limit a point-like energetic potential of denser points which radiate across their immediate surroundings (see figure XI). In a certain sense, it can be argued that any place on which vision is focused on the surface of the plane is the meeting place of a vertical/horizontal energy, thus intensifying the dynamic effect of any perceptual centration.

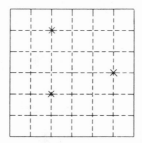

Figure XI: Energetic Checkerboard Grid of the Basic Plane

4.5. Other Formats of the Basic Plane

The potential passage of peripheral energies from the corners and formative lines will vary considerably according to the establishment of different proportions between the peripheral vectors. In other words, the transformation of the format of the plane from the square or other gestaltian primary forms to the most idiosyncratic ones will produce less stable or neutral equilibrated types of Basic Plane.

In increasing the length of two of the parallel sides in relation to the other two, the rectangle will stress, to a greater degree than the square, the potentialized force of the vertical or horizontal axis, whichever the case, thus creating the instability of a circular movement of the longer axis on the

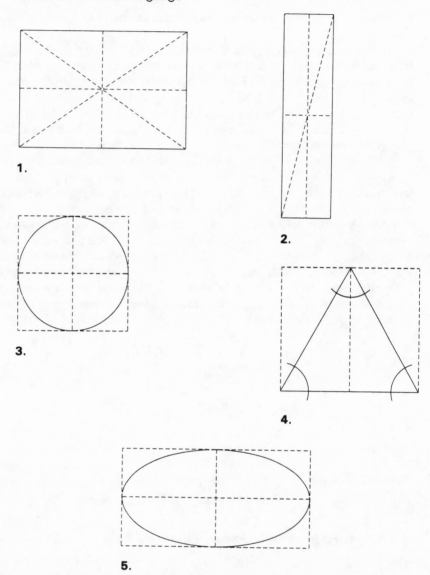

Figure XII: Various Formats of the Basic Plane

other. While unbalancing the cruciform stability of the square, the rectangle will render more operative the vibrating forces of the diagonals which connect the opposite corners (figure XII, No. 1).

A striking example, in this regard, would be the very high and narrow rectangles which Barnett Newman produced in the early 1950s which effect a radical reduction of the concept of the Basic Plane, whereas this plane will "almost" identify itself with its peripheral energy. In this radical exclusion of the horizontal potentiality, the vacillation of the vertical axis, occupying in its reverberation all of the Basic Plane, is strengthened by its endless transformations into one or the other diagonal (figure XII, No. 2).

The Basic Plane of the circular format, the circle, seems in contrast the greatest antithesis to the fundamental Basic Plane in that it virtualizes all the energy of the peripheral corners and sides, while actualizing the focal energy very strongly. The four median points of the sides, where the diameters of the circle meet at a right angle, serve forcefully as parameters, imposing the cruciform energy which is not circumscribed and equilibrated by the antagonistic movements of the peripheral lines. This prominence of the cruciform structure and of the focal meeting point, whose energies will be diffused in a uniform, steadily diminishing way toward segments of the peripheral curves, produces in the circle a strong convexity of the Basic Plane. The elongation of the diameter which makes a circle an oval or an ellipse regenerates a more sustained interrelation with the energy of the horizontal or vertical sides of the subjacent rectangle (figure XII, Nos. 3–5).

Any triangular format is necessarily based on the infrastructure of the rectangle from which it virtualizes two angles and three sides, hence accentuating the actualization of the tensions of the base line in relation to its acute angles (figure XII, No. 4). As mentioned earlier, actual, potential, and virtual energies share a maximum function in the articulation of both the basic and the pictorial planes, but this level of energy is much weaker and more diffused when acting outside of the Basic Plane where it is confronted with the less organized, nonlinguistic forces of the natural environment.

The majority of irregular formats, or "shaped canvases" as they have been called, offer diverse variants which, as Kandinsky remarked, "must be classified under one basic form and, therefore, represent more complicated cases of the given basic form" (1976; 40). The virtualization realized by a shaped canvas of angular or peripheral vectors always corresponds to a stronger actualization of central, focal, or cruciform energies which are no longer subject to energetic countertensions from the periphery.

Beyond the shaped canvas or irregular format, contemporary pictorial thought has dealt with other aspects of format dynamisms which question certain properties of the Basic Plane. A first hypothesis of production, found in Pollock and later in Morris Louis and others, stated that the dimension and the final proportions of the Basic Plane would only be determined once the pictorial plane is produced. A second hypothesis, particularly defended by the support-surface movement in France, claimed that, if one refrains from using a stretched canvas in the production and presentation of the work, the representation would cease to be conditioned by the dynamics of the Basic Plane. In both cases, one could thus be "liberated" from the conditioning exercised by the format and its implications of context, limits, or predetermined energetic constraint.

In fact, Pollock's decision to delay to a later stage the determination of proportions and dimensions which will permit the pictorial plane to function with maximal intensity and unity only reaffirms the functional role of the Basic Plane in the syntactic structure of the work. On one hand, even when disposed/deposed and worked on the ground, the unrolled canvas, whether or not cut, already offers, by the orientation of its surface in height or in width, by its dimensions or its proportions, a Basic Plane endowed with given functional characteristics. The definitive adjustment of the pictorial plane on a stretcher, of which one will carefully vary the dimensions by adding or taking out a few centimeters in height or width, has the aim of making more efficient, of strengthening and adjusting the type of insertion and interaction of the pictorial plane in relation to the energies of the Basic Plane. But the pictorial production itself, on an apparently less determined support, remains essentially linked to the structural axes of the Basic Plane, that is, the horizontal, the vertical and the diagonals, as well as to the energies of the sides. Even if they are not presented and perceived with the maximum possible intensity, these energies of the Basic Plane cannot be ignored by the artist in the course of production, since they represent the fundamental matrix in which pictorial traits are inscribed. The canvas on the ground, even when unstretched, retains the energy of the Basic Plane in relation to which the artist measures the dynamism of his pictorial trajectories. This is the profound meaning of Pollock's dance, around his canvas lying on the ground, as documented by a renowned series of photographs by H. Namuth (1978).

However, when the artist refuses altogether to stretch his canvas, even in the final phase of production, and to actualize to the maximum the energies of peripheral vectors and of their angular conjunction, he removes a part of this actual/potential energy from the pictorial system. Only one part is actualized when the canvas is not entirely cut out in an irregular format. Sometimes, this canvas, hanging on the wall in a more or less loose or slack fashion, retains in the upper regions the energy of clear angularities which then dwindles in the lower regions along more or less pronounced waves. Through this actual volumetric production, the work tends to incorporate the mixed structures of bas-relief, borrowing from the pictorial and the sculptural. As a slightly irregular frontal format, it remains no less tributary, like the shaped canvas, to the 'good form' of the closest approximation of a Basic Plane. Yet, through certain of its regions, this work simultaneously calls for a sculptural dialectic in a context more linked to the production of external than of inner volumes. In addition, when these polychromatic canvases are hung far from the wall, in the 'real' space with which they enter into interaction, they are inscribed, all the more, in the syntactic organization of sculpture. We will return to this point presently.

Any element of the pictorial plane actualized outside of the 'force-field' defined by the strong gestalt of the Basic Plane cannot satisfy a dialectic as intense as that of the pictorial field's tensions and countertensions, because it would be grappling with unorganized, nonlinguistic energies of the spaces of reality. More often, occasional extrapolations from the main format summon the perceptual projection of a second, somewhat larger virtual Basic Plane, encompassing the first in a field of more subdued energy.

4.6. The Pictorial Plane and the Effect of Periphery

Beyond the dynamic structure which constitutes it, the Basic Plane undergoes at its physical and plastic boundaries an ensemble of interactions with the field of forces surrounding it. In a proxemic manner, this field of surrounding forces—even if it sometimes takes the angular form of corners—is essentially constituted by a level plane, a wall, or a portion of a wall on which a work is affixed or hung. Before any inscription of visual variables, but even more so when the work is begun, the pictorial support (canvas, masonite etc.) undergoes a particular effect in its interaction with the surrounding wall, which we will call the "effect of periphery." It consists, first of all, for the still-unpainted canvas or monochrome canvas, of a tonal contrast. This is established through the action of a more luminous or darker environment which illuminates or darkens, by contrast, the peripheral layer of the Basic Plane. These tonal contrasts will either be accentuated or not by the specific action of textures offered by the surrounding wall in relation to those of the pictorial support, as well as by the closest position of the pictorial plane to the lighting source, since it is situated in front of the wall on which it is hung.

Added to this effect of periphery, there is a second specific factor modifying visual variables placed on the pictorial support and rising from perceptual interpretation. We allude to the particular contrast between the relative homogeneity of the surrounding wall and the heterogeneity of the plastic components or, again, between the least energized state of the wall and the most energized state of the pictorial field.

The confrontation of the system of the pictorial plane with the system of the wall is strongly marked in the area of transition between the peripheral layers of the basic or pictorial planes and the surrounding wall, producing a maximum or a minimum of antagonisms which will be reverberated perceptually as a constituent of the pictorial plane.

A minimum of antagonisms results from smaller differences between the plastic components of the wall and those of the pictorial plane, for example, a white peripheral layer, of a texture similar to that of a whitish wall. A maximum of contrast can be obtained by the use of large and ornamented frames, separating the fictional linguistic system from its factual surroundings. But this new intermediary zone of the frame will have a strong interaction with the chromatic, formal, and vectorial components of the representation.

More specific effects of separation between the pictorial plane and the surrounding surfaces result from the pictorial decision to activate the

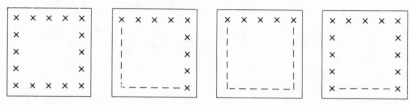

Figure XIII: Pictorial Effects of Periphery

energies on the peripheral layers of the Basic Plane, on one, two, or all the sides of the plane (figure XIII).

This peripheral effect is strongest when all sides are markedly differentiated from a uniform wall. This has led some artists, such as Seurat and Mondrian, to extend their painting to the very frame, and other artists to substitute for the framing device the chromatization of that part of the canvas covering the side thickness of the stretcher. This liaison of the pictorial field to the environment outside of the dialectic of the Basic Plane tends to give a sculptural or architectural/environmental dimension to the physical support of the work.

When the wall is itself invested with plastic energies, such as textures, chromatic contrasts, and so on, the energy within the pictorial plane will become less perceptible or will be interpreted in a sort of indefinite interaction with the stimuli offered by surrounding walls, more as a sensorial than a linguistic experience.

At its limit, this generalized integration of the pictorial plane in the colored reality would relieve it of all linguistic function to make of it only an object, a thing, in external reality. Its apprehension would resemble that of a closed book, resting somewhere on a table, still existing, but at another level than that of a linguistic proposition.

To summarize, the energy of the peripheral layers of the visual representation is influenced by: (1) the vectorial infrastructure of the Basic Plane; (2) the effects of the visual variables produced by the pictorial activity; (3) the various simultaneous contrasts of color and tonality, of textures and vectorialities, produced by the interaction between the pictorial plane and the surrounding walls.

The effect of periphery will be particularly noticed in a monochrome work, that is, a pictorial work which presents one single color in an homogeneous and smooth texture, which excludes any potentiality of plastic structuration. The peripheral layers of a totally red work, for example, appearing on a surrounding field, be it white, grey or another color, would immediately be subjected to: (a) the effect of tonal contrast and (b) the effect of simultaneous and successive chromatic contrasts which will lighten, darken, or somehow tint this peripheral layer in relation to more central layers which constitute the overall work. The specific energies of the central regions are relatively protected from interferences from the surrounding wall. But still the central region will differentiate itself from intermediary layers serving as a connection between the center and the periphery by a more moderate activation or vibratory modulation. Thus, when perception recognizes the transformation of visual variables in the periphery and the greatest density of the region stabilized by the cruciform energy, the intermediary layers will remain the place of the greatest mobility; this will apply in relation to both the infrastructure of the Basic Plane and to the general structure of envelopment which characterizes this pictorial plane.

Most often, however, such monochromes are not presented under the aspect of the above-mentioned condition of an ideally smooth and homogeneous texture, but are characterized by the production of a pigmentation which offers, even finely, effects of texture. Their specific tonal and chromatic vectorialities will become determinants for the organization of the work. Despite its peremptory affirmation of a color, the monochrome organizes itself not only through its chromatic aftereffects, but also through the infrastructure of its format and its dimension in relation to the surrounding wall and its textures.

4.7. Energizing of the Pictorial Plane

The syntactic organization of visual language is thus defined as a network of various intensities resulting from the interaction of the energies of the Basic Plane and those of the visual variables of the pictorial plane. As accrued intensities are determining factors in the positioning of regions more or less distant in depth, the grammar of visual language is to be understood as covering the rules of production of specific spatializing effects.

The energies carried by visual variables operative in the production of the pictorial plane are multiplied when they are anchored in the reservoir of the actual, potential, or virtual energies of the infrastructure of the Basic Plane.

This reaffirmation of the infrastructure of the Basic Plane is carried out according to the dictates of diverse modalities that are more or less efficacious and important. They are called:

—*Accentuation:* when the regions of the pictorial plane are inscribed precisely and in a large expanse, on a component element of the infrastructure of the Basic Plane.

—*Punctuation:* when a region of the pictorial plane is inscribed in a smaller expanse on an element of the Basic Plane.

—*Redoubling:* when a region of the pictorial plane repeats, in a large expanse but in a shifting position, an element of the infrastructure of the Basic Plane.

—*Reiteration:* when a region of the pictorial plane repeats, in a smaller expanse and in a shifting position, an element of the infrastructure of the Basic Plane.

—*Punctuation of Corners:* the formative corners are punctuated when a neighboring region reiterates one of its formative sides or when there is a formation of a virtual triangle through the orientation of a neighboring element in the pictorial plane.

—*Virtual Division:* when the vertical and horizontal axes of the Basic Plane are virtually inferred from several puntuations of the pictorial plane.

—*Virtual Reiteration:* when an element of the infrastructure of the Basic Plane is inferred from a position or a connection between shifting regions of the pictorial plane.

4.8. Specificity of Various Visual Linguistic Fields

The various types of visual language (painting, photography, drawing, video, sculpture, architecture, and so on) do not differ in the utilization of the visual variables which are in fact common to all. They are rather differentiated in their syntactic and semantic structures by analytical hypotheses which provide them with particular infrastructures. These are: the *Basic Plane* in the case of painting, photography, or other visual representations carried by a so-called two-dimensional support, the *Virtual Cube* in the case of volumetric sculptures, and the *Environmental Cube* in the case of architectural installations.

As seen above, the proposition of Kandinsky concerning the Basic Plane is as fundamental to the development of visual semiotics as Troubetskoy's phonology, establishing the differences between sounds in general and phonetic sounds, was for verbal linguistics. It is in effect only through the structure of a Basic Plane that the visual variables contributing to various forms of visual representations cease being pure material data and acquire linguistic functions.

It is important in each case to distinguish sharply between the Basic Planes of painting, sculpture, and architecture and their pictorial, sculptural or architectural planes, the latter referring to the level of the effective material production of a work in these fields.

As an energetic infrastructure antecedent to any actual production of the visual discourse, the Basic Plane presents a potential spatial distribution of energies allowing visual variables, which are physical quantities/qualities belonging to any visible reality, to be inserted in a context where they can contribute to the elaboration of a "fictional" linguistic representation of a variety of organic spaces: visual, tactile, postural, kinesthetic, thermal, and so on.

By contrast, the pictorial or sculptural planes are terms used to designate the level of energetic material organizing various visual variables according to topological and gestaltian rules, but in interaction with the structure of the Basic Plane.

In painting, sculpture, or architecture, the Basic Plane or Virtual Cubes are derived from the dynamic structure of their gestalt, as manifested by their support or format, or by the closest approximation to a unifying gestaltian figure.

Chapter Five

Effects of Distance and Perspectives

One has to define as categories of the syntax of visual language, pictorial or sculptural, the various modalities of representation used and developed in different cultures and subsumed under the rubric of *perspectives*. They belong to the grammatical organization, as they appear as constant syntagmatic junctions of coloremes, carrying each particular symbolic meaning.

Like every notion involved in the dialectic of perception, perspective depends upon a subjective and an objective dimension. Subjectively, this term designates the presence of a point of view, a 'sighting', an aiming, a form of relation with a field of reality resulting from a unique position. In the visual field, it refers specifically to the *distance* taken by the perceiver in relation to his object (Panofsky, 1975; 37).

Objectively, the systems of perspective offer precoded programs of selection of the visual variables and of their organization into specific spatial interrelations corresponding to a more or less exclusive spatial, sensory, and conceptual hypothesis.

The perspectives are supersyntagms inasmuch as they imply a necessary regrouping of a certain number and type of coloremes, observable as concrete marks or distinctive traits, produced according to fixed and relatively precise organizational schemas. Historically, any transgression of these perspectivist codes has been experienced, given the expressive requirements of an epoch, as a "blunder," a "fault," or an "inventive deviation" when the need is sufficiently strong and conscious to transform the previously dominant perspectivist structures. They can also be seen as 'modal propositions' in that they offer a concrete inscription of the subject *qua* subject in its various positions in relation to the visual field.

In one of his most significant works, Erwin Panofsky has established how the diverse perspectives used in Egypt, Greece, Rome, and during the Renaissance constitute in themselves symbolic forms by which common spatial structures are expressed in diverse collectivities.

Even though he drew on the "strong and successful terminology of Ernst Cassirer" to extend the notion of symbolic form to the history of art, Panofsky modified its definition in a very significant way.

He wrote that perspective can be designated "as one of these symbolic forms" owing to which "a signifying content of an intelligible order is ascribed to a concrete sign of a sensible order for clear self-identification" (1975; 78). From a semiotic point of view, one can wonder at the exact meaning of the expression "signifying content," suggesting a possible identification of the notions of "signifiers" and "signified."

Confronted with this notion, the iconology of Panofsky undertook a similarly parallel development, first studying the concrete signs of the objective organizations and then the immanent meaning or content, which he assimilated to Riegl's "Kunstwollen," or impulse/drive to produce forms (Riegl, 1978). He further proceeded to interpret the latter as a "Weltanschauung" (or vision of the world) only intelligible by recourse to the study of the most important verbal texts in a given period (1975; 221).

This may appear quite different from the intuition of Cassirer who suggested a more "immanent" meaning in symbolic forms, one that has to be grasped in a somewhat more phenomenological experience of the concrete symbolic signs: "But the symbolic signs that we encounter in language, myth and art, 'are not' at first to acquire next, beyond this being, a determined signification: all their being, by contrast, derives from the signification" (Cassirer, 1955; 48).

Indeed, Panofsky comments too briefly on the immanent meaning of linear perspective in the Renaissance, which Spengler had already identified as the emergence of an intuition of the infinite within the new Faustian sensibility. He comments even less on the contrasting perspectives of Northern European countries that he describes as presenting: "the mass of a painting as a homogenous material at the interior of which luminous space is experienced with almost as much density and 'materiality' as the bodies which are distributed there" (1975; 178). However, confronted with Wölfflin's formalism, he always reaffirmed his hypotheses concerning the symbolic or meaningful character of formal systems of representations and the need for art history to distinguish and study their particular characteristics:

> That an artist chooses the linear mode of representation instead of the pictorial one signifies that he limits himself, often under the pressure of the all-

powerful epoch of which he may not have conscience, to certain possibilities of representation; that he draws his lines in such or such a way means that he chooses, amidst their always infinite diversity, one alone of these possibilities and realizes it . . . One could then rightfully consider the different elements of this general form as a system of particular categories. And here we must decide in favor of Wölfflin, when he says that the first task of art history is the discovery and development of these categories. (1975; 195)

It is only when general structures are known, not only of a style, but of a perspectival system, at any given moment in history, that one can appreciate the way in which individual sensibilities adjust, modify, or deviate from a model offered by this supersign, and whether or not they contribute to its transformation. Through the intermediary of a code or a group of rules for the selection and arrangement of plastic elements, these hypotheses of spatial organization translate multiple conceptions of reality, experimented within different value-systems.

5.1. Perspectives of Perception of the Natural World

Developments in the cognitive sciences in the later part of this century make possible for visual semiotics the tasks defined by both Wölfflin and Panofsky, and as yet unfulfilled. In particular, they permit us to understand the so-called artistic systems of perspectives as representational constructs based partially upon the perspectives of the perception of the natural world.

A basic postulate in the study of systems of perspectives is the observation that each human being occupies a particular point in space-time and that, by virtue of this unique and different physical and psychological position, one necessarily perceives, *stricto sensu*, a different aspect of reality from that which is perceived by one's neighbor. In effect, the activity of perceiving reality is realized only through a perceiver's occupying a particular position, permitting him to establish an immediate and unique relation with reality. It is only through a denial of the perceptual process on the abstract plane of concepts that several individuals can claim to see the same thing, when they look at the same object. An existential position can yield only a particular point of view in space-time, revealing only certain aspects of things and leaving others concealed.

A second postulate is that perception of reality is successive, made up of the accumulation of various sensorial centrations on different aspects of phenomena. The egocentric and partial character of all perceptual centrations obliges the human being to adopt the largest possible number of points of view of objects, (that is to multiply centrations from different positions in a more or less gradual temporal unfolding) if access to the most adequate informational data on specific objects or environments is desired. The necessity of such an active and plural interrelating with reality does not, however, exclude some similarities between the *mechanisms* of perception, adopted by individuals relative to various sensorial fields.

As far as apprehension of natural objects in space is concerned, important factors influencing the perceptual constructs can be related to the observer's position and visual apparatus as well as to specific characteristics of the object apprehended. The psychologist James J. Gibson (1950) has called the constant regrouping of typical information according to different categories of factors "perspectives" of natural perception. These thirteen varieties of perspectives have been summarized by E. T. Hall (1966; 191) and classified into four different principal classes, as follows: 1) The perspectives of *position* (by texture, dimension, linearity); 2) *Parallax* perspectives (by binocularity and movement); 3) Positions *independent* of position and movement of the observer (aerial or atmospheric), shuffled, relative location in height, linear space by textural change, modification of double images or acceleration of an object, transition between light and shadow; and 4) Perspectives produced by *completion* or not of contour. Although Gibson has devoted extensive research to the perception of the world through vision, each of the senses could be described as establishing different points of views/perspectives on reality. These would lead to the construction of various sensorial organic space representations.

The term 'perspective', which we would like to use more in relation to concrete modes of representation, refers in Gibson's context to particular aspects of perceptual determinisms. It is nonetheless particularly efficacious for expressing the way that ambient reality appears extremely different according to how particular modes of relating to the world are used and valued.

These perspectivist modes of perception produce particular channels which assemble the elements of reality in a more or less constant way. At more local levels, the continuity or prevalence of certain perceptual attitudes, within these perspectives, also produce regular percepts and modes of interrelation with limited features abstracted from reality. No one of these "images" produced by only one of these perspectives can be considered as equivalent to reality. From different points of view or perspectives, other aspects of reality can also be regrouped in regular and significant ways, sometimes conflicting with the previous, or with perspectives that have been deemed more important in different cultures.

The multiplicity of organized points of view or perspectives developed by the perceiver to provide different information about reality obliges him/her not only to proceed to accommodations with a plural visual field in constant transformation but also to attempt to conceive a possible unification of these heterogeneous groups. According to Piaget, the coordination of perspectives "raises three sorts of conflicts, that can be surmounted only by dialectical syntheses" (1980; 189).

The first conflict results from the duality between the identity of the object, presumably existent and permanent, and "the multiplicity of its observable forms in function of changing points of view."

The second conflict corresponds to the need to conciliate our points of view with those of others. It invokes: " . . . the necessary passage from the absolute to the relative, no perspective being privileged and each remaining relative to the position of the observer" (Piaget, 1980).

The third conflict arises from the need to complement actual perceptions by anticipations, that is, by perspectives that will be required to represent changing phenomena. This would mean the production of a synthesis between the differentiations and their integration "into a grouping assuring the existence of an all new invariance; this will be of a transformational nature and not any more static as was the initial identity of the object conceived as having to keep an apparently constant form" (Piaget, 1980; 190).

This synthesis or integration of distinct sensorial/perceptual points of view into a new "transformational" invariance is achieved in the elaboration of more complex spaces which permit the unification of the diverse organic spaces. By virtue of its immediately spatializing nature, visual language is the privileged linguistic tool through which the organism is able to experiment and produce "spatial dialectical syntheses" that establish relations not only between the fragments of actual emotional and conceptual experience, but also between these and fragments that are retained, consciously or unconsciously, from past conceptual, sensorial, or imaginary experience.

However, whatever the spatial model used for representing groups of elements experimented with by perception, the most fundamental point to emphasize is that the spatializing model of semiotic representation, that is a representation constructed with material components, cannot be the same as that of perception or conceptualization. These are formed by totally different constituting elements, reunited in a context heterogeneous to that of actual experience. Just as words *are not* the things they represent, so visual representations, spatial models, diverse perspectives *are not* of the same order, and do not possess the same existential status as elements which constitute reality. If certain acquired codes of perception allow us to recognize certain images as resembling real external objects, it does not render the space of representation that constructs the visual representation the same as that of reality and any more "real." This fruitless opposition, in this respect, between pictorial movements, from one generation to another, results from shifts in the definition of what is the essence of reality: static substance, movement, hidden structures, light, and so on. It should have terminated from the moment, as Lessing tells it, when the ancient author Lucien discovered that he did not know how to decode a painting of Zeuxis, which was of so "natural" a complexion that it could deceive the birds. Not only did the animals seem better tuned to the concept of the real, but they were better semioticians than the writer who admitted his incapacity to distinguish whether a given figure was placed behind or over another (Panofsky, 1975; 86).

Even if certain natural perspectives used in perception maintain an influence in the construction of spaces of representation, these two sorts of spaces cannot be assimilated one to the other. The first offers a dynamic and substantial discontinuity, whereas the second attempts a symbolic function in terms of a continuity requiring a basic homogeneity in its constituents. Panofsky well understood this:

> In the space of perception, the concept of homogeneity cannot be applied as it is in representation, where at each point of space, it is believed possible to effect similar constructions in all places and in all directions. In the space of immediate perception, this postulate can never be satisfied. We do not find in this space any homogeneity of places and directions; each place has its own modality and value. The visual space and tactile space, agree on one point: at the inverse of metric space of Euclidean geometry, they are 'anisotropic' and 'unhomogenous'. In these two physiological spaces, the three principal directions: before and behind, top and bottom, right and left, are not equivalent. (42–43)

And following Cassirer, he underlined the fundamental difference of value between "solid bodies" and the intermediate expansions of the void between them in a tactile field, which is not in fact observable in a pictorial work, since it is everywhere occupied by visual variables.

It is necessary, furthermore, to remember the great difference that exists between the act of perceiving an object in external reality and the perception of an artwork. The pictorial work, or the sculptural work which we will discuss further on, is not made up of objects possessing the structure of external objects, but rather by paradoxical objects that are determined by their linguistic function as specified in the representational visual field.

Visual works are indeed real objects, whether or not suspended on a wall or installed on a pedestal, and subjected in this regard to the normal perspectival constraints in the so-called natural space. But at the same time, instead of being constituted simply by relatively planar marks affixed to planar supports, these works present the effects of depth and distance, as used in a fictional space different from that of natural space. This has been demonstrated by experiments conducted by R. L. Gregory. "Among other things, (these experiments) tell us that seeing pictures is very different from seeing normal objects. This means that pictures are *not* typical objects for the eye, and must be treated as a very special case" (Gregory, 1980; 50).

5.2. Perspectives of Semiotic Representations

If the perceiver must transform the usual mechanisms of visual perception, which are regulated by survival and functionalism, in order to be able to enter into a relationship with the visual linguistic field that constitutes a work, he finds there another order of major difficulties. Not only is this work not a simple object of reality, but it is also a symbolic place where another human being organizes a representation of his own experience of reality, of his own perspectives and points of view. The perceiver is called upon to confront or compare, *volens nolens*, his own perceptual mechanisms and perspectives with those that are used by the producer of the work in his apprehension of the world. The perceiver can only infer these as they are represented in the work by the instrumentation of certain visual variables.

Models of various sensorial perceptions of reality, or models of internal perceptual representations, always interrelated with sensori-motor, emotional, and conceptual elements, must not be confused with the modeling potentialities of the material, visual language. At the same time, it would be hazardous to identify the perceptual and referential constructs of experience and language produced by one individual with the positions, points of view, and perspectives of another individual. All visual works propose, therefore, a simultaneity of sensorial perspectives, more or less integrated or for that matter, integrable: the natural perspectives of the producer, which are inscribed more or less adequately in the work, and those of the perceiver, issuing from his own possibilities and habits of sensorial spatialization, acting on the actual stimuli of the work in a temporal succession of points of view taken on that work.

This confrontation of the points of view and of the organizational systems of the perceiver and the producer in the visual field can only multiply and intensify the conflicts and heterogeneities that the perceiver had already discovered within himself, as referred to earlier. These have now to be confronted with those of another human being. Without recourse to Freud or Lacan, a simple psychological hypothesis about the emotional development of the human being and the intensity of his 'mechanisms of defense' would explain certain difficulties of the perceiving public in placing themselves in a fruitful relation with works which upset their own acquired schemas of reality. This hypothesis would also explain how the occident was able for a great length of time, to persevere in the belief that there was only one single true visual perspective on the world, namely its own, and that all others were inferior, underdeveloped or simply incapable of producing works of art.

Indeed, the observation of forms of visual representation produced by diverse groups or human societies obliges us to recognize more than two dozen of systems of perspectives, favored at one time or another. These representations are accessible through museums, collections, and general information, to any producer of the visual artwork today. They offer an extremely large number of modalities of spatial structures that may respond to new needs of thought and communication. This richness in grammatical resources in visual language is to be contrasted with the rigidity of natural verbal living languages, reluctant to borrow from or to revive grammatical categories used by dead or foreign languages or to create new ones.

One cannot insist enough upon the multiple meanings of the term 'perspective', in view of a certain usage which would still pretend that it may only refer to the system of artificial perspective that the Renaissance, following Brunelleschi and Alberti, opposed to medieval "natural" perspective. Hubert Damisch has pointed out how the new perspective of the Quattrocento appeared revolutionary, indeed "as a rupture with the very idea of tradition" (1979; 113). It took a long time before this system of representation was accepted by the popular sensibility, which was more familiar with the structures of representation of natural perspective inherited from the Middle Ages and with those of northern societies.

The artificial and calculated character of this linear perspective was embarrassingly obvious. It required from the perceiver a single and motionless position, in a prescribed area in relation to the visual field; it demanded a viewing with one eye closed and held immobile, and so on. In fact, it tried to identify spatially the perceiver with the producer of the image. One may recall from Damisch analysis the curious process of production of the perspectivist apparatus by Brunelleschi, with his arbitrary recourse to a mirror in order to produce figures on the upper part of the work. This subterfuge, he wrote, "made perspective appear as a structure of exclusion, in which coherence was based on a series of refusals" (Damisch, 1979; 171).

One has stressed less often the exclusion that it placed on all visual representations involved in a medium or near distance, because of its incapacity to resolve the lateral distortions that its mode of representation imposed. As much as his contemporaries, Leonardo da Vinci recognized that the works representing objects at a short distance had a particularly strong power of illusion. But the painter had to renounce this point of view because it could not be rendered by linear perspective:

> If you want to represent a thing nearby which produces the same effect as natural objects, then it is impossible that your perspective not have a false air . . . Otherwise, do not undertake to represent a thing without the distance that you adopt being at least twenty times greater than the largest height or width of the object that you must represent; then your work will content every spectator in whatever place he finds himself. (Panofsky, 1975; 46–47)

Wherever he finds himself, except close to the object! Elsewhere, da Vinci (who will be followed by Lomazzo), established that the distance where objects are placed in a field of representation must correspond to the largest dimension of the artwork multiplied by a factor of three (Panofsky, 1975; 169).

This is still recognized as an important constraint in visual representations today: "One assumes, by convention, at least since Leonardo da Vinci, that occidental artists create a painting with a perspective appropriate to a visual distance ten times greater than the size of major depicted objects" (Hagen, 1984; 33).

This artificial perspective developed by artists—and, as Damisch noted, more so by architects than by painters—is applicable more to the constructed or built object, or even better "to the space of the town such as it is defined by the buildings which enclose and delimit it" (1979; 22, 124), than to the pictorial space.

This system describes "the effects engendered by distance, not only by relation to the object, but in relation to the plane of projection" (Damisch, 1979; 130). This notion of plane, as mentioned earlier, was a substitute interpretation of the Basic Plane and reveals itself here as fundamental, in the geometrical construction of volumes on a flat surface. But the adjunction required of points of distance, of several vanishing points along the horizon line, of calculations of foreshortening scales, as well as the introduction of rules pertaining to the atmospheric perspective, the exploration of different points of view, and the juxtaposition of double horizon lines explain the pluralistic character of perspectives in use between the 14th and 16th centuries, as demonstrated by the studies of P. Francastel (1965). Other systems of perspectives were elaborated from the baroque 17th century up to our time. These have not been duly studied and described, since they were seen as superficial and accidental deviations from the one "true" system of perspective that appeared at the Renaissance.

For our part, we will define perspectives as those organized groups of sensory marks placed on the Basic Plane, offering parameters for the suggestion of distance and depth in visual representations. These parameters depend as much on the characteristics of visual variables as on their modes of junction.

In other words, the perspectives are constructed, on the foundation of perceptual data, as different systems of spatialization, so as to interrelate a multiplicity of coextensive elements in a simultaneous context, according to certain needs of feeling and understanding. However, even in those works offering a dominant perspective, one will often find another or several other perspectivist systems, translating diverse sensorial experiences, seeking unification through a more abstract spatial model. This complexity will be perceived as harmonious and well integrated in certain instances, and as chaotic and discordant in others.

Other types of contradiction appear as well in some mimetic perspectives that claim to account for certain codes of perception of natural objects. The perceiver is engaged in choosing a hypothesis of recognition of objects able to correspond to certain visual stimuli, so that the work can be interpreted in terms of a similarity of objects as seen in external reality. He must therefore necessarily appeal to visual memory in order to identify, starting from several parameters, certain agglomerates as corresponding to real objects hypothetically posed in a particular situation. Visual memory, however, as Richard L. Gregory has pointed out (1980; 86–87), furnishes only fragments of rough objects or larger aggregates of these, with no information about their context, namely the particular distances between these objects and others, or their orientation, their movement, or even their objective dimension. These spatial characteristics can only be constructed through pictorial representation itself. Even visual mental images must accommodate or adapt to the points of view adopted by the producers. If it is true that the first human made visual representations had as their function the reproduction of mental visual images rather than the production of images resembling perceived reality, one will recognize with R. L. Gregory that it "is not so very surprising that representation of distance and orientations occurred late in art history" (1980; 120).

What is important to remember is that the perception of distance in three dimensions has to be made from the sensorial data offered by a particular pictorial work, and not from the recollection of mental visual images as such. As for isolated visual variables, certain references can be established between the color, texture, and dimensions offered by certain pictorial stimuli and the recollection that is associated with them in the perceptual souvenirs of objects in reality, where they were inserted into the widest possible variety of contexts.

The relativistic character of the notion of perspective has been known in the theory of art for several centuries. It reached a culminating point, for example, in the proposition of Charles Blanc who opposed a utopian 'geometrical' image to that of natural perspective: "The geometrical is the image of an object seen by an eye as large as itself, in its real dimension: all that is larger than our eye is seen in perspective, that is, in its apparent dimension" (1880; 513).

In this regard, the perceived coloreme in a foveal angle, equivalent to the dimension of the source of vision, would be the most truthful object of perception, other objects being subject to distortions of perspective. We believe it is more heuristic to recognize in the "geometrical" of Blanc that which depends on parameters of topological geometry constituting a type of perspective or specific point of view structuring the object, whereas other sorts of perspective will refer to different geometries: Euclidean, projective, and so on.

Reapplying its primary meaning to the term 'perspective', as handed down from the ancient Greeks, namely, "the science of the transmission of light rays" from a reflecting surface up to the organ of sight, we would define perspective as any unified system, implicitly coded, that determines the choice and use of visual variables in precise interrelations, with a view to producing different types of "distance effects" (Klein, 1970; 237).

While retaining the terms 'points of view', 'positions', 'sightings' and 'aimings' to describe the physical and mental characteristics of the producer of the visual representations, we apply the term 'perspectives' to those representations of points of view that are realized materially by visual variables in visual texts.

In the context of this interpretation, perspectives are organized forms, codifying not the position required of a given spectator, but the position chosen by the producer in relation to the object of his representation. It is by no means necessary that the spectator physically occupy the position of the producer which he has to infer from the syntax of the text. Indeed this exigency would seem a virtual impossibility—either on the theoretical or physical plane. This postulate of the Renaissance perspective attempts to reduce or negate the plurality of points of view in human experience and to construct a hypothetical universal subject.

What the work presents to the spectator's view is an ensemble of relations established by the producer between the different elements that he himself has chosen as means of representation and by relation to which elements he situates himself. Consequently, a duality always exists between the position of the spectator of a work and the position occupied by the producer, reflecting their existential statuses. This maintains a psychological distance between the two and requires a specific strategy, more or less successfully accomplished on the part of the spectator, in order to imagine himself experiencing the perceptual position of another subjectivity. This psychological distance is masked only when, in a frontal or oblique trompe-l'oeil, as in the case of a vertical panel the height of a person or of a distant perspective taken on a ceiling, the producer stipulates that the perceiver imitate his own fixed position, by way of which he intends to prolong the natural perspective of perception. But as Ernst Gombrich has explained, this illusion requires the mental suppression of a very large number of characteristics of natural perception; soon enough, the illusion is rejected as inadequate by the perceiver who regains his free mobile point of view on the representation (1960).

The various systems of perspectives can be regrouped according to their aptitude to model a spatial experience close to the body of the speaker/producer, or at a great distance from him. This distance constitutes one of the fundamental factors defining the potentialities of one's body in obtaining informational data about the world within specific organic spaces.

Distance has been given different names in the domain of visual representation. The distance established in one dimension is called length; in the second dimension, it is called height and width, whereas the distance observed on a perpendicular axis in front of or behind the body is called depth.

As a constitutive element of the "construction" of space, this quantitative notion of distance is not necessarily measurable mathematically. That notion of distance defined by constant metric length is an operational concept developed in an epistemological and conceptual human context which is relatively foreign to amorphous and continuous matter in movement, and the more so to mental subjective phenomena. Non-Euclidean geometries will consider points infinitely close to each other, within a continuity ruled by field-laws and distant actions.

Mental spaces of representation, concerned with experience or knowledge, are not amenable to metric quantification, except for the indirect accompaniment of minute electric discharges. As such, they have to be modeled with qualitative quantifications, establishing continuity between particularly dynamic events.

Once integrated in pictorial space, the concept of continuity will require an analogous transformation of the notion of distance-in-depth, which remains an indispensable parameter of any spatial experience. Thus, the parameters of distances which will be utilized in the description of depths in visual representation must remain as hazy and shifting as the field of reality that they designate, that is, the tactile, olfactory, thermic spaces, and so on, that have become the subjects of the representation. In fact, visual stimuli, strictly understood, are the only sensorial data that lend themselves to both measurable and unmeasurable interrelations in distances of depth. The other sensory stimuli are more related to a very close internal or external range of experiences that constitute the range of the "proxemics."

These notions of distance will play a major and multiple role in the development of perspectives, since they derive from the position taken by the producer in relation to distinct and indistinct objects which form his representational field. This distance will be evaluated from four principal parameters:

(1) The distance instituted in the three dimensions by the type of ocular vision (foveal, macular, or peripheral) demanded by the characteristics of coloremes in the visual field;

(2) The angle of ocular vision adopted by the producer in relation to the represented field;

(3) The distance where the producer is situated in relation to the representational field that he constructs;

(4) The effect of distance inserted between the represented elements/regions constructed in the field.

These effects of points of view and of distances find a syntagmatic expression in varied historical systems of perspectives. These latter present themselves as coded and normative superstructures, defining the use and position of diverse visual variables for the principal purpose of producing different levels of depth. They range from topological proximities to the extreme distances dealt by Euclidian or projective spaces.

5.3. Topological Depths and Illusory Depths

Any definition of space as a three-dimensional construct postulates that the perception of any visual field can be articulated in three planes, whatever the mechanisms of perception or the perspectives utilized: 1) the forefront plane, 2) the background plane, and 3) the intermediary planes. These notions will serve to describe the effects of distance in visual representation.

The forefront plane is the region of the visual field that seems the nearest, the closest to the perceiver. Inversely, the background plane is that region which seems to correspond to the furthest point from the perceiver in the visual field. An indeterminate number of intermediary planes are staggered between the forefront and the background plane, connected to these and to one another by various types of liaisons: superimposition, parallelism, linear oblique, vectorialities, contrasts, and so on. The forefront and background planes are thus conceived as the equivalents of a nearness and a remoteness, but always in a relative context. Thus, the distant one can be located in a relative proximity, as in certain close-up portraits, still-lifes, or certain interiors, when it refers to different hypotheses of objects, such as skins, clothes, walls, mirrors, and so on, or it may seem to recede into an indefinite or very remote distance, sometimes called infinity.

The different systems of perspectives will radically differentiate themselves as to the distance in depth which will be selected and treated and the specific interrelations established between the various groups of planes mentioned above. This articulation in depth is obtained through a great many devices using a mnemonic reference to natural perceptual processes, even if they introduce some symbolic conventions. For instance, the staggered perspective system divides the global visual field into various superimposed stripes, from bottom to top, assigning to those on top the function of signifying the furthest point in space, and often in time. The fundamental perceptual triad of the forefront, background and intermediary planes always reconstructs itself at the interior of each of these stripes, creating the rhythm of the visual field.

The distances between regions both in the two and in the three dimensions have also been called 'intervals'. If 20th century artists, such as Hofmann and Albers, have emphasized this notion as an important dialectic element in the elaboration of continuity between the categories of planes, the tradition by contrast has habitually connected this very notion to that of Euclidean discontinuity or illusions of voids between objects and planes. Thus, according to Wölfflin (1950; 150), Leonardo da Vinci insisted on the introduction of distances between the objects he was representing: "Although things in front of me are all replaced in a continuous relation, I will not maintain any less my rules of 'distances,' of 20 and 20 aunes like the musician has established between tones, of which each holds nevertheless to all the others, a scale of several degrees going from one tone to the next (the intervals)."

5.3.1. Topological depths

As we have just mentioned, various distances in depth can be regrouped into two distinct categories: proxemic or topological depths and distant or illusory depths.

The proxemic depths, as they are called by E. T. Hall (1966), can be described as pertaining to the narrow distances surrounding one's own body, in an intimate or personal distance. In the realm of perception, they refer to the virtual totality of organic spaces which seem to invade even the endodermic regions of the body (thermic, tactile, kinesthetics, and so on). The characteristics of the more polyvalent auditory and visual spaces undergo a complete metamorphosis at near or far distances. As a rule, the stronger the intensity or energetic aspect of sensorial percepts, the closer to oneself its source will appear. In the same way, perception of intensities of energies, endowed by internal dynamics and continuous volume, will be basic for the construction of depths in the representational field.

On the grammatical plane, one must emphasize that topological depth, or the intuition of the internal volume of a mass, is contained in the parameters of the Basic Plane in which the periphery, strongly energized by the formative elements, opens at the center—through a concave/convex movement—a potential state of oscillation around the hub of the internal axes and the reflux of the periphery. The Basic Plane can thus be represented as an undulatory space of depth, both narrow and shifting in character, determined at all its points by a potential/virtual energy. This depth in the visual field is fabricated by the perceptual mechanisms of centration and attention which multiply the field energies, producing chromatic adaptations, effects of figure-ground and so forth, according to the interactions between the energies of the Basic Plane and those added by the pictorial plane.

To a hypothetical lateral vision (sighting by the side), the Basic Plane thus presents itself as a space of extendable depth which cannot be precisely, mathematically measured, but immediately offers to perception a distance of proxemic depths (figures XIVb, XIVc and XIVd).

This undulation or this "push-pull" effect, produced by the interactions between percepts of diagonals and cruciform energies emanating from the mass, remains as a characteristic of the visual field in any other type of sighting: frontal, horizontal, oblique, etc. This is a fact of perception and not a metaphoric or codified symbolic connotation. Kandinsky already described this perceptual experience, insisting in particular

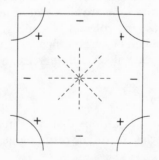

Figure XIVa: Energetic Structure of Space in the Basic Plane

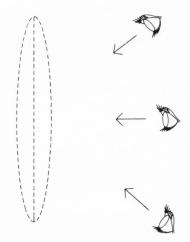

Figure XIVb: Proxemic Space of the Basic Plane Viewed from Side, Frontal, and Oblique Sightings

on the role played there by what we will call in the following paragraphs the optical perspective: "The elements which go backwards or forewards expand the Basic Plane towards the spectator and away from the spectator, as an accordion does. It is primarily the color-elements which possess this force" (Kandinsky, 1975; 226).

Indeed, interrelations established by perception between whatever visual variables (dimension, texture, vectoriality, etc.) will involve this movement of aggregates of coloremes foreward or backward, modified further by the influence of one or several hypotheses of integration or of continuity. Often, as Arnheim noted (1954; 226), to avoid the possibility of a perforation or an interruption in the spatial continuity, the perceiver will establish a maneuver in depth, which maintains the integrity of the whole.

Arnheim's analysis of a woodcut by Arp, in *Art and Visual Perception*, is particularly enlightening in this regard. The work is constituted, according to a gestaltian regrouping of its whites and blacks, as three regions which envelop one another. At the periphery, an irregular form—curved, black, speckled with white marks, and oriented to the right—envelops another irregular form—a white curve oriented according to the disharmonic diagonal. This second form envelops in turn a third irregular form of the same black speckled texture as the peripheral form, but oriented on a more horizontal axis.

Arnheim does not, unfortunately, specify the dimension of the Basic Plane that he will use in the determination of the planes of varying depths that the elements described above can occupy. A two-dimensional organization cannot be proposed, as it would suppose an absence of the white colored material in the intermediate layer, since visually this white can only be situated in front of the surrounding white. Arnheim describes four different types of superimposition of elements in depth which require different perceptual modes of cutting-out energetic planes. The selection of the criteria will vary from tonality or an accrued privilege attributed to the closing of forms, and so on. Arnheim will point out that this type of fluctuating space—which we will qualify as being of a reversible order—has been explored by certain modern artists as they question the material solidity of the visible world.

He also adds that it would be wise to analyze in the same way the spatial structures of paintings, relief sculptures, free-standing sculptures, or buildings belonging to different stylistic periods.

One could discover characteristic differences in the number of levels of depth used as well as in their arrangement. The number of objects assigned to each level of depth would be examined as well as their type of distribution in the frontal plane. One would find there varied types of reliefs in depth: the global relief could be concave with objects at the center located at the greatest distance or, to the contrary, a convex relief offering a protrusion from the center. The effect of the factor of interruption versus that of coherence and continuity could be studied equally well in dimensions of depth as in the two dimensions (Arnheim, 1954; 227–228).

It is solely through this systematic analysis of depths, in effect, that spatial fields can be described in their proper structures as to the relative positions of their elements. Only in such a way can the very structure of the pictorial statement be determined, which is to say the particular spatial curve which interrelates the elements, following their interactions/interventions in the global visual field.

The disclosure and naming of these various levels of topological depth will be accomplished by semiotical analysis in relation to coloremes and their insertion into the infrastructure of the Basic Plane through a more or less minute or extensive scale, according to particular needs. These means of measurement constitute the development of a system already carried out by Edward T. Hall, for the notation of all behaviors of a proxemic species (1972).

The proxemic depths, inherent in movements produced by percepts in the visual field, play a fundamental structural role in the syntactic development of any visual text, whether or not it offers a further iconic or mimetic function. It is not unusual, however, that the spatial energetic infrastructure that they construct should modify or contradict dialectically those visual causalities brought about by other regroupings of visual variables in the same work, which would be oriented towards illusory depths, thus complicating the syntactic structure of the whole. But if a visual work may present only proxemic depths or topological depths, the illusory depths themselves can only be developed on the basis of topological movements in depth and surface, without reducing their efficacy, which is irremediably wed to the very process of perception.

5.3.2. *Illusory depths*

Illusory depths result from movements suggested over larger distances in the visual field, not by mechanisms specific to visual perception itself or the structure of visual variables, but rather by specific organizations of these, associated with interpretations resulting from a code of specific cultural learning.

The representation of a large distance in the depth of a visual field does not stem from the energetic structure of the Basic Plane, nor from that of coloremes as vibratory energies. It is the product, rather, of an interpretation of a certain group of marks or signs dependent upon conventional codes (Eco, 1970; 12). These metaphorically constructed depths refer to the social, public, and remote distance where the producer situates himself in relation to an imaginary perceptual field. The greater the distance that a producer chooses to be from the object or the environment he calls forth, the less sensorial stimuli will be accessible to perception. In addition to this elimination of organic proxemic spaces, great distances nullify the experience of volumetry in the object. The potentiality of volumetric perception disappears indeed after five meters, and objects appear as cut-out silhouettes on a background. Visual space itself, the only one establishing a relation to remote objects, becomes more and more confused since it induces mainly peripheral vision. Paradoxically, the very remote space—indefinite or to infinity—which offers far less precision of stimuli to perception, will frequently borrow, in a semi-visual or informal organization, the organizational structures of proxemic space, experimented with here in a putting-in-distance. This is what is revealed by an analysis of skies and clouds, in which respect Damisch pointed out that it instituted a perspectivist duality in Renaissance painting (1972; 29).

The dualities or pluralities of perspectives in a given visual work are more often the rule than the exception, given the multiplicities of points of view from which the producer endeavors to form a synthesis in his visual discourse. They result also from the fact that the constituting elements which are interrelated to form an organic space (auditory, kinesthetic, buccal, and so on) present a different structure which must be modeled by different types of spatialization.

In this context, the determination of the distance taken by the producer in relation to the object of his representation is a syntactic modality that is as revealing as the uses of tenses in verbal language allowing for the identification of categories of signifiers. As in a novel or other work of fiction, the analysis will identify in the visual text, at different stages of the treatment granted to aggregates of coloremes, structural traits which the positioning of other elements in the distance often contradicts.

Thus, some characteristics of foveal vision, which are only realized at distances less than five meters, are sometimes attributed to regions theoretically situated according to other marks at further distances, such as the

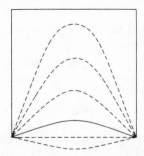

Figure XIVc: Topological Depth (Continued Line) and Illusory
Depths (Dotted Curves)

effects of proxemic textures to remote elements. Or, contiguous objects are
defined by heterogeneous and contradictory perspectivist parameters. The
production of a spatial synthetic unity in these complex visual fields seems
to have been the aim of a certain number of ancient artists, still esteemed
today, whereas producers of less scope or merit are often content with
having recourse to a verbal metaphor or label, which unifies logically but
not spatially the works in question.

For the requirements of the analysis, a system of notation of medium
and remote distance, evoked by an illusory depth, can be developed, on
the basis of those categories of distance determined by Edward T. Hall
(1966). It will serve to establish the spatial curve of a representation in its
relation with topological and illusory depths. Figures XIVc and XIVd indicate models for an estimation of positions of objects in various distances in
depth.

5.4. Distances in Height and in Width

The distance taken by the producer in relation to the visual field that he
constructs determines not only variations in depth for the third dimension,
but also for the two other dimensions of height and width. These angles of
surface vision give rise to various sorts of expanses or of angles of opening
of vision and of field, which can be of a topological or illusory type.

In height and laterality, the object of representation can be described
as:

• transversal (of height from top to bottom of the Basic Plane);
• in close up (or microscopic);
• macroscopic (close vision from about one meter),
• at the interior of a room (three or four meters), or of several rooms (five or
  six meters);
• at the inside of a building (10 meters or more);
• at the exterior: urban (streets, buildings);
• at the exterior: landscape without sky;
• at the exterior: landscape with sky.

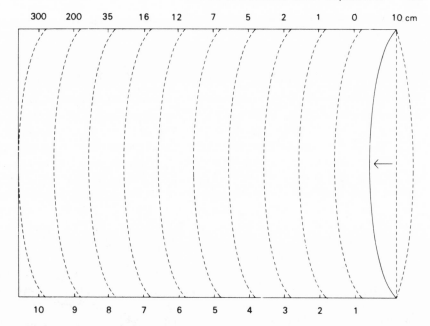

Figure XIVd: Topological Depth and Illusory Depths, Estimated in Meters, under a Representational Lateral Viewing

Any representation suggesting an object or an environment which would be measurable approximately mathematically and which would evoke a dimension in height/width larger than the dimension of the Basic Plane, would present an illusory bidimensionality. A nonmeasurable or indefinable expanse, which does not seem arbitrarily cut up inside another measurable visual field, is immediately structured by the topological and energetic limits of the Basic Plane.

Even in illusory height, as in the evocation of the interior of a house, the depth-distance can be treated as proxemic or distant. Panofsky commented on this short type of distance in the interior scenes of northern European art, in contrast to the remote distances in Italian art (1975; 169).

The distance in width instituted by the field of representation can, in the same manner, be said to be topological or illusory in the following modalities:

- Close up (an object occupying all of a field);
- Lateral transversal (from left to right);
- Macular: an angle of 15 degrees and about 10 meters;
- Peripheral: an angle of 60 to 100 degrees (70 meters);
- Very distant: an angle of 200 degrees (130 meters).

The narrower the angle of vision is in width, the more it suggests closeness and foveal vision. A similar effect is produced by a strict juxtaposition of objects in the field. Some systems of perspectives, namely the Byzantine frontal one, calls for an equally precise treatment for objects which are localized in the center and those on the far sides, thus contradicting the natural perception.

5.5. Positions of the Producer in Relation to the Field

Regions of the visual field, suggesting a plural series of perceivers, or a perceiver who occupies a multiplicity of positions at the same time, or better, a perceiver moving in front of it, are in fact making explicit the spatial positions taken by the producer of the representation. The subject/ producer of the visual discourse identifies his position in relation to a given visual field according to a set of syntactic elements that one could term 'explicit performatives' or indices of subjectivity (Recanati, 1981; 102). Thus, given that foveal vision is the only way one can see a precise detail on an angle of one or two degrees on this side of five meters, any determination of coloremes which affords such a precision indicates the distance of the producer from this object and eventually from the totality of the field he constructs. Similarly, variations of visual variables, in particular certain large textured planes or a formal confusion that implies a closer distance, can correspond to such a close proximity that it calls to mind more tactile and kinesthetic sensations than a representation of the organic visual space.

Thus, macular vision, which allows one to perceive colors but with a lesser degree of precision, still produces clear vision inside a vertical angle of three degrees and on a horizontal angle of 12 to 15 degrees and a medium distance ranging from five to ten meters. In between macular vision and peripheral vision, more sensitive to movements and tonalities than to colors, visual 'scanning' allows one to cover an angle of 60 degrees at the horizontal and at the vertical at a far distance.

The reader is advised to consult the list established by Edward T. Hall of the possible types of sensorial perception and experiences accessible, according to the different positions of objects in the distance.

Since the distance taken in relation to an object may express physical relations as well as psychological ones, it will not be unusual to find confirmation that the position of the producer can vary in relation to various objects that he places simultaneously in a given scene. We will call these 'mixed viewpoints or sightings of the ocular apparatus'. Some examples are the foveal vision on the macular field as in the *Primavera* of Botticelli, the foveal vision on a peripheral field as in the same artist's *La Calomnie;* macular vision inserted in a peripheral as in the *Erato* by Lippi, or foveal vision simulated at a peripheral distance, across macular fields, as in the *L'Ecole d'Athenes* of Raphael. If the three types of ocular vision function simultaneously within their respective potentialities, in any point of the natural field of perception, it may happen that the visual field of representation is divided into autonomous regions where the trajectories of the eye are realized differently and sometimes in a heterogeneous and contradictory manner in relation to one another.

In addition to these marks which are attached to isolated objects (mimetic or nonmimetic) by the visual process, which situate and define them, the producer can also indicate a particular position of his whole body in relation to some objects or the totality of the field of representation as such. We give the name "sighting" to this relation in the field, from above or below, sideways, and so on. This constitutes one of the most important characteristics for the differentiation of systems of perspective which have as their function to position the producer's body in his space of representation and not only the direction aimed at by the eye.

Thus, in a *frontal sighting*, the producer will situate elements of representation parallel to the vertical plane of his own body, or, again, as Wölfflin commented, apropos the classical art of the Renaissance, parallel to the plane/surface of a work, that is, to the base which constitutes the Basic Plane.

In a sighting *perpendicular* to the vertical plane of the producer, one can dispose the elements along an illusory horizontal plane in the deployment of width, height, and depth, often offering linear points of convergence on one or several horizon-lines. In this horizontal sighting, certain portions of the field may be situated, nevertheless, beneath the producer's gaze or his own body, and certain others above, producing local angular sightings.

Angular sightings can be of different types: 1) an angular sighting from the top to the bottom, as if the producer were positioned above the field of representation; 2) an angular sighting from the bottom to the top; 3) an angular sighting proceeding from the right side in gazing towards the left or from the left side towards the right, either in a horizontal or oblique path.

These angular sightings have always been present in visual representations of every epoch, used in a global or partial way, but they have taken on a new significance in the development of the baroque and mannerist periods and in various experiments with linear perspectives, such as anamorphosis. Robert Klein (1970; 171) underlined their dominant role: "But already in his epoch (Tintoretto), a new use of perspective, that which Rubens preferred, was ushered in with Veronese: the angle of taking sights plays the role there, for an expressive purpose, which today movie producers assign to it."

It is on these fundamental data that Jan Peters (1981) founded the semiotics of the cinema, invoking the basic role played by perspective in pictorial art itself.

Unfortunately, pictorial semiotics has been slow to recognize the fact that cultural norms do not assure an absolute status to the artificial perspective of the Renaissance, whose restrictive and ideologically repressive character had for a long time been pointed out by artists as well as a number of art theorists.

But, following Panofsky's research, it can be said that any system of perspective is restrictive, because it is based on a specific point of view, in relation not only to the visible but to the ensemble of sensorial experience.

It institutes a specific context in the midst of which very particular statements are developed. The partial and limited character of each is a point that it possesses in common with any modal category in other types of human language. Nevertheless, it is necessary that certain types of sighting be opened to several sorts of perspectivist organizations which thereby conserve common points, in spite of the specific modes of interrelation that each commands. The semiotical analysis of systems of perspective will allow us to define, at the same time as their specificity, their particular positioning in the group of points of views of reality that human beings have succeeded in spatializing.

5.6. Systems of Perspectives

At the level of a syntax of visual language, one must envisage systems of perspective developed by the spontaneous or learned practice of this language, as essentially programmatic schemas of organization of constitutive elements of visual texts. These vary with respect to times and societies, as well as within the genetic development of the human being. We have already devoted a book to the study of how systematically and regularly the structures of children's art evolve, relatively free from sociocultural conditionings during the child's first emerging years (Saint-Martin, 1980). Various schemas of organization of visual elements have been recognized there for a long time, but except perhaps for the "folding back" perspective, they have not been interpreted as bona fide perspectivist systems, endowed by specific elements and modes of liaisons, with a view to fulfilling different linguistic functions.

Extensive research is still necessary in order to develop the area that Panofsky opened up in *The Perspective as Symbolic Form*, but did not pursue while engaging in his remarkable works on the iconology of the art of the past. The enterprise was perhaps not realizable without the development of a theory of the grammar of visual language, given the fact that any system of perspective requires a type of variations in visual variables or interrelations between groups of coloremes, that cannot be analyzed before being identified.

But even before any further development of visual semiotics, it is necessary to present a taxonomy of this vast body of research and to describe, in however minimal a way, these essential signposts in the visual syntactic field that are the various modalities of perspectivist systems. We will endeavor to clarify a terminology and concepts that have remained until now far too confused, and to construct the first levels of description of these programmatic regroupings so particular to elements of visual language. While offering these few parameters, we are deeply aware of the volume of research still required in this fledgling area of investigation.

Let us recall that modalities of perspectives are syntactical tools and do not constitute the object per se of representation in visual language. Being always implied in the enunciation, they signal the illocutionary aim of the producer as well as his orientation within certain semantic contexts (Searle, 1970; 65). Its recognition in the syntactic structure of the enunciated corresponds also to that which Austin has called "the uptake," or "the comprehension on the part of the listener of the illocutionary force in which the speaker has invested his enunciation" (Recanati, 1981; 42). This force, furthermore, is one which cannot exceed its actual meaning since "it is the image of the force which is a part of the meaning of the enunciated, not the force itself, which must be inferred by the listener (spectator) on the basis of the speaker's intentions" (Recanati, 1981; 37).

Perspectives therefore constitute unified systems of treatment and of regroupings of coloremes, working at the level of topological, gestaltian and chromatic laws and presenting themselves as more or less rigid grids orienting the dynamisms of the visual variables. Given that their principal function is the regulation of effects of distance in the three dimensions from a certain position taken by the producer, the systems of perspective will be regrouped according to how they tend to model spatial experiences which occur close to the producer, at an intermediate distance, or at a great distance from him. A special case is encountered in distances presented as indefinite/infinite, which escape any concrete experience because they are indefinable in relation to the developed visual context, as for instance with certain Medieval blue backgrounds, or Byzantine and Chinese golds, or even Mondrianesque whites. They will be paradoxically assimilated to proxemic spaces because of a particular function of their mass, which, as Panofsky pointed out (following Wölfflin's pictorial analyses), resembles unification rather than remoteness. These organizations differ so much from the usual treatment of the effects of distance, that these depths have sometimes been qualified as 'spiritual' or 'internal' depths.

Categories of proxemic and remote systems are specific, but not exclusive. A visual text is certainly able to simultaneously present regions organized according to both of these hypotheses. They remain, however, distinctly perceptible and localizable, in one region or in another, through their own syntactic structure.

The syntactic operators which ground proxemic perspectives are *juxtaposition*, or a contiguous/distant neighboring produced most often by a system of *parallels*. The operators of perspectives at a distance are *superposition* and *oblique vectoriality*.

Moreover, secondary operations in the establishment of distances derive from variations in the treatment of visual variables, such as an enlarging or an abridging of the dimension, an accentuation of the textural effect, the treatment of tonalities, and so on. But these internal fluctuations of the spatial curve of the text must be integrated and interpreted in the general context of perspectivist systems which regulate the ensemble of regions.

The fundamental matrix level of the two systems of operators in the perspectivist syntax of visual language will allow us, moreover, to establish correspondences and similarities between styles of visual representation which have been seen in the past as foreign to each other.

5.6.1. *The proxemic perspectives*

We use the term 'proxemic perspectives' for those perspectives which organize the visual field in a close distance to the organism. These have been defined as "intimate" and "personal" regions by Edward T. Hall. These perspectives can aim at the spatialization of endo-epidermic (under the skin) experiences as well as to an illusory evocation of objects resembling those of the external world or belonging to an imaginary universe. But all are seen as being near the viewer's own perceptual apparatus, that is, with the precision of linear variables, saturation of color, minimalization of the environment, and so on. These illusory allusions to things that are nearby in reality frequently involve, as noted earlier, conflicts with rules of perspective that regulate the seeing of things in the far distance.

The narrowest depths constructed by proxemic perspectives stem from an overt dialectic and use of energies belonging to the infrastructure of the Basic Plane in the organization of various regions. Thus there is a reiteration of the energetic reverberation of the formative parallel sides or corners; of the horizontal, vertical, and diagonal axes; of the checkerboard grid; of harmonic and disharmonic triangles; or of the cruciform juncture. Dynamically energized and virtually contained in the depth of the Basic Plane, these depths are essentially topological and not metrical.

The most fundamental among them are here described first: the optical perspective, which underlies all the other possible proxemic or illusory perspectives, and the parallel perspective, which offers an organizational matrix for a large number of modes of visual representation, in primitive, oriental and occidental art. In addition, they have played a major role in the classical art of the Renaissance and have known considerable development in the art of our own century.

5.6.1.1. THE OPTICAL PERSPECTIVE

This perspective designates the variations in the position in depth of simply juxtaposed plastic elements, resulting from their chromatic/tonal, textural, vectorial, or size interrelations, the most potent factor being chromatic disjunction as described in our remarks on the interactions of colors. The well-known effect of a figure which detaches itself from a ground because of a greater density of its visual variables is a product of the optical perspective, since it is a movement of distancing between parts of the field inseparable from the visual process.

Usually the latter is not reversible, as it has a tendency to immobilize perceptually the levels of ground and form, to provide the figure with a metaphorical "thingness," which prevents further perceptual movements. Proper optical depth, which is more fluctuating and less 'substantialized', endows the visual field with more supple energetic phenomena which are open to transformations. Distances between two regions constituted by optical perspective are proxemic and topological, although an intense contrast between a black and white plane has been called "infinite," as in the case of the artist Borduas's working vocabulary (1978). As long as the "infinite" cannot be an object or a referent for a perception, it might better be called "indefinite," or better yet, "indefinitely close or distant."

5.6.1.2. THE PARALLEL PERSPECTIVE

Based on a topological order of succession in depth parallel to the Basic or pictorial plane, the parallel perspective strongly relates regions which may differ as far as some variables are concerned. It establishes them as neighbors in spite of the intervals which seem to keep them at a distance. These elements are seen as aligned in a series, at a more or less equal distance from one another, and while strictly parallel, they can be projected in frontal or oblique points of view, in a vertical or horizontal superposition. This continuity can be reinstated at another level of depth by other series of parallel planes, but always in a depth which suggests closeness.

The parallel perspective partially reconstructs a potentiality of the layered spatial structure from the Basic Plane. The effect of proximity produced by this perspective results from the repetitive frontal and foveal visual orientation of the producer toward his various objects, whatever their particular location in space happens to be.

In this perspective, the intervals between the more gestaltian regions no longer help to distinguish, differentiate, and reject these regions farther from others. On the contrary, they seem to be inherently endowed by vectorial energies which connect the elements and place them in a strong neighboring. By the dynamic effect of the topological relation of neighboring and by the parallel disposition, the intervals acquire a new role which does not stress the individuality of the elements, but allows them to be massed together in a strong homogeneity. A continuum is established between regions, not through metaphorical or logical considerations but as a result of a cohesion which is produced by the distribution of regions along the main axes of the Basic Plane.

The spatializing effect of this perspective is partly similar to Panofsky's description of the kind of renewal which Gothic works of art presented in relation to those of antiquity: "Their tri-dimensionality and their substantiality is, on the contrary, that of an homogenous substance constituted from an aesthetic point of view through relations between undissociated elements, complying in their extension (infinitely weak), their form and their function ('particles') to a principle of uniformity" (1975; 111). But it is not necessary for elements to be isolated in order to be put in form by the parallel perspective.

The parallel perspective can be achieved by the partial or total superpositions of elements vertically, horizontally, and diagonally. It serves as the foundation for the development of symmetries and asymmetries around the central axis, as long as the components retain a parallelism with the formative energies of the Basic Plane.

The effect of proximity produced by the parallel perspective derives in large part from the fact that the producer as a perceiver adopts a similar position and a sighting in relation to variously located elements, as if he/she displaced himself/herself in order to grasp each of them in a frontal way. This abandonment of marks attributed usually to lateral objects can only serve to reinforce the proxemic effect of frontal perception.

Parallel perspectives have served as a matrix for a large number of proxemic or intermediate representations of distances: in children's art, in primitive societies, Egyptian, Greek, Byzantine, Chinese, medieval and Renaissance artworks, as well as in the myriad proxemic spaces of 20th century abstract art.

5.6.1.3. T HE ARABESQUE PERSPECTIVE

This perspective derives from an application of the optical perspective to linear, parallel, or crossing pictorial marks, juxtaposed or superimposed, which alternately uplift or push back the topological mass of the Basic Plane from the front toward the back. It is an immediate, more or less reversible product of the figure on ground construct. Capable of infinite developments, diversifications, and ramifications, this perspective has been used in all kinds of formats and contexts, as documented by E. H. Gombrich in *The Sense of Order* (1979). The choice of symmetric and vectori- alist elements may be considered as ordered topological representations, which may lend themselves to psycho-sociological interpretations, as attested to by Claude Lévi-Strauss's analysis of the corporal art of Brazilian Caduveo tribes (1973; 203–258).

While excluded from a representational status by the hegemony of narrative structures since the Renaissance, this topological perspective was widely used in primitive, Oriental, Persian, Egyptian, medieval pictorial, sculptural and architectural productions, as well as in most of the so-called minor decorative arts. Most of feminine artistic productions in the past belonged to this form of representation that Riegl has described as 'ornamental'. This perspective has since made a comeback, but without being duly recognized as such, in the works of Jackson Pollock in the 1940s and the subsequent developments of Op Art, "patterning" art, and so on.

5.6.1.4. THE FOCAL PERSPECTIVE

One can define as proxemic the focal perspectives which establish in the representation an object across the breadth of the pictorial plane, occupy- ing almost its entirety, save for a narrow band at the periphery, and constituting the object as a central and mostly closed form. A very large number of portraits have been so structured, advancing the model forward in a personal distance from the perceiver/producer. In many cases, gar- ments, when seen very close up, with an abundance of detail in the fabrics and textures, point to tactile and kinesthetic sensorial percepts. A dualism may be produced by a slight recession or diminution of the size of the head, thus inducing more visual percepts. This perspective of a closed, more massive central region contrasted with a more opened, linear environment, served as a crux for Joseph Albers's late production. The representation of the nude, favoring the whole of the body, is subjected to another sort of perspective; since it has to be positioned at a greater distance to be seen in its entirety, the central figure has to enter into stronger interrelations with a more distant environment.

5.6.1.5. THE REVERSIBLE PERSPECTIVE

The reversible perspective is an optical perspective which regularizes an alternation backward and forward of the elements that it links. Thus, by a simple continuation of the gaze, a region which had been seen in front, as a figure, slides toward the rear, and the region which was situated at the rear advances as a new figure toward the front. At times this reversible space lends itself to the gestaltian fabrication of different mimetic images in what was at one moment given as a form and what seemed to be the ground. This perspective is, however, used more in the 20th century in a more global trajectory which aims to destroy the fixity produced by positionings in depth by traditional linear perspective.

5.6.1.6. THE UNISTIC PERSPECTIVE

The "Unistic Perspective," elaborated upon by W. Strzeminski (1977), has the objective of producing a "homogeneous mass of forms," through the rigorous juxtaposition of internal elements within a strict definition of the format of the Basic Plane: "Thus the dimensions of the work become the most important element, and not a secondary element, existing in some way outside of our consciousness, as was the case in the Baroque; they are fundamental and are dictated by the construction and its character" (1977; 78).

Most contrasts of color and tonality, as well as contrasts of forms, dimensions, texture, are banished, along with the central form of construction. This regular uncentered construction is based upon "a line linking all colors of equal saturation," principally through their luminosity. In avoiding separations caused by contrasts, the unistic perspective aims to produce an equally energized mass at all its points, by way of "a concordance of all elements of the work with its primary data" (Strzeminski, 1977; 78), a concordance which will be elaborated upon by calculations and numeric proportions.

Although it is produced through different semiotic means, the unistic perspective is related to the "all-over" perspective seeking to extend and equalize the pictorial energy across the totality of the canvas, so as to create an energetic plenum or rigorous continuum. The same organization prevails in some periods of children's art where large sections of the visual

field are filled up by regular or similar types of visual variables or coloremes often interpreted as, say, snow, birds, clouds, or flowers.

5.6.1.7. THE TACHIST PERSPECTIVE

Whereas the syntactic mechanisms of optical perspective based on juxtaposition apply to all visual texts, figurative or nonfigurative, geometric or
informal, the term 'tachist' is reserved for the application of the optical
perspective to ensembles of informal regions with closed or diffused frontiers, stressing particularly textures, tonalities, and vectorialities. This perspective appears mixed when it permits the operation of superimposition
in addition to juxtaposition, more capable of evoking illusory depths. Even
if it uses the disjunction of figure/ground or of multi-oriented levels of
depth, this perspective produces masses sharing elastic topological internal volumes occupying indefinite distances in depth. It then offers
marks of textures, better apprehended in proxemic distances.

5.6.1.8. THE CHECKERBOARD PERSPECTIVE

The checkerboard perspective is constructed upon the internal or, as it has
been called, the deductive reiteration of the formative straight lines and
corners of the Basic Plane, forming a focal or nonfocal grid. These regular
and orthogonal bidimensional coordinates can be actualized over all of the
pictorial plane, but some may remain virtual. They regulate the localization
of elements in staggered levels, while maintaining their proximate or
'indefinite' distance. The position in depth of the segments is regularized
by the optical perspective, as well as the vectorial effects of contiguous
series.

   This very strong matrix which corresponds to the bidimensional surface of the Euclidean grid forms the infrastructure of the principal modes of
representations used in children's art before the adoption of the oblique
deep-setting of an horizon line and vanishing points.

   It generates potent symmetries/asymmetries, various lateral parallel-
isms, or juxtaposition in height, regular orders of succession, dynamized
by the virtualities of the diagonals. Given a privileged role in the work of
Mondrian, this perspective has been subsumed under the rubric of "mod-
ernist grid" (Krauss, 1986) as one of the most important substructures
evolved in contemporary art.

5.6.1.9. THE MICROSCOPIC PERSPECTIVE

This notion evokes a variety of visual representations obtained by the optic
use of magnifying glasses or mixed lenses, producing an enlargement and
bringing near of the components of matter which are regrouped in indefinite topological spaces.

   Chromaticisms are illusory there, only added in with a view to a
recognition of distinctive aggregates. Allowing for a spatial visualization of
internal organizations of ultimate and minute constituents of matter, these

perspectives do not constitute new repertories of visible matter, but are the products of specific points of view enabling the analysis of internal volumes. They present similarities with the perspective of arabesque.

5.6.2. *The intermediate or middle distances perspectives*

5.6.2.1. THE SPHERIC PERSPECTIVE

In connection with Greek art, Panofsky (1975; 55) described a correspondence between certain structures of representation and an intuition of "real" space as being finite, closed, and spheric. From empirical experience, still accessible to the average man, the Greeks identified space with the "image" of the natural curve of the world around the perceiver. This seemed to be corroborated by the fact that in perception, straight lines are seen as being, at a distance, curved, and curved lines as straight, the right angle at a distance as roundish, and so on. In this perspective, distance is not signified by any variation in foreshortenings, but by the result of a different aperture in the angle of vision.

Furthermore, the modes of regrouping elements in this perspective are aggregative in the sense that these elements remain autonomous from one another, independent in their relative proportions, freed from the spectator's point of view or the particular evocation of a remoteness. Neither a vanishing point nor a horizon line was instituted although, at times, various earth lines were added. This perspective is structured, additionally, inside a parallel succession of focalized, isolated elements, devoid of any environment which accentuates an effect of nearness, in spite of the predilection for figures to be seen in full, that is, at an intermediary distance from the viewer.

5.6.2.2. THE AXIAL PERSPECTIVE

Panofsky has also identified and described an axial or "fishbone" perspective which was used in late Greek art, in Roman paintings, and throughout the course of the Middle Ages. This structure simplifies the previous parallel perspective in dividing the field in two through a virtual central axis upon which converge at regular or graduated intervals a series of oblique vectors, originating from the front or from the background. For a long time, this axial perspective applied only to circumscribed regions of the field and not to others. When the whole field is submitted to this perspective of organization, the way is open to convergent perspectives, not on the central axis but on one or several points on the line of horizon. This perspective, however, was never global, the elements maintaining therein an autonomy of aggregates and the effects of distance of peripheral elements being still submitted to the parallel perspective.

5.6.2.3. THE FRONTAL PERSPECTIVE

Derived from the parallel perspective, it proposes one main vertical and continuous plane as mostly parallel to the surface plane, or to the inferior side of the painting, as observed in Byzantine art. If the recession of parallel planes toward the background establishes a more remote depth than that which we classify as proxemic, the force of cohesion and regrouping of these elements in parallel establishes, above all, a strong interrelation which emphasizes their neighboring and indefinite positioning. Other uses of frontal perspectives are also more or less proxemic, such as presentations of objects reflected in water in a strict verticality which eliminates all the marks of distant spaces. On the other hand, Malevich's suprematism and Mondrian's neoplasticism developed frontal perspectives, often monumental, as can also be seen in the work of Barnett Newman, Clifford Still, or the more recent works of the Quebec Plasticiens and the Minimalists. This perspective is widely used in children's art, Byzantine and Egyptian art, in Greek reliefs, and in the art of the Canadian northwest coast Indians.

5.6.2.4. THE FOLDING-BACK PERSPECTIVE

Panofsky called this organization "perspective by echelon." Frequently used in Egyptian, Persian and medieval works, it is also one of the most extraordinary facets in the development of children's art. 'Invented' by all children at around the age of five years, it will be used more extensively in following years. It involves a high and frontal point of view where some elements, oriented differently in the same spatial field, see some of their contours elevated in a perpendicular plane in relation to the projection plane, while others are folded back on the ground. It places the elements within a strong parallel continuity and symmetrical relationships, in refusing any allusion to a void in the intervals. While the emphasis is on the energies of the 'corners', as Panofsky observed (1975; 83–85), this enveloping structure, affirming the external limits of the field, generates a strong intensity in the central regions. This is the result of the vivid vectorial contrasts created by its relations of angularity and perpendicularity.

Whereas Dubuffet borrowed this perspective from children's art within a definite proxemic representation, Mondrian developed, in an indeterminate distance, the structural dynamism of potential folding-backs of asymmetrical and orthogonal planes.

5.6.2.5. THE CAVALIER PERSPECTIVE

Often used in the pictorial organization of the still-life and particularly developed in the work of Cezanne and the cubists since the beginning of this century, this perspective presents a relatively close view of the object, seen from above in an angular vision. It often creates conflicts with the marks used for distant surrounding objects; it emphasizes the contiguity of elements, of precarious pilings, of slanted surfaces, and so on. It produces a fully dense space where regions of passages are as dynamic and signifying as the closed clusters forming the 'iconic' objects. Instead of a frontal view, it is here a plunging and oblique view which subjects volumes to a pressure which freezes them in a sort of equivalent distance, in spite of their "objective" different positionings.

5.6.2.6. THE PERSPECTIVES OF CUBISM: ANALYTICAL
AND SYNTHETIC

The analytical cubist perspective may be the first one to be recognized in art history as aiming at the construction of a narrow distance in depth, or in Robert Rosenblum's words: "an extreme shallowness of the space" (1976; 32). Although its depth distance is clearly limited by a vertical or dark background, analytical cubism has maintained the method of superimposition, oblique vectorialities, and the contrasts of tonalities, common to the production of distant perspectives. But proximity is accentuated by the piling of variously oriented vectorial elements which seemingly reveal the internal mechanism of gestaltian forces which constitute the volumes. In cubist analytical perspective, the representation is focalized, constructed as in a low-relief and enveloped by a peripheral oval layer, often dark and diffuse, which neutralizes the Basic Plane's peripheral energies and reinforces the focal affirmation.

In some works constructed in a topological distance, contours dissolve themselves in vibrating textures and optical perspectives; reversible effects are at work, pushing into the foreground that which was perceived as the background. As R. Rosenblum observed: "In the new world of Cubism, no fact of vision remained absolute. A dense, opaque shape could suddenly become a weightless transparency; a sharp, firm outline could abruptly dissolve into a vibrant texture; a plane that defined the remoteness of the background could be perceived simultaneously in the immediate foreground." (1976; 14)

The "synthetic cubist perspective" is radically different from the analytic cubist perspective. Except for linear allusions to volumes and mimetic objects, this synthetic perspective deals mainly with interactions within the topological parameters of the Basic Plane. It strongly juxtaposes closed and open chromatic planes, angles, straight lines and curved vectorialities, contrasting textures in a series of parallel planes, frontal and susceptible to the effects of symmetry and folding-back.

5.6.2.7. THE PROJECTIVE PERSPECTIVES

This expression is largely polysemic when used outside a strictly mathematical context. It may refer, as Panofsky said to the decisive step when the occident saw the limits of Renaissance perspective and began to transform it. It gave birth:

> following the researches of Desargue . . . to a general projective geometry, and—owing to replacement, operating for the first time, of the unilateral 'visual cone' of Euclid by the multilateral 'geometrical cluster of rays—achieving a totally abstraction of the direction of the gaze and opening thus uniformly all directions of space. (1975; 174)

Instead of focussing on already existing, stable properties, this geometry studies relations which permit the production of forms, mainly from a point of view postulated at an "infinite" distance. Developed by Poncelet, Felix Kline, and others, and having become one of the important non-Euclidean geometries, this new conception of space was disseminated in Europe at the beginning of the century by the theosophist and scientist, Rudolf Steiner, who was also the first to offer an English translation of Goethe's *Theory of Colors* (Whicher, 1971). Adopted by Russian suprematists and constructivists, it influenced Mondrian's and Kandinsky's spatial intuitions. It received considerable elaboration in El Lissitsky's works. In a space defined as a homogeneous continuum, and from various points located at a point in the infinite in all directions, an ensemble of elements coexist, produced by heterogeneous points of view or distances. These forms or volumes were seen from below, from the side, and from above, according to various orders of juxtapositions, successions and superimpositions regulated by multiple and 'discontinuous' positions adopted by the producer.

No rationalization of this mainly visual type of arrangement can be offered through the traditional mechanisms of the production of illusory far distances. Dimensions, for instance, do not obey laws of foreshortening, and contradictory viewpoints are juxtaposed in the same spatial field.

On the other hand, Jean Piaget determined within the evolution of children's modes of representations a transitory period, called 'projective', interposed between topological and Euclidean constructs. This stage is characterized by the child's intuition of the notion of his own personal point of view in the construct of the 'straight line', a prerequisite for the setting up of the 'spatial box' of Euclidean space. While still pre-Euclidean, this projective perspective differs entirely from the one described above. It does not incorporate the mathematical notion of the infinite. And in the latter perspective, in spite of some contradiction among viewpoints, strong textural effects point to a still tactile proximity.

5.6.2.8. THE BAROQUE PERSPECTIVE

This angular or "baroque" perspective, described with beautiful lucidity by Wölfflin (1961), deploys in a proximate or intermediary distance an entanglement of planes with accentuated chiaroscuros, in a harmonic or discordant vectoriality. Even when it signals a distanced lighted region in one of the upper corners of the work, this perspective is more involved in an accumulation of elements in the foreground, strengthening their dimensions, color densities, tonal contrasts, and sudden foreshortenings. It produces a "kinesthetic" excess in the proxemic levels in relation to the treatment of elements in the medium or background levels.

5.6.2.9. THE ISOMETRIC PERSPECTIVE

One can situate within the intermediary distances the isometric perspective which may reveal the internal volumes of the polygons it represents, while maintaining the parallel vectorialities and thus excluding the impact of the environment and the effects of perceptual vision in a far distance. It is used particularly in architecture and industrial design, and is sometimes borrowed for particular effects in pictorial works.

5.6.3. The far distance perspectives

5.6.3.1. THE LINEAR OR CENTRAL PERSPECTIVE

Under various labels such as legitimate, artificial, convergent, central, or linear, this syntactical organization of the visual field has been the subject of many analyses. It has also been erroneously identified as the sole perspective true to reality and as the unique pictorial space. As summed up by J. White (1972), it is characterized by an infrastructure composed of a group of lines, regularly distributed on the inferior side of the painting, converging on a vanishing point located on a horizontal line whose height may vary, called the 'horizon line'. This frame serves to calculate the proportional foreshortenings or gradual decrease of the dimension of the elements in distances approaching the vanishing point. It defines the represented objects as endowed with a noncompressible external volume requiring a contiguous 'empty' environment in order to achieve and maintain 'roundness' and constant contours. In the case of landscape, this grid is applied only to the earth's plane; the portion treating the sky and clouds is submitted to heterogeneous forms of perspectives. It imposes a rigid selection and hierarchy of objects to be represented since, owing to the superimposition, only relatively small objects can be positioned on the first plane. All objects in reality of a large dimension (cities, mountains, etc.) are pushed toward the background, to be then rendered in quite reduced dimensions.

This perspective, based on a planar conception of the Basic Plane, tends to establish the illusion of very far distances, which would coincide with the perceptive experience of natural perspectives. Its longtime acceptance as the 'true' and unique form of representation of space is linked to the postulate that perception of far distances is the more common or valuable sensorial experience of man, and should be established as the paradigm for all intuition of space. Though it may present objects in a foreground, its organizational structures prevent the possibilities of representing not only proxemic visual experiences, but also other forms of sensorial experiences that unfold strictly in the proxemic distances. Its artificiality in representing perceptive vision as a whole has led artists, as early as the Italian artists of the 15th century, to correct, by various means, the specific distortions it produced with regard to binocular and peripheral vision. Like the photographic camera, which was constructed in order to produce an image in a similar perspective, it is not able to appropriately accommodate various focuses and peripheral vision. It is seldom used without the accompaniment of the atmospheric perspective with a view to realizing a better illusion of great distance.

5.6.3.2. THE INVERTED PERSPECTIVE

Developed before the central or linear perspective, this perspective offers a reverse organization where lines converging toward a unique point are not directed toward an illusory depth in the background of the representation, but to a point in front of the projection plane, often below the inferior limit of the Basic Plane.

This point of convergence may be located in the region where the producer/perceiver of the work would stand or upon any arbitrary point on the side or the front of the picture plane, in the same way distance points were distributed in later constructs of the linear perspective. This perspective has also been called the 'oblique perspective', notably by Julia Kristeva (1972) in her remarkable analysis of the organizational structure of Giotto's works.

5.6.3.3. THE OBLIQUE PERSPECTIVE

We apply the term 'oblique perspective' to those implying a particularly distinct oblique sighting from the producer himself which, while unfolding horizontally in a field defined by linear perspective, opens to a very large extent its angle of vision toward upward illusory heights in order to create the illusion of highest buildings or mountainous reliefs, for example. These regions belonging to the most extreme heights are often described as seen frontally in a degree of precision and neatness of detail which are inappropriate for their remoteness or inapplicable to peripheral vision, the only instrumentation that can in fact apprehend them.

This oblique perspective is differentiated from the perspective in height, which amplifies the vertical angle of sighting in the same way by a continuity maintained between high and low regions.

5.6.3.4. THE ATMOSPHERIC PERSPECTIVE

Although the organ of sight is the only one of our senses that can give us data about the environment situated at a great distance from us, this information is extremely reduced compared to the data offered by vision at a close or average distance, since it stems only from peripheral vision.

The perspective known as atmospheric 'mimics' the transformations which objects perceived in external reality undergo, when situated at great distances. Visual foreshortening, as well as atmospheric layers which are interposed between object and spectator, reduce the distinctiveness of their visual variables, rendering them more and more intractable to perception. This perspective therefore introduces the dissolution of the contours and chromaticity of objects and the reduction of intervals between them, stressing their dark character and formal masses. It provides distant representations with marks not unsimilar to those used to represent objects in a close proximity, or objects referring to nonvisual organic spaces. This perspective is also frequently called the 'aerial' perspective, because it is linked with the air or atmosphere, but the expression may be misunderstood to refer to a bird's eye or perspective taken from a high point in the sky. It provides distant representations with the marks of peripheral vision, reducing chromatic properties and precision of contours and accentuating both blurred effects and dark tonalities.

5.6.3.5. THE BIRD'S EYE PERSPECTIVE
As its name implies, this perspective proposes the point of view of the producer being positioned at a very great distance in height from the surface of the earth. Though it may have acquired a realistic connotation in the aeronautical era, it was first developed millenia ago. It frequently produces an effect of flattening of the earth's curvature under a direct or oblique vision. At other times, it provides for simulations of reliefs or concave-convex undulations of the pictorial plane which assimilate its syntax with that of low reliefs.

5.6.3.6. THE STAGGERED PERSPECTIVE
This perspective, frequently witnessed in early forms of representations in western and oriental cultures, suggests very large distances in depth by the simple superimposition of more or less horizontal bands or layers from bottom to top of the Basic Plane. Metaphorically it produces an illusory path from the front toward the background, endowed with correlative spatial or temporal connotations. When confined to geographical connotations linked to various layerings, it may preserve a strong unification of the visual field.

5.6.3.7. THE PERSPECTIVE IN HEIGHT
In contrast to the bird's eye perspective, this perspective positions the producer not completely above the earth, but at the height of highly elevated terrestrial elements as in the case of very high mountains. It was widely used in Chinese art, where, however, it was rarely used alone, but most often juxtaposed with an 'eye-level' perspective, as many commentators have demonstrated (Cahill, 1977). The perspective in height situates the producer at very elevated levels from which some linear perspective is either spaced out or not, possessing its own horizon line and various curved trajectories at fixed points.

However, if the linear and atmospheric perspectives are easily integrated in the occidental's point of view, the two perspectives used in oriental art appear to stem from a duality in the position of the producer in relation to his field of representation. First, in a medium height looking down upon a vast region and then, secondly, in the upper part of the visual field, in a horizontal confrontation with the most elevated objects possible. These visual discordances, often attenuated by a uniform monochromy, may result from an aleatory definition of the limits of the Basic Planes of representations, horizontally or vertically unfolding in the scrolls of painting, in accordance with the aesthetics of asymmetry that is the basis of much oriental art.

5.6.3.8. THE ANAMORPHIC PERSPECTIVE

In medium or distant depths, this perspective modifies in a gradual way the dimensions of one of the coordinates (height or width) of the Euclidean grid, without applying the correlation defined by the law of foreshortenings in the linear perspective. Destroying the strict proportionality of the grid, it allows for a reconstruction of an iconic resemblance from a particular point of view on the side of the visual work.

Chapter Six

The Grammar of Sculpture

6.1. Preliminaries

In 1956, the art historian Herbert Read wrote that sculpture did not truly exist before the turn of the century, as it is only since 1900 that it has become conscious of its own "autonomous fundamental laws" (1954; 28). While clearly defining the syntactic structure, these laws would shed light on the process by which an object is constituted as a sculpture; that is, as a linguistic object differing in its functions from any other objects of the natural or human environment. The lack of semiotical foundations for the decoding and interpretation of sculpture is certainly still felt to the present in a most distressing way. And the task of providing such foundations has by no means been entirely achieved to this very day, as Rosalind Krauss, another historian of sculpture, pointed out more recently: "The issue of what might be properly considered a work of sculpture has become increasingly problematic" (1977; 2).

It should be recalled that it is only through a conscious understanding of the role played by the Basic Plane that painting can be constituted as an autonomous system of representation and not merely as the attenuated mirror image of a mimetic reference. Introduced by Kandinsky, the semiotics of the Basic Plane allows for the definition of a system describing the necessary fictional (since it is linguistic) space of pictorial representation, as well as those syntactic structures which regulate the energies of plastic variables in spatial depth.

However, in developing the syntactic hypothesis of the Basic Plane, Kandinsky did not believe in extending its application to sculpture. Furthermore, he denied the possibility of the autonomy of this artistic medium. He said: "The identity of the basic elements in sculpture and architecture explains in part the victorious subjugation of sculpture by architecture today" (1976; 83, n. 1). And if some decades later, the developments of sculpture in minimal art have been accompanied—and then principally on the part of the producers themselves—by interesting theoretical work, it was mainly constructed on the basis of the fundamental findings of Gestalt theory, as we see in the case of Donald Judd, Carl Andre, Robert Morris, and others (Battcock, 1968). The absence of a hypothesis such as that of the Basic Plane seemed to render questionable the whole discourse on sculpture, if one listens, for instance, to the nostalgia expressed in this regard by Carl Andre:

There is no sculptural space before the elements are projected. There is no canvas and no field of retinal vision, only empty space. The block of brute marble is not the space of the empty canvas . . . The sculpture has no interior (1980; 13–14)

The need for a rationale for the description of sculpture led to the postulate that there can be no syntax without the definition of a smaller particle, discrete and nonsignifying in itself, that acquires meaning through specific modes or organization. The sculptor Carl Andre proposed, under the name of constructivism, a theory of sculptural forms as structured from an accumulation/repetition of discrete elements such as cement blocks that generate their own field, akin to the modular elements of Seurat, the atomist touch of Cezanne, or the mode of production of concrete poetry (1980; 18, 3).

On the one hand, as the constructivist Strzeminski had previously remarked, the principle of repetition cannot constitute a system of construction, but at the most a mode of production of arbitrary aggregates: "When the requirement is limited to the necessity of repeating the same segment on demand, there is no construction, there is an almost total freedom" (1977; 119). This freedom can be asserted, but more under the name of an informal art than that of a constructivist one.

On the other hand, the temptation to come to terms with the sculptural system in determining the basic particle or element, and then of performing a leap to the syntactic level remains aleatory. We have noted Chomsky's observation to the effect that nothing at the level of the phoneme, or verbal sound unit, can reveal the organizational modes of verbal syntax. Verbal linguistics has also shown that the determination of a basic element is always questionable, since it results from a certain number of analytical hypotheses which are only justified by virtue of their heuristic character. Thus, as demonstrated by research measuring the aptitudes of infants in recognizing linguistic sounds, it is now suggested that the syllable be substituted for the phoneme as the first element of perception/ comprehension of audible language, despite the convenience of the notion of the phoneme in the learning of alphabetic writing (Mehler, 1981; 36).

If one can speak of an epistemological failure in the attempt to construct a syntax of sculptural language, it certainly follows from the complexity of perception of what visual semiotics would constitute as the 'semiotic' material of this medium; that is, volumetry defined as real three dimensionality. As described by Edward T. Hall, depth is a "hidden dimension" which cannot be the object of direct perception, but can only be a product of a cortical synthesis of many visual percepts. Similarly, the eye cannot perceive a 'volume' in any one centration, but has to multiply its positions and angles and establish relations between them in order to "reconstruct" the notion of the "invisible" internal volume. In any horizontally-sighted perspective, the eye cannot perceive volume as such, but rather a semi-volume or a semi-relief on the background plane. The restricted depth of this relief can itself be determined only through a complex mental elaboration.

The notion itself of a three-dimensional volume or object—which one would often consider as the most concrete characteristic—is the result of a perceptual synthesis effecting a leap in relation to the perceptual data given. In Strzeminski's words, "from whatever vantage point that we observe the work of art, depth is hidden from us" (1977; 115) Or, as expressed by Herbert Read:

> The volume, the notion of tri-dimensional mass, is not given by direct visual perception. We see objects from several points of view and we retain a particular and significant aspect as mnemonic image . . . Also an imaginative effort or, at least, a mental effort is necessary in order to move beyond the mnemonic image to construct a tri-dimensional image. (1964; 27)

This construction of volumetry requires further the contribution of specific signifiers, in mnemonic images, to evoke a volume, particularly those of modelling or tonal differences (light/dark) in certain regions of the object. As previously noted, from a distance of more than five or six meters, the eye is not able to perceive the marks of the fullness of the human silhouette, which appears similar to a cardboard-cutout figure. This means that the perception of sculpture involves certain strategic approaches that are not required for the apprehension of pictorial representations.

Information about volumetric perspectives, acquired in the 19th and 20th centuries, can help us in clarifying the various orders of development of the many-sided meanings of the word "sculpture." Without a doubt, confusion about this subject reached its apogee in the Dadaesque and conceptual era which applied this term to all existing objects, visible or invisible, concrete or not, through a metaphoric liaison between things. Not only does the hypothesis of Tristan Tzara and Marcel Duchamp, which says that "all that man does is art," complete symmetrically the hypothesis that nature can create art, but one has also added that "any portion of the universe," delimited by an artist who affixes his signature to it, would belong to art and to sculpture, since it presents itself in a tridimensionality foreign to painting. This hypothesis, a legacy of theories of *Einfühlung*, perpetuates a confusion between the expressivity of things and the expressivity or the power of representation of a language. The simple projection of subjective phantasms, imaginary or emotional, on various objects constructed by perception in reality, is not sufficient to constitute these things as elements of a given linguistic system. Colors, forms, and constructed images such as those which Leonardo da Vinci advised us to recognize or project on a wall serving as a "paranoic screen" (that is, a neutral surface made the recipient of purely subjective projections) do not belong to a linguistic system until they are recovered and inserted in a structure of representation which endows them with specific syntactic functions.

This identification of perceptual products with elements of a system of representation is at the very foundation of the semiotics of the natural world as developed by A. J. Greimas. This theory does not establish any distinction among: (1) the natural world, which, unless one is a solipsist, exists before being the object of a perception; (2) the visual percepts that one can construct from this reality; and (3) the representative or symbolic function of a language whose function is to model the relation of the organism to reality. Proceeding from the basis of a naive realism, which maintains an identity between nature and our perceptual constructs, as well as a similarity and uniformity of the visual percepts produced by everyone, Greimas wrote: "The natural world is a figurative language in which figures . . . are made up of perceptible qualities of the world and act directly—without linguistic mediation—on man" (1979; 234).

How a language can function without being "a linguistic mediation" is not apparent, but one can also ask who in this context is supposed to be speaking, of whom and about what, when for instance the temperature rises or falls, when a fly bites us, or when the law of gravity hinders us from lifting too heavy a weight?

Perceptible qualities of the world cannot as such form a language, except in a metaphoric sense. They can acquire a semiotic function only when they are used as elements in the construct of a linguistic structure, where the level of expression can be distinguished from that of meaning. For instance, a red element, or a circle, or a wooden component in a work, which are visual variables carrying specific dynamisms, cannot be said, as some doubtful theory of auto-referentiality would demand, to have redness, roundness or woodenness as meaning or reference.

These visual variables are parts of a linguistic system trying to represent a wider scope of human experience rather than drawing attention only to the immanent material quality of its sensorial, perceivable semiotic constituents. A word expressed in a high pitched voice is not intended to refer to a point in the sound scale, but to a semantic network different from the auditory reality. The case is the same in visual language, whose meaning cannot be identified with one or another of its visual variable components. This was the lesson offered by the artist Magritte, when he wrote under a drawing whose contours and colors resembled a pipe: "Ceci n'est pas une pipe" (This is not a pipe). Many similar occurrences in the work of the Belgian surrealist do not raise, as M. Foucault said (1968), the problem of nomination in both verbal and visual systems, but that of the structures of both semiotic systems in relation to the production of meaning.

In addition, how from Greimas point of view can this semiotics of the natural world propose a language when it offers nonindividualizable and nonlexicalizable percepts? What is a cloud among thousands of clouds specifically saying to us, or a portion of a lake in which one swims, the gait of a horse, the trajectory of a balloon? To project in such instances an association or an anthropomorphic interpretation does not make these natural phenomena elements of a language. To experience an emotion at the sight of a natural phenomenon or to speak of an object in this way (to refer to a sea as "angry" or to steel as "cold" or, again, to a landscape as "sad") does not make of this object a language. As is the case with sound phenomena, visual phenomena must present particular properties if they are to become flexible functions in a coherent syntactic structure, aiming at representation and communication. A. J. Greimas had realized the dead end character of a semiotics ultimately based on percepts already lexicalized and semanticized by verbal language, when he protested against a visual semiotics based on iconicity, that is, on a global analogy with the world. He offered many arguments against this approach which have remained unheard:

> At the same time, it is also to deny visual semiotics, as such, since the analysis of an articulated flat surface will consist of, in this perspective, identifying the iconic signs or symbols and lexicalizing them in a natural language; it is not surprising, then, that research on principles of organization of signs thus recognized, is led to be confused with that of their lexicalization; and that the analysis of a work, for example, is transformed as a matter of fact into an analysis of the discourse on the work. The specificity of visual semiotics is diluted, then, in these two macro-semiotics, which are the natural world and natural languages. (1979; 177)

It seems to us that not only has this danger not been avoided by certain visual analyses inspired by Greimasian semiotics but also that it is inevitable in any context which understands verbal language as the only complete and universal language.

Without recapitulating discussions on the nature of aesthetic experience and the fact that it can be more general than the relation with so-called artistic objects or discussions concerning the definition of art itself, it appears to us that one can only affirm that an object is part of a linguistic system (which permits it to convey messages other than its own immanence or simply be the target of verbal projections of a perceiver) on the basis of a specific linguistic hypothesis. Furthermore, we think that, historically, the particular problem of sculpture has always been the resolution of this dilemma concerning the conditions under which an object ceases to be a thing among other things in order to become a representative linguistic object called sculpture.

Another of the many difficulties encountered in the development of a theory of a sculptural object derives from the credibility that is still ascribed to the unfortunate distinction made by Lessing, in his *Laocoon* of 1766, between the 'spatial arts' (painting, sculpture, architecture) in which objects are perceived in a global and instantaneous way, and the 'temporal arts' (music, poetry, dance) which are perceived in a successive fashion. This concept takes into account certain characteristics belonging to the manifestations of these two types of objects but effects an abstraction of the human subject that constitutes these objects in a perceptual event which, in either case, occurs always in time. As René Thom wrote: "Now every symbolic activity is displayed necessarily in time . . . We will localize, therefore, temporally, the signifier at the moment where the interpreter perceives and interprets it; in contrast there is often ambiguity as to the temporal localization of the signified" (1980; 195).

The accumulation and diversity of gathered data at the time of perception raises the problem of the constitution, of the manipulation, and of the integration of mnemonic images, that is, memorized mental, visual images through which the signifiers/signified of these perceptive ensembles are retained and connected in the cortex, to be elaborated upon in successive *tempi* of the experience of the object. This perceptual memory is twofold: a short-term memory, retaining several instances of actual perceptual experiences, and a long-term memory retaining and connecting them as accumulated mnemonic percepts in the cortex. This essential mechanism of the relationship with any visual work, this putting of the multiple actual percepts resulting from different perspectives and sightings in relation with mnemonic percepts, is not necessarily a feat easily accomplished by the majority of human beings. It corresponds in fact to the difficult task of constructing a mental space of representation, the term 'space' being defined, as mentioned earlier, as the simultaneous coexistence of multiple stimuli, which may be quite heterogeneous to one another.

If the almost uniquely frontal position of the perceiver before a pictorial work and the potentialities of peripheral vision give him the illusion of an instantaneous perception, the reality of the perceptual process is quite different. Contrary to Lessing's proposition, the pictorial work can require a longer perceptual time than a sculpture or an architectural facade, and the perception of these visual works can demand a longer time than listening to a musical or theatrical work, whether that time is successive or continuous. In a general way, however, as we will see here, the perception of a sculpture requires particularly protracted and complex perceptive trajectories, which explains without any doubt the epistemological difficulty relative to its study.

But, before explaining the nature of the perceptual trajectories required by any sculptural object, let us repeat that the use of the organ of sight in the apprehension of a sculpture does not put into play only visual percepts, or only tactile percepts, such as a fruitless opposition between painting and sculpture would like to establish.

This opposition is often reasserted by common sense which does not possess, however, any instrument to determine what distinguishes the tactile from the visual in the perception of reality and, in turn, their differences within the visual representation itself. This discrimination requires a specific knowledge of the processes of perception and of the modes of representation of visual language. In this matter, one can fully agree with the phenomenological observation made by Merleau-Ponty: "And, inversely, any experience of the world that has always given to me, in the context of movements of the gaze, the visible spectacle, belongs to touch no more or less than the 'tactile qualities' themselves. We must become used to thinking that anything visible is shaped in the tangible . . ." (1968; 165).

In his *Historical Grammar of the Plastic Arts,* which is more of a semiology of styles than of visual language, Riegl nevertheless needed to define some basic elements of the work of art in order to establish semiotic variables by which these styles are perceived and recognized. If volume, which he called simply the 'form', constitutes the basic paradigm, Riegl knew enough to distinguish, and in an exemplary way, its tactile and visual constituents:

> All things in nature have a form, that is, they are extended in accordance with the three dimensions—height, width and depth. Only touching them permits us, however, to directly assure ourselves of this state of fact. In contrast, that of the five senses which serves for man to receive impressions which exterior things give to him—sight—is rather prone to induce in us error about the three dimensions of what we see. Because our eye is not in a position to see through bodies and sees therefore, only one side presented to it as two-dimensional surface. It is only when we have recourse to experiences of touch, that we complete in mind the two-dimensional surface perceived by the eyes in order to make it a three-dimensional form. This process is effected much more rapidly and easily when the object contemplated presents aspects which evoke memories of experiences of touch. (1978; 121)

We will return to the consequences of this structure of the perception of volume through bidimensionality.

However, one must add that senses other than the tactile and visual are involved in the apprehension of a sculpture: kinesthesic, postural, buccal, and so on. This will widen the problem defined by Reigl in the perception of the natural object as well as in that of the sculptural object.

In effect, one must insist on the facts that: a) one must not identify the mechanisms of perception with those of visual representation; b) this semiotic representation does not have as an unique reference visual perception and, even less, its products in external reality. We have already explained how visual language, by its spatial characteristics, serves to represent experiences issuing from all organic spaces. Visual variables are thus used in order to represent experiences as different and heterogeneous as those which are linked in buccal, postural, auditive or thermal space.

Vice versa, different perceptual systems may concur in gathering similar types of information, but within different intensity, context, and treatment: "Of further importance is the idea that a particular kind of information is not necessarily the special domain of a particular perceptual system, but rather that different systems can detect the same information, either singly or in combination" (Turvey, 1974; 168).

If one easily admits that words, in which the semiotic material is audible, can refer to nonauditory objects (such as, say, an apple or cancer), one identifies, again mistakenly, visual language with the unique representation of the visual. Indeed, if human beings resort to visual language, it is because its spatializing character is directly suitable for the modeling of a reality which is deployed simultaneously in three dimensions but across different sensory spatial levels.

Therefore, one must recognize that the eye is as important in the perception of a sculpture as it is in that of a painting. Furthermore, its role is more important than that of the sense of touch, contrary to widespread belief. Sculpture is mainly revealed by the visual variables which constitute it, texture being only one element among many others. Indeed, the most important differences between painting and sculpture reside in the different and much stronger way in which the other sensory organs besides vision and touch are called upon. Thus, the postural dimension, which operates in relation to the proportion and vectorialities of the body itself with those of a painting or sculpture, stakes more of a claim in the modes of perception of sculpture. Kinesthesic experience, whether it deals with the projection of possible movements in reality or the felt awareness of the results of a prehension and manipulation of certain parts of a sculpture, is more important perhaps than that of the tactile experience which prefers the exploration of the object's surfaces by the body or the hand. If tactility is important on the plane of reference, when vision recognizes certain types of textures, the tactile sensation most often plays a minor role in the perception of the work. At times, distance, most often the fragility of materials, even of marble or bronze, prohibit this type of sensory relation between the perceivers and the sculptural work.

This leads to the consideration that, with respect to the pictorial and the sculptural fields, the basic mechanisms of perception are the same.

Perception can only be realized by an ocular fixation or centration in the visual field, which, when foveal, gathers a given ensemble of visual variables which we have called a coloreme. Any centration can only establish a dynamic correspondence with one section of a visual region, which is itself animated by energies conveyed by the visual variables which have been used and whose nature we have previously explained. Parallel to the number of centrations, the coloremes multiply and form more or less strongly interconnected regions, of subgroups diversely integrated or separated. Every time the perceiver modifies the angle or the direction of his view or positions himself differently before or around the work, he is confronted with an ever-changing disposition of stimuli with respect to their structure, their density, their energy, and so on, which modify their spatial interrelations. Perception does not provide information only about characteristics of individual objects, but as stressed by J. J. Gibson (1966), informs about the spatio-temporal relations between dynamic perceptual events in the three dimensions of space.

The greater complexity in the perception of sculpture as opposed to that of a pictorial representation stems from the fact that the physical movements of the perceiver before the pictorial field place him/her in relation to given data which, from the containing properties of the Basic Plane, appear in immediate relation to other data of a similar field, whereas the different positionings of the perceiver before the sculptural object can allow him/her access to regions of the visual field which appear completely different from the previously perceived ones, these having become inaccessible to centrations because they are situated at an opposing angle or because certain elements in relief hide what was previously apprehended.

Not only must the perceiver proceed to a precise imbrication of coloremes which are provided by each region, as in pictorial experience, but he/she must also put into relation what appear as completely heterogeneous regions. The perceiver has to organize, in a constant process of transformation, a type of infrastructure which can reveal the nature of their dynamism and function in the construction of the global object. Each of the regions so interconnected in the perception must be relayed to perceptual memory in proportion as the displacement of the perceiver opens him/her to new percepts which will transform the equilibria or groupings already realized, by the insertion of actual new sensorially active percepts. These will transform in the perceived field and in memory the groupings or subgroupings already established. Not only are these interconnections between the coloremes and regroupings of coloremes necessarily produced by the perceptual mechanisms, and liable to be continually modified by later movements of the gaze, but the coloremes that are not linked to others can with great difficulty be entrusted to memory so they can serve in the construction of the object to be perceived, as research on memory has revealed (Pribram, 1971).

Perception can result only from a lengthy accumulation of centrations producing percepts which are always different, constituting subregions, each interlinked to the other in regions or superregions, suited to integrate them and the subsequent percepts into a unified totality. This temporal sequence, where the accumulation and organization of anterior percepts soon takes precedence, despite the constant afflux of new percepts, must be reconverted into a spatial ensemble, or in other words, into a simultaneous coexistence of percepts, through the development of a dynamic three-dimensionality or volumetry, as the unifying spatial structure of sculptural representation.

This integration of the innumerable regions, subsystems of regions and of superregions, of which the interrelations and dependencies are engaged in continuous transformations, is already a lengthy and very complex operation in the perception of the pictorial plane, requiring operational projections which stem from the dialectical structure pertaining to the subject who perceives. But this equilibrium is much more difficult to realize for the sculptural object, because the changes in points of view are not only those which are chosen by the eye with respect to a given field and which can be integrated by assimilation/accommodation. The changes in position of the perceiver who strolls around a sculptural object imply transformations which the object itself offers, in a volumetry to which one relates through completely different perspectives. The perceiver must proceed to accommodations to a visual field different from one position to another, in order to arrive at the conception of a possible perceptual unity of these dissimilar ensembles in one and the same work.

Thus the perception of a sculpture hardly differs from that of a pictorial work in the need for the development of a lengthy series of percepts of regions and of interactions between regions which, according to their respective positions, dimensions, colors, vectorialities, and so forth, define the different quantities of energy and the intensities which bring them together or dynamically separate them, thus creating effects of depth. But to the effects of depth produced by perceptual mechanisms involved in one single positioning of the perceiver, the sculpture requires the integration of the percepts and the effects of depth, multiplied by numerous points of view, in order to construct its rotundity. The perceiver must occupy multiple positions around the object in order to obtain the data with which he can construct the global object—unless the object itself is in mechanical rotation around its axis—and from these, look at it from a multiplicity of angles. This physical movement has as an immediate consequence the production of kinesthetic percepts in the endogenous or internal space of the perceiver, of a different order from those which result from visual percepts and which can come into conflict with the dynamic relations that the latter tend to produce. In addition, one must recall Merleau-Ponty's observation: "Touching . . . is to touch oneself" (1968; 308). If the tactile senses give data, mnemonic or actual, about the endo-epidermic reality as much as about the external object, one can hence suspect the magnitude of the sensory-motor and kinesthetic experiences aroused, which can present an obstacle to the apprehension of other kinesthetic movements inscribed in the semiotic materials themselves.

The reflections of Strzeminski on sculpture have underlined some of these complexities of perception: "The optical impression of a plastic three-dimensional work of art presents itself as a sequence of projection planes which are quite numerous, different and separated from one another. Each plane is separated from the others by a certain lapse of time corresponding to the movement of the spectator and the positions from which he chooses to observe the work."

He concludes from this description that one can thus:

> compare to a chain the impression of the ensemble which results from the observation of a three-dimensional work of art:

> The verticals represent the visual impressions (projection planes) and the horizontal lines the lapse of time which separates these visual impressions from each other. (Strzeminski, 1977; 113)

If the temporal sequence is well illustrated in this diagram, we cannot accept the linear and regular character of the model as representative of the process of production of percepts. This process must instead be conceived as a dynamic activity which transforms some elements inside the perceiver as well as the global unity of the work being perceived. On the other hand, the linear chain thus evoked cannot properly account for the diversity of the interrelations and the heterogeneity of perceptual networks, con-structed in different and successive changing networks which are always at work in the perception of a sculpture.

6.2. Networks of Perspectives

At a first level, the sculpture presents itself to perception as a physical object belonging to the natural macroscopic world and which, whether or not labeled as an object of art, is understood in its relation to the physical objects which surround it according to the perspectives of natural percep-tion. Situated in a given space, the sculpture is necessarily apprehended according to the network of parameters which ordinarily defines any natural object, from a view at a near, medium or far distance. In certain cases, explicit indications must be given so that this object is isolated from others and recognized as a work of art. It is the case with any of the so-called "ready-made" objects, as Duchamp called those more or less modified prefabricated objects borrowed from external reality, that would not have any symbolic function without the subjective affirmation of the artist. But whatever the perceptual treatment accorded to a three-dimensional object and the particulars of its symbolic structure, it will always already have been first understood according to the perspectives linked to the perception of any physical object. These will have to be compounded with the different perspectives which will be established or recognized in the course of a perceptual trajectory, constructing the volume as a linguistic object.

In the majority of natural perspectives, from a horizontal viewing, objects in reality appear as demi-reliefs against their background as long as changes in position inform us, not of a perceivable rotundity, but rather of different facets of the object, always in demi-relief on a plane, with which we construct the notion of volume. Even when the contrasts of chiaroscuro are used to construct the depth in demi-relief presented by the front of any object, the conclusion that the object is round, rather than in demi-relief, results from a conceptual leap and not from any direct perceptual data.

Indeed, the recognition by the perceiver of the fact that an ensemble of percepts can be identified as the "good gestalt" of a tree or a house, that is, a known volumetric object, constitutes most often a permission he/she gives himself to perceive no longer the visual variables which constitute the object. The economy of pragmatic functions devalues the perceptual trajectory which is no longer essential to the "substantialist" identification of the object, to the benefit of a quick interpretation where what one knows of the object is more important than what one actually sees. The decoding of the visual language, serving symbolic representation, requires for its part an active perceptual relation with all visual components, of which the modes of interaction constitute the specific syntactic network. As observed by K. Bühler:

> "The structure of any particular language is largely field-independent, being determined by its own convention rules, but the field determines how the rules are applied" (Blumenthal, 1970; 56).

In this context, empty or redundant visual variables do not exist, since each contributes to the specific structuring of the visual fabric, according to its organizational rules.

One must, therefore, not confuse the natural perspectives of perception with the pragmatic behaviors and functions which have been added to it, and which forsake as much as possible the steps of the perceptual trajectory under the pretext of an economy of efforts, time or energies. The natural perspectives of physical reality cannot be constructed through nonvisible data, under threat of becoming abstract perspectives. One cannot maintain, as it has been done to certain minimal sculptures, that a work can be seen instantly and globally in a single moment of perception (Judd, 1964; 36, 37). The fact of "recognizing" a cube in the *Black Box* of Tony Smith, from percepts obtained in a given position, does not reveal to us in any way the particular aspects that a strolling around it, requiring time and made at different distances, would reveal, such as successive angles and proportions, lightings, surfaces, always-changing vectorialities, which all lead to volumetric syntheses in continual transformations. The perceptual data have the farthest removed relations from the form that a certain geometric representation or a mental visual image would give to a cube.

Furthermore, when the perceiver moves nearer to the sculpture to obtain an appropriate distance from which he feels he can best perceive it, he will adopt various sorts of positionings and of visual orientations and will multiply these angles of vision in an active movement, producing a certain number of fragmentary percepts from the zones on which his centrations will be made. Locally, these percepts of regions are regrouped into subensembles and consigned to memory, continuously being added to other subensembles resulting from different points of view, leading to a more or less fragmented apprehension of the ensemble of stimuli presented by the totality of the work. Whereas it is difficult to evaluate the mnemonic impact of percepts produced at the first level of natural perspectives, which position the object in its environment, the more proxemic and extraordinarily varied perceptive paths of the second level have to be actively interconnected with them, so as to represent the structure and the characteristics of the work at the cortical levels.

In addition, on a third level, the perceiver must also take into account the points of view, sightings, and perspectives that the producer has himself inscribed in the work. These are apparent in his choice, treatment, and organization of the visual variables constituting the objective observable marks defining the object of the representation. Certainly, in order to become a language and stop being a simple thing, the sculptural object must not only be endowed with a syntactic structure allowing material signifiers to acquire permutable functions in the ensembles, but it must also be able to incorporate in the object organizational schemas of perspective stemming from the intentions and needs of the producer. This means that besides the natural networks of perspectives in which it is necessarily inserted as a physical object, the sculptural object must find the possibility of integrating a network of foreign perspectives, sometimes contradictory to the first perspectives, likely to signify and represent sensory and spatial organizations of a different order.

In both a natural and semiotic attitude, the sculptor Cellini defined in the sixteenth century eight points of observation for a sculpture, corresponding to points issuing from the main vertical, horizontal, and diagonal axes. While prescribing or programming a minimal path of perception—which is not spontaneously taken before a natural, physical object—the artist was still describing only an abstract theoretical schema, applicable to any physical object. This requirement was, in fact, minimal, as this schema should ideally extend to the 360 degrees of rotation and of possible transference of the object, if one wished to have an adequate knowledge of it.

This is particularly the case of the small discrete sculptures that can be held in the palm of one's hand, which by their autonomy and perceptual openness seemed for some time to correspond to the very paradigm of sculptural art.

The aesthetics of the ancient Greeks emphasized the sculptor's need to harmonize the points of arrival of the mobile path of the eye around an object, in relation to the fundamental axes. Contemporary thought has particularly questioned the absolute and static character of these perceptual sightings, oriented in an arbitrary manner on a few points only of the object's periphery. They do not seem to correspond to the nature of usual human mechanisms of perception nor to other types of intentionality governing the production of the sculpture whether they are mimetic or nonmimetic. Besides being a three-dimensional physical object, the sculpture would appear the vehicle of particular messages which must be read in a linguistic or symbolic context and not only through simple physical or static structures of the object. The origins of sculpture in human societies—curiously still somewhat inscrutable today—certainly indicate the intention not of producing without reason other physical objects to be juxtaposed to natural objects but rather of transmuting physical materials into semiotic materials, as carriers of a particular language.

This path of "syntaxicalization" was developed over time in an extremely varied way by artistic production. It corresponded to the fundamental parameters of space as near distance and as remote distance: "The distance from which sight perceives things is therefore of primordial importance for the reception of things in nature by the inner senses of man and, consequently for the competition with these things in which man is engaged when he forms plastic works" (Riegl, 1978; 122).

Given this finding, we will proceed to distinguish the syntactic correlatives of this basic dimension of distance in all the heterogeneous objects subsumed under the same label of "sculpture."

6.3. Proxemic Sculptures

The hegemony of the free-standing sculpture that emerged in the Renaissance, as well as that of styles of painting reflecting it, singularly obscured the possibilities of an analysis of a sculptural phenomenon, all the more since it was linked to an illusory mimetic function whose magical aspect seems to still fascinate our contemporaries even one century after the invention of photography (Gombrich, 1960).

Historically, sculpture seemed to have sprung up from two totally different syntactic sources: (1) the 'kleinplastik', the small sculpture, the figurine or amulet, that is, an autonomous and small round object which one could hold and turn in one's hand, and (2) the low-relief obtained from the hollowing-out of a slab or plate in order to obtain a series of concavities and convexities. Even if these two types of sculpture posit most frequently a field of proxemic representation, they are ultimately capable of creating illusory distances.

The small sculpture which can be manipulated seems to obtain an autonomy in relation to the surrounding milieu because, in a perspective of height, from a more or less oblique sighting, the distance which is established between two opposing points on its circumference, multiplied in continuous rotations, offers most rapidly the experience constituting a volume or rotundity.

It seems to define itself by the system of its external volume, closed and constant, by the particulars of the visual variables of its surface, where inclinations and variations in texture multiply its accidental relations with surrounding illumination. Its autonomy is rendered possible, however, only by the consideration of its external volume seen as isolated and constant, while its relations with visual energies which dynamize the surrounding milieu are placed between parentheses and disregarded.

The diverse vectorialities and the inclinations in the peripheral contour of the small sculpture allow us to "imagine" an internal structure of the volume which could explain the variations in the external regions. This internal structure remains, however, always imagined and not perceived; what is given to be seen/touched only constitutes the external volume. Without repeating our earlier reflections on this notion, let us recall the definition of Jean Piaget of the system produced by a dominance of this concept. The 'external volume', he wrote, makes of the object that it envelops "an indefinable solid in the sense of being incompressible and nondilatable" in radical opposition with the properties of "interior volume" (1980; 189).

The internal regions of an object conceived from the notion of external volume remain in a state of "coalescence" for perception, according to the term used by Piaget in order to stress the absence of the previous separability of a field, where one could determine similar/dissimilar factors capable of being coordinated into subensembles. Indeed, these undifferentiated regions correspond to the notion of a topological point, being a region inaccessible to experience as well as to knowledge.

A sculpture which centers its structural constituents on the properties of external volume puts into play signifiers which cannot be transformed or interrelated and interact in perception in a way that will produce the tools of a syntactic structure sufficiently developed to construct representations other than their immanent images. The external volume tends to freeze the object as a "thing", and no longer as a medium where syntactic functions result in a mobility of positions and interrelations between the constituting elements.

The small sculpture that one can hold in his hand, as well as the more recent kinetic sculpture which turns on itself under the action of the hand or a motor, necessitates most often only a frontal position on the part of the spectator in a more or less oblique viewing. But it does induce an integration of visual, tactile, kinesthetic, sensory percepts in an actual or virtual spatialization founded on one of the fundamental topological relations—that of envelopment. Tactile/visual percepts of linear and planar regions confirm that the hand/eye has returned or could return to its very point of departure. In this sense, the experience of external volume is always that of a closed-in object limited by a closed form.

However, archeological residues of primitive or historically ancient societies lead us to believe that the small sculpture was, since the very beginning, accompanied by another type of sculptural production—that of *low-relief* realized in sand or clay or on the walls of caves. The most ancient productions of India or Egypt have reached us in the form of reliefs, at first slightly marked, then more obtrusive, obtained by hollowing out a surface, which constituted the very support-plane of the work.

This artistic production was overshadowed in the theory of art by free-standing sculpture, a state of affairs against which Wörringer has vigorously protested, but it seems, in vain:

"But it is still the history of Greek relief, of which we have underestimated for too long a time the meaning and the decisive role to devote exclusive consideration to free-standing sculpture, which does show how the flat presentation was chosen for itself and not following external requirements, because it was that which responded the best to the artistic wish" (1953; 107)

We would say rather that representation in low relief offered more possibilities for the development of sculpture as a language than did free-standing sculpture. In effect, low-relief seems to borrow its syntactic possibilities from pictorial art, since its support constitutes, like the pictorial Basic Plane, a dynamic gestaltian data, already strongly structured, in which the interior volume and mass play with the semi-rotundities produced by the artist. It produces a fictional space suitable for structuring an indefinite series of spatial representations. Low relief also resembles the pictorial Basic Plane in that the perceiver's approach is mainly frontal at a relatively close distance, even if it does evoke, as well, the illusory, distant spaces of painting within the same repertoire of perspectives. Thus, sculpture in low-relief, even when situated in a vast architectural ensemble, determines its own fictional space which differentiates it from other objects of the natural world.

In an intuition close to that of the pictorial, even if tonality plays a more important role there than chromaticity, this type of representation showed a remarkable understanding of the necessity of opening itself to spatial potentialities in order to organize a language capable of saying more than the mere connotations of its materiality. It is only through the structuring of an internal volume in sculpture, which engenders in turn countless virtual volumes, that the conjunction, juxtaposition, and integration of different experiences and different points of view about reality can become representable.

What is described today as a willingness to "flatten-out" or collapse volumes on the plane in a low relief was, in reality, a coherent and powerful way of exploring the expressive possibilities of virtual or topological volumes through a structuring of internal structures.

Even when, by the accentuation of protuberances into the third dimension, these low reliefs became high reliefs, the relation of this volumetric object with the wall was maintained for a long time. In spite of the interruption caused by the emergence of Hellenic sculpture after the third century before Christ, the sculpture of the Middle Ages registered a very slow progression from low relief toward high relief in sculptures which still lean against the wall, inside a niche, or under a canopy. Panofsky queried the meaning of this curious phenomenon:

> "The incapacity of the classic Gothic statue to live without its dais is heavy with a symbolic value that is highly significant. The role of this dais is not only to connect it to the mass of the edifice but, moreover, to delimit and assign a certain portion of free space to it" (1975; 112)

Panofsky underlines the acuity with which the architect and theoretician Bertani had understood "the problematic of perspective relief, that he sees as an amalgam of fiction and reality, reprising in many instances the analyses of Leonardo da Vinci, in No. 37 of his *Treatise*" (168).

In the 15th century, the most extreme reliefs produced by Ghiberti, as well as the first free sculptures, did not exclude leaning on a side of a wall. In a less extended way, these sculptures conserve the dynamic parameters which permit them to make potential their internal tensions, to constitute virtual energies, in a word, to make their elements dialectic in a specific linguistic function.

The evolution from low relief toward high relief and semi-free standing works, and of volumes of sometimes quite larger diameters, while these were still embedded in a plane or an original slab, was without doubt accelerated by the desire of sculpture to become autonomous in relation to painting. This has been a secular conflict which still prompts Carl Andre to say that he feels "an instinctual hatred for Leonardo and low relief" (1980; 27). But once sculpture was progressively liberated from the wall and transposed to public places in a wide, complex and changing environment, it underwent a profound change. It lost the syntactic and semantic system of former bas-relief, which allowed it to give an operational structure and a linguistic function to the organization/production of potential internal volumes, and began its search for an equivalent element acting as a Basic Plane.

6.4. Sculptures Situated at a Distance

The free-standing sculpture of the Renaissance, most often of a monolithic nature, seemed to return to the dilemma of the "external volume," autonomous and unchangeable, isolated within its frontiers and in which only the axes and peripheral protruberances could offer information about its structural elements. Except for its mimetic function which defined it as a specular subproduct of which one did not know how to make a system, sculpture threatened to vanish as a linguistic system in order to become only an object among others. As such, it could be said to be perhaps more beautiful, suiting the variability of aesthetic taste, or it became endowed with a magical function, actually reduplicating or competing with the productivity of nature itself, as explained by Riegl and Gombrich.

However, on the plane of its apprehension, free-standing sculpture, larger than the previous small sculptures, was confronted with a major problem concerning its true autonomy in the milieu where it was placed. This environment offered energies vibrating from light itself, reflecting on natural objects or constructions in which the visual characteristics of dimensions, colors, vectorialities, and other factors possessed an obvious dynamic force. The first question can be readily asked: what part should the *scope* of peripheral vision, active in natural perspectives, play in the apprehension of a free-standing sculpture, situated in a public place or in a vast architecture? With which environmental elements could it or should it establish relations of proportionality, of contrast, of vectoriality? In other words, did sculpture possess a specific space in which one could apprehend it, or was it an integral part of a much larger environment, where most of its means of expression greatly lost their visual efficacy? Riegl argued that the refusal of color or its parsimonious use in the polychromy of antique statuary derived from a willingness to make autonomous the work of art of large dimensions in relation to natural objects or other objects produced by man. The small figures could better capitalize on the possibilities of chromaticism, because their "format excluded all possibility of taking them as something other than the work of man" (Riegl, 1978; 159). This would explain the refusal of sculpture to exploit the resources of color until the beginning of the 20th century, accompanied by the curious theory that the color of materials did not act as chroma, but as simple revelations of the nature of constituent materials. For a long time, the best solution for sculpture remained to define the distance within which it existed and could be seen from parameters which a wall or a series of edifices offered in the distance, these playing on a larger scale the role of the fictional wall of the low relief.

It is necessary to wait until the end of the 19th century in order for artistic practice and theoretical reflection to grasp the fact that free-standing sculpture had in fact substituted the supporting ground for the syntactic function of the original wall of the low relief. The ground is the ultimate physical support to which sculpture is linked by a base or pedestal, isolating it from an environment where it could otherwise be nothing more than an object among others. This base, already a low or a high relief, allowed sculpture to be displayed in a specific fictional space, involving a limit linked to the support, where the spatial potentialities necessary to the production of a symbolic representation could be engendered.

This global structure, however, remained dualist and fixed, the connections between the two regions being predefined. A functional role was superficially assigned to the base and a dynamic or expressive role to the upward figure that it supported. In a certain sense, this figure on a base reconstituted the status proper to the relation of the pictorial figure on a ground, where only the first element is the object of a valorization and of a dynamic development. By this fundamental nonvalorization, even if the base were the site for many ornamentations of which one denied a linguistic role (as would be the case in any ornamental art), the base of the sculpture conserved an intermediary status between that of a linguistic instrument and that of a purely functional object.

Furthermore, free-standing sculpture, with its closed external volume, does not allow any more than small sculpture any observation of how the visual variables used by the producer interconnect in the central layers where the energetic sources of the occurrences perceived on the surface are localized. The system of external volume does not permit the constitution of the material energies forming the central layers as semiotic signifiers nor the description of them by an articulation which would specify their syntactic function. Perception only exercises itself on the particulars of external volume, according to a certain number of perceptual parameters of position, distance, angularities, and vectorialities, defining the object only from the exterior. This epistemological gap will be filled in part by the development of the notion of internal volume at the end of the 19th century.

It is by returning to the mechanisms of perception that the reflection of a sculptor such as Adolf von Hildebrand (1907), whose thinking would be broadly disseminated by Riegl and Wörringer, allowed the questioning of the notion of external volume in its association with that of internal volume. Hildebrand reestablished, in effect, the fundamental distinction between what near vision sees and what far vision sees, which will revivify the notion of both the plane and that of relief in the cube.

This proposition is widely discussed by Riegl:

> If one brings totally together the object and the eye—what we will define as near vision—we have an impression that procures simply a two-dimensional surface. If the eye distances itself a little, it has the possibility of perceiving in the object aspects which awake in him the memory of experiences of touch . . . If the distancing between the eye and the object exceeds the possibilities of normal vision, it is again the opposite process which is produced: the shading disappears more and more behind the growing density of the layer of air between the eye and the object and, to finish, the retina perceives nothing more than a uniform surface of light or color; we will qualify this process as far vision. (1978; 122)

Because far vision gives the illusion of a planar surface where there actually exists a volume in three dimensions, Riegl considered this a sensory illusion and called this percept a "subjective" surface, whereas the first, obtained by near vision, which is not an illusion, is called the "objective surface."

Thus, bodies in three dimensions are all perceptually delimited by surfaces in two dimensions, which fragment in a continuous fashion the contour of the external volume, the latter always only a theoretic reconstitution from several points of centration of perception. Riegl used this hypothesis to define volumetry altogether differently, since "the surface that the eye sees from near and transmits to the interior sense is a part of an effectively existing body, of which the eye, in this precise case, cannot perceive anything other than this surface which is a part of it" (1978; 123). Indeed, the internal sense which is thus awakened by a perceptual contact with partial surfaces of the volume becomes aware of the reality of an internal volume of which the surface is only the visible limit. This interior volume is, according to Riegl, perceptibly different under an objective surface and a subjective surface: "The contents of the objective surface is larger than that of the subjective surface. Because the objective surfaces of an object do not rest absolutely in the same plane, they are bent towards the interior or towards the exterior; and partial surfaces belonging to these curves escape distant vision" (1978; 147).

This is what caused Hildebrand to conclude that only near vision could be the basis of the work of the sculptor, and not the distant vision which serves rather a purely empirical activity.

The inclinations of the planes in partial surfaces, perceived by near vision, being necessarily linked to differently oriented internal masses, reveal these as individual units, characterized by axial energies specific to each and offering, according to Wörringer, "the image of the closed material individuality," that no theory of contour or silhouette can procure, because "relations of depth had to be, as much as possible, transformed into surface relations" (1953; 70).

Wörringer used the notion of the internal limit of interior volume in his analysis of Michelangelo's sculpture: "Here, in turn, for Michelangelo, the enclosure of material is not rendered perceptible from the exterior but from the interior; according to this artist, the rigidly enclosing limits of the material are less factual than imaginary, which does not prevent them from appearing with utmost clarity to our consciousness" (1953; 109).

But this hypothesis about the organization of partial surfaces as signifiers of depth required, at the same time, recourse to a basic parameter by which these "closed material individualities" could be measured and compared, not metrically but topologically. It required the postulate of a primordial plane in relation to which these reliefs or distensions of matter were displayed. Thence a resurgence of a vocabulary linked to low relief, but with a completely different meaning, since the Basic Plane postulated for all these agglomerates of matter is now dialectic and fictional and not linked to a material support like that which the Basic Plane provides in the pictorial.

This made it possible for sculpture to resume a function of representation as a finality in the artistic act. Hildebrand, who was strongly aware of this, wrote: "The activity of the plastic arts takes possession of the object as an object uniquely explainable by the mode of representation and not as an efficient or meaningful object in itself, poetically or aesthetically" (in Wörringer, 1953; 40).

Hildebrand also remarked that the apprehension of a free-standing sculpture as a simple cubic volume does not take into account its true artistic function:

> Inasmuch as a plastic figure is made the most of, at the first, as cubic, it is only the first step of the configuration and it is only when it will act as a plane while remaining cubic that it will have acquired an artistic form. It is only by the consequent accomplishment of this apprehension of relief of our cubic impressions that the representation finds its consecration, and the mysterious benefit that we experience owing to the work of art rests only on this same accomplishment. (in Wörringer, 1953; 56)

The perceptual necessity that any region of a sculpture must present itself as a surface in two dimensions, as Riegl had said, but on a surface which possesses, nevertheless, a content, an inclination, or an internal thickness, constitutes this region indeed as a topological mass inserted in the virtual Basic Plane determining the dynamisms of its constituent visual variables. The depths behind the partial surfaces will be interpreted through the elaboration of a series of partial Basic Planes, making explicit their internal cubic volume. This interrelation will first be described as that of an undulatory plane. "All the separate judgements concerning depth must be unified in a unitary and encompassing judgement. So that, finally, all the richness of the form of a figure is placed before us as a continuity towards the rear of a single simple plane" (Wörringer, 1953; 93).

The necessity that any representation of volumetric depth be constructed through the planar dimension was reaffirmed by a number of artists. Certain of them, following Greenberg's theory of "planeity," claim even to interpret it as a true bidimensionality and no longer as the external limit of an interior depth. Hans Hofmann, for example, while affirming that we always see bidimensionally, added that a sculpture which, by the interplay of its lights and shadows, does not offer an absolute bidimensionality, expresses only an irritating tridimensional disequilibrium, because static and incomplete, through the absence of the dynamic of negative spaces, that is to say, spaces constructed from the background itself (1948; 53).

This undulatory continuity of the sculptural structure derives, according to Hildebrand, from a system of interactions of lights and shadows in the periphery of the volume, emphasizing the reliefs through the inclinations of external planes which multiply the revelatory energetic events in the near vision of internal volumes. Even if this opens to a first level of "syntaxicalization" of interior volume, the theoretical considerations of Hildebrand and Riegl remain strictly linked to the structural problem of the low relief and also to its subordination vis-à-vis the pictorial Basic Plane. It stresses also the sculpturally restricted possibility of the treatment of peripheral regions, to the scorn of the expressive potentiality of a more affirmed internal volume. It is through a more radical explosion of the external volume notion that the revolution of sculpture at the beginning of this century was realized.

6.5. Cubist and Constructivist Rupture

In a development from Degas to Brancusi, the concept of the base of the sculpture was first questioned, with the view of eliminating it or integrating it more into the global structure. With Rosso and Rodin, the notion of external contour was eschewed in favor of a more flexible and incisive treatment of peripheral layers, a multiplication of textures and angles of luminous reflection, a multiplication of axes and vectorial tensions in unstable equilibria which intensify the connection between central and peripheral layers.

The decisive rupture of cubism operated on two levels. As a first stage, the syntax of low-relief and of medium relief was introduced once more by the return of sculpture to the basic mural support. But it substituted for simple hollows the superimposition/juxtaposition of elements generating virtual volumes of projected shadow, creating a first effect of positive and negative space. This alternation creates a dialectic in the internal layers of sculpture, between zones of radiant and reflected light and gradations of shadow accessible to perception. These volumes created by chiaroscuro resulted in complete hollowings of regions at the interior of the global volume, incorporating light and air in sculptures. This revived both the hypothesis of centered construction, supported by a base, and the virtualization of the base in the disposition of various resting points on the ground.

The second stage produced a more complete rupture of the external volume in redoubling the elements, so that the intervals of real space could play a greater part. As already defined in *Les Bourgeois de Calais* by Rodin, the positive vectorialities and projected shadows multiply on the background-plane of a base lying on the ground, integrating with axes and tensions of the elements, all while maintaining by means of its base a structural boundary to the invasion of surrounding light.

In the contrast made possible by the relation between zones in relief and those hollowed out: a) in the background-plane of the wall; b) on the vertical base of the low relief; c) on the ground in the high-relief or d) in the relation of positive and negatives zones in the hollowed volumes, cubist sculpture opened the road to futurist and constructivist thought, which demanded the rejection of monolithic sculpture with closed external volume, and the necessary integration of internal space of sculpture to the ambient spaces, or vice versa (Boccioni, 1975). Once the base on ground was eliminated, several solutions for the replacement of the physical support were proposed, without always, however, being recognized as such: angularity of corners, suspension from the ceiling, and so on.

·This evolution made possible the presemiotical elaborations on sculpture conducted by W. Strzeminski in collaboration with K. Kobro. They spoke out against the persistence in cubo-futurist sculpture of the centered construction, that is, of a sculpture which maintained, in spite of excrescences or vectorialities oriented toward various peripheral points, a compact and dense central volume, serving as a substantial basis for these movements toward the external (1977; 103). The Polish constructivists questioned the fundamental nature of the site or the space which could properly be called sculptural. Through a general notion of space as isomorphic, homogeneous and stretching out toward infinity, derived from projective geometry, they first denied any dualism between the surrounding space and the space of the sculpture, as exemplified by the notion of boundaries or of limits assigned to the latter.

Sculpture did not possess any natural boundaries and it could be constituted without establishing boundaries of any other type. Sculpture would share with architecture, both arts of space, this prerogative of being able to structure themselves independently of any assignation of limits for its constituents: "Architecture and sculpture do not have bounds. To impose a limit on a spatial work of art is not compatible with its definition. What becomes spatial, plastic art is the space without natural boundaries, not limited by anything" (Strzeminski, 1973; 106).

But the tradition of sculpture had not realized that ideal. Baroque sculpture, for instance, which had succeeded in substituting the notion of a sculptural zone for that of external volume, had led "to the definition not only of exterior limits to sculpture, but to that of the interior of volume itself which is then open to us" (1977; 104). Strzeminski and Kobro recognized the importance of that stage constituted by this determination in baroque sculpture of a limit to the form. This was defined as "the limit of the zone of influence of its dynamic forms. We can define it in linking all the points which emerge from sculpture" (1977; 97). They called "limiting-limit" this sculptural zone which is opposed to the direct limit constituted by the old contour of the external volume: "The utilization of limiting-limit affords the advantage of making apparent, for the first time, the notion of sculpture as an ordering not of material but of a definite part of space". In other words, for sculpture "the formation of the space in which it appears is the most important thing and the quality of material with which one fills up the different parts of these spaces is only a secondary problem" (Strzeminski, 1977; 44). The sculptural zone reunites at the same time, therefore, a region of the sculpture localized in the central volume and "the zone of transition which is included between the central volume and the limiting-limit, partially by free space" (1977; 98).

In this perspective, "to construct sculpture is to give form to a part of space contained in its limiting-limit" (1977; 105). If Polish constructivism did not fully accept this intuition of a sculptural zone as a valid one, it did not altogether deny its worth as a replacement for the ancient notion of the limiting external volume: "As much as the union of forms found in the zone included between the limit of the volume and the limiting-limit with space can be considered, as much the union of volume itself with space is impossible" (1977; 100).

But through its opposition to any dualisms and to the values of movements, of dynamisms, or of structural asymmetries, it could not accept the persistence of the contrast between the materialized form and that form which can be called negative, circumscribed by the limiting-limit and the global space: "A work of sculptural or architectural art, placed in an illimited space, should be united with it as an inseparable part" (1973; 107). However, this inseparability does not proceed from characteristics offered by the visual variables themselves, but rather by a system of proportions calculated mathematically, which encompasses simultaneously the positive elements and the external space integrated into the global structure. What is more, Strzeminski and Kobro will transform this notion of the limit of sculpture into that of a place where action is reversible, structuring at the same time an internal space and the external space itself:

> The limit of sculpture is the demarcation which distinctly separates the space situated outside of the sculpture from the space contained in the sculpture. We can thus consider that this limit determines either the interior or the exterior space. The essential characteristic of sculpture rests in the fact that it is not uniquely the mise-en-forme of the interior space. One can entirely, for that matter, consider that its surface, its limit, confers a form on exterior space, a form in accord with that of the volume. (1977; 85)

This total opening of sculpture outward into exterior space appears to us, nevertheless, to render impossible the proportional relationship which must assure the inseparability of positive and negative elements of the very sculpture itself.

This inseparability between positive space and negative space is first presented by Strzeminski and Kobro as result of a calculation in the process of the production. It will be subsequently affirmed by later sculptural theory as a given perceptual datum, if one refers to the propositions of Hofmann, for example, to the effect that positive and negative spaces "exist simultaneously—both conditions the other—neither is conceivable without the other" (1948; 51). But this proposition valid for painting evades the problem of the limits of the sculptural object. Many sculptors have been unwilling to accept the constructivist hypothesis that the unified reality of sculpture should be achieved by the intermediary of mathematical equations and not by some proportions born from material characteristics of visual variables constituting the sculpture. This involves forgetting, perhaps, that any syntactic structure is necessarily anterior to the semiotic materials which it puts into play and belongs to specific theoretical levels. For our part, we find this mathematico-formal solution promulgated by Strzeminski unacceptable because it is not general enough to explain the structure of sculptures constructed according to different a priori assumptions.

Not that sculpture as a system should not be based on a priori concepts or postulates. This necessity has already been recognized and discussed by Wörringer under the name of 'legalism', but it was only used in reference to Gothic sculpture:

> These figures lose the arbitrary and obscure character which is attached to free-standing sculptural presentation, since having become aware so to say of their own relativity, they come to be integrated with a system of legal formation exterior to them. Maximal closure of the material and violent submission of the object to a geometric or cubic legality, these two plastic stylistic laws are valid from the very beginning of all sculptural art and remain more or less determinant during all its evolution as long as sculpture . . . can the least renounce, in virtue of the three-dimensionality, to 'stylization' and carry at the most, in opposition to the other arts, the characteristics of a need for abstraction. (1953; 49)

Whether this need for abstraction is epistemological or psychological, Wörringer recognized rightly that "no natural object can serve as a model for this abstraction" (54). The semiotical hypothesis will propose rather that this internal structure is defined by the syntax which permits the understanding of the various functionings of the linguistic system that is known as sculpture.

According to other theoreticians, the emergence of the hypothesis of a positive/negative space has given rise to a new questioning of this space which immediately surrounds free-standing sculpture. Arnheim expressed his reluctance to consider the relation between the volume of sculpture and the transparent volume of the air which envelops it as opposing plenum and emptiness or the relation of figure to ground: "It may seem more proper to say that a piece of sculpture is surrounded by empty space than by a substantial ground" (1966; 249). But how to explain then the transmutation of this empty space which, when it is perceived through holes introduced in the full volume, as in Moore's sculptures, appears an intermediary transparent substance which is added to the substance of positive materials? Faithful to the notion of the Euclidean void, Arnheim is reluctant to accept the contemporary intuition of the ambient air as plenum: "This is a daring extension of the sculptural universe, made possible perhaps by an era in which flying has taught us through vivid kinaesthetic experience that air is not empty space but a material substance like earth or wood or stone, a medium that carries heavy bodies and pushes them and can be bumped into like a rock" (1966; 253).

Even if one accepts this point of view, he emphasized, it is necessary to see if air is a substance which is added to the more material elements of the sculpture or if it makes the sculpture indistinguishable in the magma of the real, since the inclusion of the space eliminates any clearly defined delimitation between the work and its environment. The sculptural phenomenon becomes again, therefore, indefinable and unthinkable, as long as it vacillates between these notions which Focillon had distinguished as the space-limit, which limits the expansion of the form, and the space-milieu, by which the same work opens itself to a dynamic expansion in the multifaceted space of natural reality.

6.6. Syntax of Sculptural Language

Even if it depends entirely upon perceptual processes in order to constitute itself, as does any language, visual or otherwise, sculpture can only be defined as a linguistic object through specific internal structures, different from definitions of natural nonlinguistic objects. It cannot refer to its simple materiality, but this must be the instrument through which its elements and their interactions become suitable for the construction of open and complex spatializing models responding to the various needs of the visual representation.

At the level of its elements, sculpture is constituted, like any other medium of visual language, by the ensemble of the visual variables which are specific energetic sources submitted to movements engendered by perceptual processes. Even if they can in a very sporadic way be perceived by touch, in which the recording of data remains reduced, the sculptural visual variables are most often grasped by the sense of sight, as a product of the luminous rays reflected on a more or less opaque material support.

As such, sculpture is submitted to the discontinuous structure of visual perception which is effected through a succession of centrations of the gaze, itself constituted by the different perceptual levels of foveal, macular and peripheral vision. The ensemble of variables perceived by foveal/macular vision, at any given moment, constitutes a coloreme. Each coloreme structures, in height, width and depth, an aggregate of energies in a mass or a region more or less flat or undulated. The ensemble of coloremes perceived successively will be regrouped similarly in larger regions, into subensembles or more complex ensembles, through the basic syntactic rules which regulate the interactions of the visual variables constitutive of the visual language. These syntactical laws are as follows:

(1) *The topological relations.*

(2) *The gestaltian mechanisms of visual interactions.*

(3) *The laws of interactions of color.*

At this point, we refer the reader back to the preceding chapters for the explanation of the functional modes of these three first groups of syntactic regulations.

The syntax of sculpture will differ, however, from that of the pictorial through significant variations in the two last levels of structural organization, which are as follows:

(4) *The infrastructure of the Virtual Cube and its series of Basic Planes.*

(5) *The interactions between fictional and natural groups of perspectives.*

Sculpture shares with pictorial representation the impact of the structural modalities produced by systems of perspectives. But here, the proxemic and illusory systems of distance effects will have to come to terms with other effects of the natural perspectives as they have developed in perception of the external world. Perceptual constructs of sculpture will have to take into account the different relative weight opposing: a) the topological or illusory perspectives constructed by the producer through a certain manipulation of visual variables; b) the perspectives arising from the movements, points of view, angles of vision, and so on, produced by the perceptor; and c) the important dialectical function of the 'natural' perspectives resulting from the interrelations of sculpture—as a physical object—with its global environment.

The perception of regions or regroupings of coloremes in the sculptural object is realized, at a first level, in a way similar to the perception of pictorial regions. Perception can always only select an ensemble of masses in the sculpture, at first topological, variously undulating and inclined, that it must regroup in visual fields through the establishment of an actual or virtual Basic Plane. Furthermore, some limiting parameters must be bestowed on sculptures.

Otherwise, not only would they be unknowable, but nonexistent as linguistic systems since no means could assess the intensities of the energies and dynamic interrelations in this specific section of the global visual field. Moreover, as the theory of sculpture has already proposed, the eye perceives, in looking at a sculpture, only partial surfaces in which dynamisms and vectorialities can only be felt through a temporary limitation of the field and an estimation of the particular inclination on the recessed plane or recessed ground of the internal volume of which this surface is the facet that is accessible to perception.

The essential difference between painting and sculpture would appear, first of all, in the fact that all inclinations in depth (or the spatial curve) in painting are constructed in relation to a unique Basic Plane in which peripheral energies are very strong, whereas the perception of sculpture implies the perceptual construction of a series of Basic Planes in which energy is less condensed, given the virtual and more diffused character of the vectors which define it. This series of Basic Planes, in relation to which perception of partial surfaces of sculpture can be effected, could seem to be infinite, since their dimensions can vary from the reunion of several coloremes to the regroupings of intermediary or superregions. But this series is seen here as constructed to return to its point of departure, that is, to form a closed and limited configuration. If the perceptual process is made up of a succession of centrations leading to increasingly subjective reappraisals of the visual field, the temporary halts allowed after an adequate gathering of information will have to deal with more different and more numerous data in the case of sculpture than of painting. Moreover, this succession in perception of "partial surfaces" of sculpture requires a real movement, an actual kinesthetic experience of the body and not a subtle blink of the eye on the part of the perceiver in order to perceive regions which are to him/her at first virtually imperceptible or inaccessible.

Inversely, in this ambulatory movement, regions already perceived are completely expelled from the field of vision, thus prohibiting the realization of perceptual interactions between the former and the latter, except at the cortical levels of perceptual memory. At the basic level of the internal volume, the perception of sculpture already seems like a much more abstract operation than that of painting. It calls for a greater number of interactions between actually perceived regions and a series of multifarious memorized regions, made difficult by the fact that a simple change in the angle of the gaze is not sufficient to recall the anterior percepts.

However, the syntactic relations established from the external surface of the sculpture are not sufficient to explain the structure of this material object which obviously possesses a central region—perceptible or not—which regroups the most fundamental structural elements on which the surface energies depend.

Our hypothesis proposes, in the first place, to define sculpture, in a global way, as a topological mass essentially structured by vectors linking its central layers to its peripheral layers, and these two zones in turn to their immediate environment.

This definition excludes, on the one hand, the conception of sculpture as a simple external volume in which the periphery is autonomous and immutable in relation as much to internal energies as to those of the environment itself. It postulates that sculpture is always endowed with an interior volume—at once shifting and differentiated—capable of increasing or diminishing, diffusing or concentrating its levels of energy, and of transforming its vectorialities in relation to the structure of the peripheral layers and of the surrounding environment.

This definition entails the determination of the boundaries of the sculptural object, at whose interior a structural proposition can be verified. Like all material objects unfolding in types of spaces variously defined by geometries, sculpture can be endowed with an internal structure which defines its limits, even if these remain in a dynamic interrelation with the objects and intervals of its milieu. Conceived as a linguistic object, sculpture must necessarily assimilate itself to open structures of negative entropy, accentuating its heterogeneous functions, which cannot be materially prolonged in the entropy of the infinite and the radically illimited. Syntactically, it must be endowed with a basic limiting structure within which the components of the sculpture may acquire definite spatial characteristics, qualities and energies.

6.6.1. *Virtual cube*

It does not appear fruitful to use literally the notion of the "limiting-limit" whereby "the sculpture is contained at the interior by the limits formed by its extreme parts" and requiring that this limit is obtained in connecting, such as they are, "all the points which emerge from the sculpture" (Strzeminski, 1977; 97). The reasons are that the action of these extreme parts influences and transforms not only the other material parts of the sculpture that are thus interlinked, but also the intervals which separate and surround them, constituted by luminous and atmospheric material.

We propose, by contrast, that the immediate limit of a sculpture, which does not exclude the possibility of secondary limits, will be contained in a larger unit, the *Virtual Cube*. This construct finds its dimension in the contour which reunites, in effect, the extremities of the sculpture, but conceived as a regular form which incorporates the surface-planes, volumes, and vectorialities of 'positive' regions of the sculpture as well as those of 'negative' regions. This cubic, regular and virtual form, possessing its own proper internal structure, would thus interconnect actualized as well as virtualized energies, a necessary precondition for the development of linguistic functions.

This Virtual Cube also offers a basic volumetric structure, corresponding to a topological three-dimensional mass and according to which the potential and synthetic volumetrics of the structure can be constructed. In this sense, its dimension and form will vary with the parameters offered by the most extended "positive" elements of each sculpture, producing parallelepiped forms of cubic square, rectangle, trapezium, or a regular or flattened sphere, cone, or cylinder, all these forms being topologically similar. On the one hand, the fundamental continuity of a topological mass requires that this Virtual Cube be presented in a unified structure which can encompass the totality of a sculpture, even of an irregular or idiosyncratic form, without potentially severing it into two or more parts. On the other hand, this inclusive form must possess a maximum internal energy, the sum of its formative factors, that will intensify the forces generated by the components of the sculptural planes or volume.

The Virtual Cube thus corresponds to the contour of the most unified geometrical forms which as gestaltian "good forms" have a preeminent status in the perceptual process. Under each of these forms, the Virtual Cube possesses an internal structure endowed with specific energies whose pressures are equilibrated by the condensed energies in the external contour. Whether peripheral or central, the energies of the Virtual Cube are deemed to have effects on the perceptual plane analogous to the actual energies emanating from the visual variables constituting the sculptural material.

In the majority of cases, the Virtual Cube of sculptures is constituted as a parallelepiped, that is, as a square or rectangular cube. Thus, when the "small sculpture" presents one prominent axis, it is endowed with a rectangular cubic infrastructure. The low and high relief are endowed, from their highest protuberances, with planes which close their frontal and lateral expanses to form a cubic box, usually rectangular. The free standing sculpture sees its virtual cubic limits most often defined and its peripheral energies partially reiterated by the format of its base, its pedestal, or its supporting points on the ground. The cubic form issues from the points of maximum expansion in the "figure" or the base sections (figures XVa, XVb, XVc, XVd, and XVe).

Given the stability and the stronger dynamism of its internal/external equilibria, the square or rectangular Virtual Cube prevails even when the sculpture borrows relatively simple and primary forms on the geometric plane—such as the pyramid, the cone, or the sphere. But material sculptures presenting incomplete or truncated versions of these basic forms, such as the truncated cone or triangle, would, in an immediate way, obey the gestaltian pressure for the completion of its "good form," before interconnecting with the stronger square or rectangular Virtual Cube.

Paradoxically, it must be recognized that "minimal" sculptures actualizing the form of a cube have an equal need to be endowed with a Virtual Cube, to define their "hidden" internal structure. In fact, the "external" cube is poorly revealed and always deformed by the partial surfaces, which are provided by the different points of view and movements of the perceiver around the sculpture.

Determined in the first moments of the perceptual process, most frequently through widened vision and at a distance of peripheral vision, the already constructed Virtual Cube may seem inadequate for other points of view subsequently taken on other parts of the work which were not accessible to the primary perception. This first Virtual Cube developed by perception will yield its place to a more encompassing Virtual Cube which can account for the totality of vectorial expansions of material volume. Though difficult to assess, the mnemonic traces of this first global effect will interfere with the energetic functions later recognized in the sculpture.

On the other hand, the shadows cast by the strict lighting of a sculpture by its producer serve as parameters for the construction of the Virtual Cube encompassing the total work, since the virtual volumes generated by

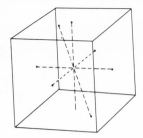

Figure XVa: Structural Axes of the Virtual Cube

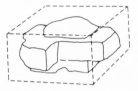

Figure XVb: The Virtual Cube of the Small Sculpture

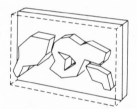

Figure XVc: Virtual Cube of a Low Relief on a Wall, Laterally, and on the Floor

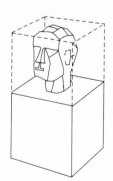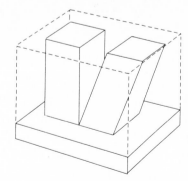

Figure XVd: Virtual Cube of a Sculpture with a Base

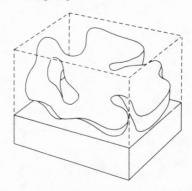

Figure XVe: Virtual Cube and Positive/Negative Volumes

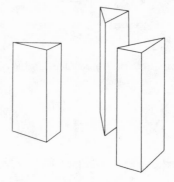

Figure XVf: Sculpture with Multiple Elements on the Floor

these shadows must be put into relation with the positive/negative volumes produced by the other visual variables.

One can only regret, in this respect, the habitual discourse on sculpture which, while recognizing the volumetric specificity of the sculptural object, reduces it always to the description of a pseudo-frontal plane on a surrounding ground, as if all sculpture could be reduced to the structure of low relief, but this time on a nonexistent background, or worse, to that of a pictorial drawing.

In an immediate way, the hypothesis of the Virtual Cube and its a priori infrastructure appears essential to unify, in a volumetric system, both the diversity and heterogeneity of the various internal/external volumetric masses with their particular dynamic characteristics. The trajectories, movements, positions, and points of view that the perceiver establishes in the various perspectives allow a complex synthesis where each plays its proper role.

We should point out that the hypothesis of the Virtual Cube does not have as a function the substitution or withdrawal of a certain external volume as paradigm of the sculpture, but rather to define and render explicit the internal energetic structure of the object. It serves to determine the grammatical functions of the parts which cannot be perceived in the apparent visual statement. In the same way as deep structures had to be assigned by Chomsky, for the understanding/description of the surface structure of the verbal phrase, the syntactic structure of sculpture often cannot be observed at the surface level of its visual variables but must be developed by way of more encompassing structures possessing a specific energy.

Similarly, the function of limits filled by the Virtual Cube must not be conceived as a metric determination, but rather as an *individuating* determination analogous to the role played by the notions of cells or atoms in the biological and physical sciences which are not strictly measurable but necessary for the development of hypotheses about the function of certain elements in the whole. If, in one sense, we agree with Strzeminski's observation to the effect that "the limits of a sculpture appear only after its execution" (1977; 87), it should not however be applied in such a manner to the variations in the dimensions or the format of a sculpture, because these differences do not radically modify the possible interrelations at the core of the Virtual Cube between the forces of the infrastructure and those of the positive elements themselves.

In addition to its individuating function, which allows for the cognition of a given sculpture without denying its environmental interrelationships, the Virtual Cube fulfills the major function of establishing and maintaining the fiction of volumetry at the heart of the sculpture. As mentioned repeatedly, volumetry is never a given in perception, but is solely deduced from partial surfaces by the cortical processes. The proposition of the volumetric structure of the Virtual Cube serves to keep present and active this volumetric notion which is too often neglected in the perception of a sculpture. It defines systematically the relations between those energies perceived on the plane or in demi-relief and the fundamental energies which structure the interior volume in a permanent way.

This syntactic matrix also proves indispensable for the apprehension of the energetic events produced in the peripheral layer of sculpture, through relations of its material boundaries with the surrounding, luminous energy at different levels. The strongest juxtaposition of a sculpture's visual variables to the surrounding luminous radiation produces two different types of phenomena. The first are constituted by the refraction of luminous rays which reach the periphery of the sculpture, causing tensions and expansions of all variables (form, color/tonality, texture, dimension, position, vectoriality) and producing varied spatial curves and inclinations. The second type of phenomena is constituted by the perception of luminous energy itself, natural or ambient, gathered and rendered dense in the so-called negative regions as well as in those regions which are contained by the formative sides of the Virtual Cube itself. This allows the material extremities of the sculpture to be interrelated with the peripheral negative regions that their expansion has incorporated into the sculpture.

Thus the orientations, pressures, extensions, and radiating expansions in which the visual variables are deployed at the periphery of the sculpture are the meeting points between the internal vectorial energies, the characteristics of the frontiers, and the light energies in which the sculpture is immersed and which it reflects. It is uniquely in a relation with the energies of the Virtual Cube that the vectorial dynamisms can be felt and estimated as well as the expansions and contractions of volumes and partial surfaces, the tangential energies, the variations in texture, the proportional relations between sections of a sculpture of which the nature, meaning, and function would otherwise be dissipated in the indefinite context of the surrounding environment.

Through the virtualization of these peripheral sides, reiterated partially or not at all by a sculptural work, the internal structure of the Virtual Cube is at first defined by its central, vertical, and horizontal axes. Hofmann already proposed these as essential parameters: "All volumes can be considered as having imaginary, vertical and horizontal axes. All volumes move around such axes. And each of these axes can be brought in opposition to the other. The result is movement and countermovement in spatial opposition" (1948; 51). However, it must be added that the diagonal axial energies constitute to a similar degree a source of tensions and countertensions at the volumetric core.

The vectorial axes can act in a linear way in the volume but can also exercise tensions of planes (or of two-dimensional units) which are not necessarily flat since they can be rippled by unequal energies. Naum Gabo has already described these planar axes as those occupying a surface in width and length in the continuity of central orthogonal axes (1964; 108). One must also include as syntactic elements the planar axes which deploy in two dimensions the diagonal energies, exerting their flat or curved pressures in all the regions of the sculpture.

The internal planar horizontal and vertical axes draw their energetic force not only from their own directional vectorialities, but also from the fact that they reiterate the condensed energies in the periphery of the Virtual Cube, that is, the planar facets which circumscribe and contain the internal energies of the cube. The planar energies of the six sides of the cube, because they are virtual and thus not as strong as the peripheral energy which forms the pictorial Basic Plane, are vividly felt at the same time as pressure on the internal, that is, on the vectorial regroupings of the volumetric regions and as limits of the system that they encompass.

In the internal global volume, the linear and planar axes, which are spread out to the sides in the three dimensions of the Virtual Cube, are in a state of constant dialectical relation to the actual energies of the visual variables realized in a sculpture, producing punctuations, reiterations, intersections, curves, junctures, and envelopments in the internal partial volumes which are juxtaposed, separated, or interpenetrated, according to topological or gestaltian rules. The Virtual Cube is the only theoretical structure which allows for the implantation of given regions in volumetric depth. Its most significant syntactic role is undoubtedly the activation of dynamic processes in the visual variables, by a continual relation between the elements actually produced by the sculptor and the energy of the infrastructure of the work.

The aim of the syntactic analysis of sculpture is to observe the nature of the energetic phenomena which are constructed at the periphery, that is, at the boundaries of the multiple, interior volumes and the interrelations of these with the infrastructure of the Virtual Cube. It will attempt to determine the spatial organization of a particular work, the type of rhythm that it conveys from the center toward the peripheries and vice versa. These internal dynamisms will be represented by syntactic analysis through a great number of vibratory schemas. Both centripetal and centrifugal, they expand in certain directions, rotate around certain axes, "breathe" along differentiated segments, react to virtual or negative adjacent volumes, and so on. Each of these dynamic structures will be the basis of reference to the perceptual field which it attempts to represent, so as to introduce it into human awareness and make it available to human communication.

The syntactic levels established by the topological and gestaltian relations and the infrastructure of the Virtual Cube account for the dynamic potentiality of the elements and structures of a given work, revealing topological and illusory perspectives that the producer effected by means of varying regroupings of the visual variables. However, like the linguistic structures of painting, these groupings of perceptual regions are interpreted first as linked inside various systems of organization of perspective, determined both by the widening of perceptual points of view and by specific relations of the work with its global physical environment.

6.6.2. Perspectives of perception

By no means can the perceiver of a sculptural work declare nonexistent or redundant the regions of the works he/she does not take the time to perceive. On one hand, we have already proposed as a postulate that the principle of redundancy cannot exist in the field of a visual work, since the effect of the smallest regions, and even of individual coloremes, can modify and disrupt all previously established relations between regroupings of the visual elements. On the other hand, if this postulate were rejected, how could one designate as redundant an element that one had not yet even perceived and whose influence on neighboring regions and consequently on the global structure could not be established? This principle of completion in perception requires taking into account not only elements and regions always organized in a perspective modality by the producer, but also the perspectives that result from the points of view taken on a given work by the perceiver.

It is the role of semiotical analysis of sculpture to determine the type of perceptual program that can insure a minimal and sufficient knowledge of the sculptural, visual text, since the subsequent semantic interpretation is normally dependent upon it. It is obvious, however, that the trajectory of perception of a sculpture is much more lengthy and complex than that which is operative in the perception of a painting, both by the multiplicity of factors contributing to the development of an intuition of volumetry and by the action of the natural modalities of perspective established by the perceiver, which must be integrated into modes of perspective inscribed by the producer in his particular treatment of the visual variables.

In contrast with the perceiver of a painting, who usually positions himself/herself in a frontal point of view (or in several frontal or oblique sightings when the work has large dimensions) which, in relation to a given format, will relate the totality of the visual field to the same Basic Plane, the perceiver of a sculpture has to multiply different frontal positions, giving him access to different visual fields, with wide angles of vision vertically and laterally offering constantly changing partial surface dynamisms. If one hypothetically reduced these surface fields to the four lateral faces of a cubic volume, those of the bottom or top being most often imperceptible as surfaces, the internal volume of the sculpture would be defined by the integration of these data in depth, in the central regions of the masses. However, not only will the dynamic pressures emitted from top and bottom transform the structure of this hypothetical lateral cut, but the faces of the sculpture organized along their various Basic Planes could not be reduced to the number of sides of the Virtual Cube. A sculpture does not possess four faces or "frontal planes," but as many as the distances and positions chosen by the perceiver will produce. The syntactic structure of the Virtual Cube serves only as a theoretical parameter, with a view to the integration of these multiple faces and their respective depths in a synthesis where their differences can still be recognized.

Without entering into a detailed discussion of the possible inscriptions of the different types of perspectives enumerated earlier, one can point out that the same regroupings of objective visual variables will be perceived differently when the perceiver sees them from a different angle which modifies their context with their specific field. By a change in position, from frontal toward oblique, different percepts are produced in the same objective place by successive centrations which will require an integration at levels no longer sensorial, but operative and abstract.

Even in an approach which always remains frontal, which is rarely the case, the perceiver of a sculpture is also called on to multiply sightings toward the top and bottom which put into play the kinesthesia of his/her body itself, and not only his or her eyes. This generates different perceptual fields and perspectives which must be put into relation with the volumetric infrastructure of the Virtual Cube through a process of continual transformation and integration.

In addition to the perspectives resulting from different positions and movements on the part of the perceiver, in part conditioned by the producer since they are linked to his very manipulation of the visual variables, one must add, as a perceptual component, the natural perspectives which the sculptural object commands as one physical object among others. These perspectives cannot be entirely controlled by the producer.

The first natural perspectives are developed as the perceiver gets nearer to the sculpture which he has first perceived in a far or medium distance as part of a wider environment. The first percepts developed during the process of localizing the work are necessarily submitted to the structures specific to the perspectives of far or intermediate distance. Stored in memory, these first percepts will influence subsequent percepts developed at a more personal or proximate distance, establishing a level of ambiguity in the experience of sensory data, interpreted in a variable way as part of a spatial context. The effects of far distance are, moreover, often reiterated by the trajectories of the perceiver who, instead of maintaining a more or less close distance to a sculpture, moves himself/herself further away at times in order to reevaluate the work at a much greater distance, where foveal vision and sometimes even macular vision are no longer effective. Thus, in addition to the multiple topological and illusory perspectives resulting from the proxemic trajectory around a given work, which are already difficult to integrate into a dialectical unity, completely dissimilar perspectives must be added to the first, sometimes in an antagonistic context.

If the reflection of luminous rays constitutes the vibratory and energetic material that determines the nature of the visual variables, in any given visual language, it follows naturally that any change in the natural or artificial lighting of a work will transform it in all of its characteristics. This is certainly at odds with the status of the verbal text; the grammatical structure of the latter does not vary with a change in lighting, but only the potentiality that the text possesses to be or not to be the object of a perception. Lighting itself does not establish the syntactic structure of a visual work, but influences its apprehension. The effects of lighting on a pictorial work may generate different artworks according to its own variations. This fact has been put aside, so to speak, inasmuch as the lighting used in the locale of presentation of a painting is believed to correspond to the intentions of the producer.

This is rarely the case in the public presentation of a sculpture. Not only is it very difficult to reconstruct in another site the sort of ambient light and the system of lighting which exist in the producer's studio, but the places of presentation (museums, galleries, and so on) use types of lighting whose chromaticity, intensity, angle of projection, and so forth, differ most often from the lighting which served in the production of the work.

One should then ascribe to the category of natural perspectives the modification of the visual variables and the total transformation of their modes of interrelation, resulting from the effects of various sorts of illumination the sculpture is subjected to when it is put in the open air or in diversely lighted interiors, as long as the producer cannot reproduce the light in which the work was created. The transformations of the work caused by these different light contexts are often radical, imposing on it specific syntactic interrelations in accidental perspectives. These vary with each place of presentation. Lighting, considered as a neutral and objective element in the case of a painting, is crucial in sculpture. The direction of the light sources, their intensity and chromaticity must be incorporated as elements in the description of the sculpture, since they establish types of perspectives which do not necessarily depend on the action of the producer nor on the perceptual process of the spectator, but which are derived from data in external reality.

Semiotics classifies in a different category the environmental propositions that, in refusing the postulate of the limits of sculpture, propose that a sculpture should be perceived in the globality of its physical or natural environment. In order for this kind of environment to enter into the perceptual field, it is necessary for the perceiver to position himself/herself at a remote distance which affords perception the unique advantage of peripheral vision. Having become an object of lesser dimensions with reduced visual characteristics, sculpture is distinguished in a more or less efficacious way from the objects which surround it. A selection of its more undifferentiated and macroscopic dynamisms, the largest, are compared to those of natural phenomena (sky, lake, mountain, trees) or to architectural instances which, even when reduced by distance, are generally more spacious and affirmative. Just as it occurs in the architectural environment itself, sculpture becomes only one region among others, subject to the logic of architecture or design which renders the dynamic of its visual variables to a large extent inoperative. These sculptural elements, thus integrated in a wider physical environment, receive considerably more light from the semiotics of architecture, or of environmental or garden design, than from the semiotics of sculpture.

These foregoing remarks do not deny the sculptural character of monumental sculptural constructions, the limits and dynamisms of which are incorporated in elements sufficiently affirmed so as to be accessible to vision at a medium distance. Paradoxically, in effect, these gigantic works often seem to present themselves to perception at a medium or relatively close distance, if one considers the proportional dimension of the surface of the ground which is deliberately circumscribed to serve as their base or environmental support.

Chapter Seven

Semiotical Analysis

If the decoding of visual language can only rest on specific syntactic hypotheses, the actual apprehension of a visual work which reveals how a particular producer has used the potentialities of this syntax also requires a particular method. Just as verbal linguistics has found it expedient to do, we borrow from scientific methodology the instrument of "analysis." This method is defined, however, in a unique manner according to the particulars of our object of study.

This analytical method aims at bringing to light the interrelations between elements—rather than their hypothetical essence—in the totality that is the visual work. Whether it concerns a painting, a sculpture, a photograph, or an architectural edifice, the work considered as a totality "does not consist of things but of relationships," as Hjelmslev has already proposed for the analysis of verbal language. In this context, "not substance but only its internal and external relationships have scientific existence" (1963; 23). We will also borrow from this linguist a definition of the process of analysis:

> The analysis thus consists actually in registering certain dependencies between certain terminals, which we may call, in accordance with established usage, the parts of the text, and which have existence precisely by virtue of these dependencies and only by virtue of them. The fact that we can call these terminals parts, and this whole procedure a division, or analysis, rests on the

fact that we also find dependencies of a particular kind between these terminals and the whole (the text) into which they are said to enter, dependencies which it is then likewise the task of the analysis to register. (28)

In a manner that is again more apparent here than in verbal language, it appears that the visual text is constituted in time by the continuous transformational process of perception, which generates movements in elements and changes in the interrelations of the energetic properties linked to these same elements. This process can only be described in the analysis by an intuition of the system which conditions it, as Hjelmslev further explains: "The process comes into existence by virtue of a system's being present behind it, a system which governs and determines it in its possible development. A process is unimaginable—because it would be in an absolute and irrevocable sense inexplicable—without the system lying behind it" (39).

If we agree, further, with this linguist that "the characteristic proper to a process, and by consequence, to a text, is that it is submitted to the general rule of the order of positions" (89), we will propose that this characteristic, (which we assimilate to the topological notion of the order of succession) must be completed in the visual text by the determination of transformations that the process engenders in the elements themselves. If a minimal dimension of homogeneity is required for the elements of the visual language to enter into any relation, one must not conclude that the variables interrelations must necessarily lead to a homogeneity of the work itself as a totality. The function of spatial continuity must itself be revealed by analysis, the heterogeneity of visual elements remaining a component whose unification will always be only a provisional step in the analysis and one destined to yield to disjunction. As expressed by Kurt Lewin: "Homogeneity results from a unifying action of perception, as well as from the 'data' itself, and maximal heterogeneity is the inverse function of the unity of the group" (1941; 105).

For Hjelmslev, the idea of homogeneity is posited as one of those indefinable concepts that his linguistic system requires (besides the notions of "description, object, dependence" (29) or of "presence, necessity, condition, function, functive" (35). Semiotical analysis will have as a central objective the illumination of the possible meaning of the concepts of "homogeneity" and of "continuity" in the visual language.

We recognize fully, with Hjelmslev, the necessity of interpolating in the description the presence of certain "fonctifs" (or operators, latent magnitudes) that are inaccessible to knowledge through channels other than the process of analysis itself.

Therefore, the description which is the result of semiotical analysis will make use of dynamic and structural concepts, issuing not from the obvious surface properties but from the underlying structures.

To this end, and through the methodology instituted by Kurt Lewin, when he discerned those attitudes that opposed Galilean and Aristotelian thought-processes (1935), topological semiotics intends to use classificatory principles that are based on concrete objects observed situationally. This will not result in dualisms, but rather in dynamic seriations which serve to support an awareness that the intermediate stages are always active and present under the rarefied poles of perceptual reference (Kaufmann, 1968; 21–22).

It rejects as inadequate any intuition of classificatory concepts seen normatively or which grants both undue importance and a permanent character to the fact that an object belongs, at any given moment, to such or such a category. It refuses to consider as the only intelligible and determined objects those occurrences that are produced frequently, in a statistical sighting which denies the heterogeneity of the real to the profit of the aleatory existence of constant averages, substituted for the concrete situation. And, in contradistinction to linguistic semiology, it refuses to establish polar oppositional tables or dichotomies too abstract to fit or reach the complexity of the visual field itself: "As in physics, classification of phenomena and objects in opposite pairs and logical dichotomies disappears. It is replaced by a classification using concepts of series allowing for continued variations" (Lewin, 1935; 32).

This description, which has to be a classification, must necessarily be abstract; that is, conserve only certain dynamic elements disclosed by perceptual activity in view of elaborating a unified understanding of the diversity. But it must be concerned with the recognition of the most important structural functions that allow elements to interrelate in the totality of this environment that the visual work constitutes. To this end, it must be unceasingly open to unknown properties, those which have not yet been perceived because of the approximative and temporalized character of all operations of perception.

Before we continue, it appears necessary to stress the radical difference between semiotical analysis, as we have defined it, and a method which has been given the same name and which has been developed, particularly in France, in the course of recent years.

7.1. Typological Semiological Analysis

A method that is called "semiological analysis," linked to computerized data analyses, has been used for many years, particularly in Europe, in researching the archeology of art, sculpture, painting, and ancient architecture, wherein it appears more immediately fruitful than in its applications to the domain of anthropology proper (Salomé-Lagrange, 1971).

However, in spite of its name, this form of analysis does appear to depend more on general typology than semiology, as a science of signs, because it is not founded on a specific theory of structures of the visual language. Moreover, the art objects which it treats are not defined as in any way differentiated from any other objects of human fabrication, except for the fact that they form part of the repertory of art history. From the verbal categories developed by that discipline, the objects are classified into groups, subgroups, and so forth. This simple classification is sufficient, apparently, for confirming or disproving earlier classifications and chronologies, definitions of types and styles, diffusion of models, and so on. That is to say, it is sufficient to verify the pertinence of the verbal discourse that has been applied to the same visual works by various authors.

According to Marie Salomé-Lagrange, this approach has as its target the verification of the validity of an already existing interpretation by confronting it with a list of pre-established distinctive traits:

> This means, in particular, to try to find anew all the descriptive criteria used by the author to differentiate classes and to verify that they are not contradictory, aleatory or abitrary in relation to the ensemble of the description furnished by the author. To examine its significance is for us to know if it is compatible with external information: chronological or geographical distribution (1973; 16).

In the first stage, which consists in identifying distinctive, minimal and mutually exclusive traits belonging to subdivisions of diverse categories of verbal information, this analysis proceeds to an enumeration of occurrences of these distinctive traits in various classes of objects belonging to the repertoire of the history of art. At this point, it constitutes a form of typological analysis such as that defined by J. L. Chandon and S. Pinson: "It is a method of the analysis of facts which permits the grouping of objects, characterized by an ensemble of attributes or variables into classes not necessarily disjointed two by two. These classes must be, on one hand, as sparse as possible and, on the other hand, as homogenous as possible" (1981; 4).

This form of classification endeavors to establish classes of distinctive traits and associates them with other classes in order to verify external hypotheses, and not to develop any possible model of internal syntactic structures by which observed objects would be distinguished one from another. It responds to the following objectives:

> What are the descriptive traits (or properties or attributes) which, being regularly or constantly associated, permit the distinguishing between types of objects? What types (or classes) are regularly associated in a way to constitute characteristic assemblages? What assemblages present a continuous and evolving sequence of traits and can be placed in relation with a chronological ordination? (Chandon, 1981; 26)

This type of analysis, as Salomé-Lagrange observed, requires a certain number of preliminary precautions in the choice of an homogeneous collection of objects of limited complexity, so that they can only be put into relation with a relatively short verbal text. This necessary reduction of variables and of classes, dictated by typological analysis, limits at a first level the application of this method to the analysis of visual language as such in a proper semiological manner.

Moreover, the classifications which serve typological analysis are based on strongly substantiated and individualized abstract conceptual schemas, for which it is relatively easy to adopt the basic analytical criteria of similarities and differences. In effect:

> The method of typological analysis rests on the simultaneous taking into account of similarities and differences between objects. It is concerned with the regrouping of objects in such a way that elements of a group are "strongly similar," whereas elements belonging to different groups are "relatively dissimilar." The multitude of typological analysis methods come from the fact that each of them gives a different sense to the terms "strongly similar" and "relatively dissimilar." (Chandon, 1981; 4)

Following procedures analogous to those of graphic semiology—which itself cannot be classified as proper semiotics of visual signs—this type of analysis is founded on lexicalized notions, carriers of stable distinctive traits which must, like the objects to be described, be present in small numbers. Modeled on a substantialist and static conception of verbal linguistic process, this "semiology" can be adapted to the quantitative procedures of computer systems, but only after having excluded the consideration of the countless characteristics of visual reality.

It has been put to the test, at first manually, then by computerized treatment, with the matrix of the scalogram, assembling distinctive traits by proximity and remoteness. "The scalogramme is a configuration where cruxes of matrices are grouped in a more or less regular escalation in the diagonal zone" (Salomé-Lagrange, 1973; 24). This disposition allows the visual estimation of distances between classes in relation to three privileged positions: the two extremities and the center of the scalogram. The classes corresponding to extremities have no descriptive element in common. While allowing to see immediately separations between the series of classes, this matrix of the scalogram allows examination of "the distribution of descriptive elements in all classes, and in particular, to distinguish by sight the most discriminating associations of traits" (24–25). In addition to the scalogram, this analysis can use other types of matrices, like those of clusters, which define groups or classes of elements linked by graded coefficients of similitude (33).

But visual semiotics analysis does not consider fruitful this kind of typological approach presenting a yielding to the logic of identity and of the static substance in the description of its proper object of knowledge. On the other hand, the abundance and the variability of data in the visual language may require the instrumentation of the computer, as well as of the graphic representation of spatial curves that perception constructs in the visual fabric, but more under the form of analogous than digital symbols. But it does not seem, until artificial intelligence research is more developed in the visual field, that computerized systems can be of an immediate help for theoretical research in this field of semiotics (Saint-Martin, 1989).

It is not only by virtue of its basic connection with the analogous nature of perceptive movements that the semiotical analysis we propose finds premature the recent efforts in "formalizing visual language, in the sense of contemporary logics" (Gips, 1975). A clarification and simplification of the basic elements and operators in the visual language appear to us impossible as long as the theory of the grammar of this language has not been further explored, as has been the case for mathematical formalization or that effectuated on verbal grammar. In this regard, we share the view expressed by Kurt Lewin who, although he did not hesitate to introduce geometric and topological formalization with respect to certain zones or contexts where psychological phenomena are deployed, wrote: "However we would produce an empty formalism if we forgot that mathematization and formalization can operate only in relation with the maturity attained by the material of the object to be studied at a certain moment" (Lewin, 1951; 1).

7.2. The Ocular Circuits

In the case of painting, semiotical analysis accounts for the perception of the pictorial plane, being that energetic mass of coloremes integrated by the producer in the dynamic structure of the Basic Plane. It bears, therefore, on the organization of specific physical materials as they are perceptually constructed by human vision.

This description cannot be based on the spontaneous movements of the gaze across the canvas which has itself raised a problem, since these movements are potentially infinite and open to aleatory unfoldings leading to opposite conclusions (Marin, 1976; 113). As we have already noted, the ocular fixations only produce a problem when the centrations are not sufficiently numerous to allow for the greatest possible number of coloremes to be perceived and explored for their dynamisms and interactions, their differentiations and regroupings. Only when this does happen do the interactions produce temporary and transformable syntheses finally destined to be integrated with vaster and more comprehensive units.

The process by which centrations unfold does not rest, however, on a hypothesis concerning a supposed normal trajectory of perception, nor on the hypothesis of the existence of privileged zones of perception in the image, as proposed by C. M. Tardy and taken up by René Lindekens (1971; 56). Following some studies on the perception of images by given subjects, a relatively constant itinerary of the gaze has been proposed that would organize, in a stable way, the system of iconic signification. In particular, it has been argued that the eye has a tendency to move in the sense of the hands of a clock, and that it actually spends more time on the left half of the field, the inverse being true for left-handers. As for the succession of pauses, their points of application would seem to have a tendency to be concentrated on the same region of the image, almost necessarily to the left, and upwards in the projected image (if it is concerned with slides or film), whereas they would disperse on different shores in opaque photographs (Lindekens, 1971; 57). Obviously, these perceptual behaviors would not permit a true apprehension by the spectator of the totality of the pictorial field, of which certain regions are thus completely neglected. These behaviors correspond even less adequately to the multitude of centrations effected by the producer in the process of production, since he interrelates each minute region of the visual field to a multitude of others in a trajectory continuously recommencing in all possible directions.

These observations of Tardy would seem to corroborate the experiences of G. T. Buswell (1935) when he proceeded to record the movement of the eyes during the contemplation of a print by Hokusai; he collected a series of 70 consecutive points of fixation. But, as Molnar observed (1966; 140) the eight fixations of the eye that are produced during the first two seconds do not correspond to those elements susceptible of being associated with a possible interpretation. In fact, he commented about the group of fixations, "we can hardly count more than fifteen which fall on something." These movements do not copy, therefore, the apparent structure of an image or of its "iconic" configurations, but correspond more to the structural locales linked to what we have called the Basic Plane. Arnheim (1954; 364) was categorical when he said that "there are very few links between the order and the direction of the fixations and the compositional structure of a work," a structure established here by the traditional codes of the iconic reading.

Moreover, this succession in visual perception would seem to assume a different order and function, according to the linguistic medium considered: "The temporal order of our perception is not part of the composition when we look at a sculpture or a painting, whereas it is a part when we look at the dance" (Arnheim, 1954; 343). It appears that the method of appropriating those elements that constitute the visual text is not to be derived either from the usual behavior of perceivers or from a previous theory of the composition of a work, since this itself must be elaborated from the perceptual trajectory.

One must acknowledge, indeed, that the ocular paths are not neutral and that what has been perceived previously, from the left to the right, from the bottom to the top, from the center toward the periphery and so on, influences the characteristics of the elements which will be next perceived. The order of succession of perception is hardly indifferent with respect to the types of dynamisms and interrelationships that are retained in order to form the composition of a painting or a sculpture, at least in the rapid and partial apprehension with which a large number of perceivers are satisfied. Visual semiotics proposes that the composition, or rather the structure of the work, can be deduced only from a series of equilibria established between the elements. The energies and the regions they form, which are taken up and modified with a view to producing superior and more complex equilibria, can finally produce a state where the ensemble of movements and transformations produces a system which can then be offered provisionally as an adequate synthesis.

The semiotical description of the pictorial plane must thus offer a *representation* of the equilibrated system of transformations that structure the visual field, following sufficient centrations to explore the totality of the dynamic field. These multiple centrations have taken up, corrected, and modified the first experiences of tensions and visual movements, verifying all the possibilities of interdependence and interaction of the elements, and testing the attractions and the disjunctions and their effects on position, dimension, depth of various regions, and so on.

These circuits, which are extremely numerous and which ceaselessly construct new interrelations between the elements perceived in the first centrations and deconstructed in subsequent centrations, transforming the qualities and dynamisms of regroupings, do proceed according to certain rules. They do not lead to a type of experience where all would endlessly transform itself in all directions, as suggested by the entropic aesthetics of Umberto Eco in *L'Oeuvre ouverte* (1965). To the contrary, the very structure of the process of perception, which is not atomistic or associative but integrative, leads to the elaboration of global systems of equilibrated transformations proper to a given visual field. In Peircian terms, some "final interpretants" are periodically produced on the syntactic levels.

In effect, by the very mechanism of perception, a threshold of equilibrium of the systems of transformation of the elements is eventually offered to the perceiver with a certain quality of necessity. The field may conserve it at the time of subsequent centrations or it may be modified by the enrichment of further visual trajectories. Thus, the semiotical description always corresponds to a provisional halt in the process of perception, when the perceiver believes he/she has reached a more or less invariant equilibrium in the dynamisms of his perceptual movements and of those which animate the work.

Jean Piaget already explicated the function of this invariance which always represents a certain synthesis: "The fundamental property of this latter is not to be 'left' unchanged, as is often expressed, but rather to result from the composition of modifications themselves which must be constructed, whereas it did not appear at the heart of initial observations" (1980; 119).

The character of necessity of such an equilibrium, produced by a given perceiver, can appear to another observer as justified or unjustified. In the latter case, another type of system of transformations—more comprehensive and accounting for more in the dynamic of the pictorial work—should be furnished to replace that which is found to be inadequate.

If, by contrast, a certain necessity in the system offered is recognized, this does not imply in any way that this structure ascribed to the work is immanent in it and that it has now been disclosed to the profit of all, after having been hidden for some time. This structural necessity does not correspond to a hidden character of the work; it is only the outcome of a set of perceptual operations that alone can produce it. Genetic epistemology has examined this problem, one that can be resolved neither by some kind of innateness nor by an objective immanence of the constructions of the perceptual dialectic: "How to explain that the construction of new relations in the course of processes of equilibration lead to results of which the internal necessity seems to imply that they were preformed or predetermined in anterior situations where the subject still did not perceive them or, more simply, did not yet become aware of them" (Piaget, 1980; 10).

The supergestalt that constitutes the integration of multiple stimuli in a field of perception is not found in the work through a simple search, but is constructed through continuous modifications of what seemed originally to be the first stimuli of a work. It exists only in and through the perception, while being this very text that semiotics must analyze in its actual constituents. However, if this semiotical description must aim at taking into account several structural levels, the parameters and the principles of analysis cannot remain the same when the levels of abstraction, which are necessary to the synthesis of awareness, become more and more elevated.

We would like to point out, finally, that the kind of ocular fixation required by semiotical analysis, if it is altogether a normal one, and does not require any "tour de force" of the eye, remains distinct from the habitual regard which we turn on things, with its more or less attentive and personal involvement. Inattentive centrations, in effect, even statistically numerous, which are not accompanied by sufficient motivation for the perceptual processes to be realized are practically equivalent to an absence of centrations or to a nonperception.

This type of gaze must, moreover, differ from that which regulates our daily activities, where, as J. J. Gibson remarked (1966), it is of primary importance to know or to interpret as quickly as possible the visual objects which are presented before us, that is, to reduce them to an object already known or to that which, in our previous experience, resembles it the most. This behavior, dictated by needs of survival, has become so automatic that it renders perceivers at times unable to perceive visual elements objectively. Thus, the majority of subjects before whom one projects on a screen an empty field in a weak luminosity, when asked "What have you seen there?" recognized a vast repertory of common objects with a precision all the stronger as the time of perception was prolonged (Frances, 1975; 225).

The sole requirement put forth to the semiotical gaze is to undertake an activity of perception vis-à-vis a visual text that one cannot presume to know before having read it. But the reading of a visual text, well before any possible repercussions of its semantic contents, constitutes a lived-experience which not only requires all the emotive and conceptual capacities of the perceiver, but also involves him in a relatively exacting process of personal transformation.

As is the case with the syntactic analysis of verbal language, the semiotical analysis of visual language is empirical, not only because it attempts to account for a reality which exists independently and outside of the perceiver, but also because it implies more extensively a sensory instrumentation. It depends, therefore, strictly on a theory of perception; as expressed by Paul Bouissac, any theory of the sign, explicitly or not, can only be linked to a theory of perception (1984; 8).

However, this necessarily experimental dimension does not permit its assimilation to advances made in experimental aesthetics. In this field, experimentation turns, above all, on the attempt to measure the reactions (surprise, interest, pleasure, or distaste) of perceivers of works. As a result of these reactions, the amount of originality or banality which a work can convey is assessed. But as such, the structure of the work remains an unknown.

Semiotical analysis aims, on the contrary, at a knowledge of the structures of organization of the works themselves, independently of the reactions, evaluations, or interpretations which the spectator adds, while imagining at times that he contributes thus to the semantic dimension. Syntactic analysis desires neutrality, in the sense that Molino wished it (1973), that is, to account for the phenomenon which any perceiver can observe who applies the given syntactic rules. It is only when this reading of the visual text is truly effected that semantic hypotheses can be intelligibly discussed, as can also the diverse evaluative reactions of the aesthetics.

7.3. Steps of the Semiotic Analysis

The study of a visual field which is offered as a phenomenon of language is necessarily started through a first approach submitted to *peripheral vision*, assessing the distance at which the work can be found, its dimension, and its general aspect. The desire to become acquainted with an object requires habitually the use of a greater angle of vision than that which macular and foveal visions can cover. The perceiver attempts, in the first place, to gather a variety of stimuli in a rapid scanning process, which institutes a certain number of links between points of aleatory centration. Foveal vision may choose to rest on these points but without attempting to inform itself in a particular way about these reduced zones which are directly accessible to it in its angle of vision. Macular vision will also contribute, at angles of 15 degrees, assembling particularly the general chromatic information offered by the field.

These multiple traversals recognize, mainly through gestaltian laws, a certain number of regroupings and disjunctions between the visual variables, their focal or peripheral distribution, certain major vectorialities, chromatic characteristics, and so on. This first scanning represents indeed the type of perceptual attempt with which the majority of perceivers of visual works are usually contented. It involves a certain number of perceptual reactions which will remain attached to later perceptive trajectories to a variable extent. However, this level of scanning, more or less strengthened or prolonged, must be considered as presemiotical, as it segments the field by blurred mechanisms of peripheral vision in regions manipulable by analysis.

We will call semiotical analysis a process which prolongs this first contact in a specific way and at two different levels. The first level, of a more phonological than syntactic nature, studies the nature of the basic elements of visual language, the coloremes. We call this study exploratory or corematic analysis. The second level, properly syntactic, studies the way in which the elements regroup themselves to form functional ensembles in a given spatial globality, according to the operators defined by the syntax of visual language.

This form of analysis is derived from the very structure of visual grammar which, like verbal grammar, is made up of two sections: one dealing with the properties of the constitutive elements of visual language and the other with the syntactic laws which specify their interrelations and sequences in possible statements. The fundamental difference between the two grammars is that the laws of perception are an integral part of the syntactic structure because they alone contribute to the actual or possible modes of interrelation of elements in a field. At more fundamental levels, concrete relations exist only between given coloremes, regrouped by topological and gestaltian rapports, at the heart of a previous energetic structure, that of the Basic Plane or the Virtual Cube.

The semiotical analysis necessarily develops, therefore, at different structural levels. It can be represented and unified through a certain number of grids which are superimposed according to larger and larger degrees of abstraction and of synthesis in relation to the concrete characteristics of coloremes. But from the permanence and importance of foveal vision, it follows that even when the analysis is related to the more synthetic levels of regroupings of coloremes, the ocular centrations are endlessly reengaged in the perception of coloremes. Even if these have already been made the object of experimentation at the exploratory level, any new context in which they are perceived can modify the nature of their visual variables and their proper dynamisms, while multiplying their interrelations with more distant regions in the visual field. These relations are always effected, however, through basic syntactic rules. But let us first deal with the presyntactical level of analysis which describes the organization and function of the basic elements of visual language.

7.3.1. Analysis of coloremes

The colorematic (or coloremic) analysis describes the aggregates of the visual variables which correspond in the visual field to that which is perceived by the foveal centrations. After having analyzed the very components of each of the perceived coloremes, this analysis describes the transformations which a coloreme undergoes by its interrelations with the other coloremes of its immediate entourage through macular centrations. The analysis proceeds thus at a first regroupings of coloremes through the topological relations which establish the first perceptual construction and structure the energetic exchanges between coloremes. This exploration of the "building blocks" of the spatial construction must theoretically be carried out on the totality of the field offered by the visual work. Nothing can let us presume that the producer has used the same visual variables in the same way in two different places, and no region of the field can be defined as empty or denuded of any specific energetic information, resulting from the particular reverberation of luminous rays on opaque matter.

The colorematic analysis has as its aim the recognition of the dynamism and the tensions specific to the first unit of perception, before they are inserted in a more elaborated syntactic structure. It determines, therefore, the characteristics of the visual variables used in this basic unit which is the coloreme, such as their mode of integration, their potentiality of expansion, their vectoriality, their vibratory energy, and so on.

On the subjective plane of the production of a percept, this analysis has a primordial function: it permits the beginning awareness of visual events correlative to perception and of the energetic experiences they cause in the organism of the perceiver as well as in the visual field. By this awareness, we mean the act of retaining in short-term memory, for several seconds, the energetic effect produced by these visual tensions perceived in the coloremes, in opposition to the process of ordinary visual perception, which is largely unaware and nonreflexive concerning the material causalities to which it is linked.

As noted previously, any centration in the visual field puts especially into action the energy specific to foveal vision, the one which is richest, most precise, and particularly suitable to reacting to visual energies present in the region which it establishes, within an angular opening of two or three degrees. If foveal vision alone can on this register and at a medium distance, see with precision minute visual elements, this does not imply that foveal vision ceases or cannot be used when less distinct organizations of visual variables are offered to it. Suitable to perceiving all variables present in its point of centration, color as well as textures, vectors and forms, the trajectories of the fovea are necessarily surrounded by elements perceived by macular vision; but these two types of perceived masses do not possess the same type of differentiation and precision, if perceived by the first or second type of vision. Further, foveal vision and macular vision cannot entirely exclude from the visual field the effect of perception by peripheral vision. However, the normal functioning of the eye easily permits attention to characteristics of percepts produced by foveal/macular or peripheral vision.

The visual variables which constitute the coloreme, (or the correlative region of the centration) necessarily differ from one coloreme to another even if it is only by the different effects produced by the variation in their position. This means, among other things, that the intensity and energy of a coloreme will be modified by its later insertion in the proper syntactic networks. But as such, the coloremes can be the object of the semiotical description, accounting for the nature of the visual variables that constitute them, their organization and function, their possibility of expansion, their vibratory energy, potentiality of junction or of disjunction, and so on. Structured as a topological mass, the coloreme will offer in addition different characteristics in its central and peripheral layers, in the structure of their boundaries, and so forth.

This analysis of the visual variables does not have as its aim a purely physical or taxonomic description of the characteristics of elements. The simple enumeration or accounting of the modes of appearances of the visual variables (color, texture, dimension, form, etc.), juxtaposed in a neutral inventory, without a priori notions concerning their functional possibilities of liaisons/disjunctions, could not deliver any information about the discourse that they serve to construct. Regrouped in the unit of the coloreme, these visual variables are already inserted in a minimal syntactic structure, that of a topological region capable of entering into energetic relation with other units. The visual variables are therefore immediately perceived at the level of the tensions that they produce inside the coloreme and secondly at the level of those which arise when they are reconnected or regrouped in an ensemble of coloremes.

We have already noted that even when more abstract structures of organization have been elaborated upon in order to take into account the interactions between ensembles of coloremes, the inevitable perceptual return to the work will always be at the level of the coloremes, as a full experience, replete with concrete energy, where the pregnancy or the real pertinence of larger and more abstract structures and their capacity to transport the more profound tensions issued from the work, may be either verified or contested.

Semiotical analysis, therefore, must linger at this stage of experimentation with the visual dynamisms which constitute the coloremes, which indeed appear as a microcosm of the particular syntactic structures used by each artistic producer. The internal/external structure of coloremes perceived in a work by Cézanne, Kandinsky or Mondrian, will be very different from one another and from the basic units that may be perceived in Matisse or Pollock. Without a doubt, this study is the sole instrument which can permit us to expand our knowledge, so rudimentary to this date, of the energetic structures of visual language.

In order to regulate this pursuit, and to permit communication between researchers, we propose a procedure which can serve to identify the perceptive constants and the first interrelations in the heterogeneity of visual percepts.

7.3.2. Systems of partition

The observations of colorematic analysis will be recorded in a theoretic grid of partition placed upon the visual work. This grid intends to provide only external parameters, situating the description, and not to implement a real division of the field or of the visual or pictorial process. The visual field can only be known in its globality or any of its subdivisions, following an integrative accumulation of perceptive centrations, that is, at the end of a syntactic analysis of the work.

Not only does the organization of this preliminary grid not attempt to mimic a possible hypothesis about the composition of a visual work, but its most immediate objective is the deconstruction of the perceptive interpretations that usually arise from the recognition of such or such aggregates of visual variables when recalling previously known or imagined objects.

Rather than being founded on these hypotheses of objects and on the verbal discourses that they make possible, the perception of the visual text must attempt to produce the experience itself of coloremes constructed by the producer to precise energetic ends. Any new tension, in effect, of the visual variables forming the coloremes involves a significant transformation in the discourse of the work.

It must be noted that theoretically this grid of partition must be used in a confrontation with the visual work itself, and not in relation to a reproduction of any kind. Any reproduction modifies, in an essential way, all the visual variables that the analysis of coloremes proposes to study in a given work. Even though certain printed color reproductions of the best possible quality can serve as a memory aid once the work has been observed in its concrete and physical reality, it is necessary to prohibit the use of slides which by their transparency misrepresent, in an irremediable way, the memory of percepts obtained through the actual experience of the work. If for reasons of semiotic training, reproductions of visual works are used, it should be well understood that information gained thereby cannot be attributed to the original work, but only to its deformed "translation."

The use of grids of partition is common in typological types of analysis, the choice of a partition of more or less compressed meshes being left to the discretion of the user, provided, of course, that it leads to fruitful results. This decision is always arbitrary if one recalls, for example, that the partitions which can be established between a group of about 15 objects to be analyzed add up to 1.4 million possibilities. However, in practice, it has been verified that the analyses carried out on ensembles of 30 to 350 objects favor the production of nine groups or fewer, the average being six (Chandon, 1981; 163). The grid used in the colorematic analysis has the particularity of determining, by itself, the number of objects which will indeed be observed, that is, the number of coloremes which will be examined and the number of surrounding coloremes with which they will be put into relation.

The only type of grid of partition which appears to us to be necessarily excluded is that in which certain coordinates could be identified with the most important internal structure of the Basic Plane, being the cruciform, horizontal and vertical axes, in order not to obscure, in taxonomizing and underscoring them, the dynamics specific to these fundamental axes in the pictorial or sculptural production.

Thus the exploratory analysis can use grids formed by ensembles of vertical/horizontal coordinates in a square or rectangular format, forming nine compartments, or again, ensembles of coordinates producing 15, 20 or 25 compartments (see figure XVI).

We propose the use of a grid of partition of 25 compartments identified from left to right and from top to bottom by the letters of the alphabet. Each of these compartments will, in turn, be divided into five zones identified by the figures from 1 to 4 according to the hourly sense (in quarters of an hour) in order to be terminated by a return to the center marked by the figure 5. These zones can therefore be described as: A1, A2, A3, A4, and A5, as in figure XVII.

These five zones correspond to the localizations of centrations effected by one or more observers in a way that permits a comparison between the results of perceptual processes of various individuals. A tighter grid—one of finer interstices—or one of wider character could establish an equal or greater number of loci of fixations. Broadly speaking, the number and the disposition of five internal zones seems a bare minimum for the study of any given compartment.

In each of these zones, the analysis describes the aggregate of the visual variables correlative to a foveal vision centration. Theoretically, this

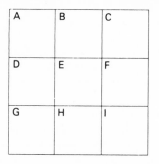

Figure XVI: Partition Grids for Exploratory Analysis

A 1	B 1	C 1	D	E
4 5 2	4 5 2	4 5 2		
3	3	3		
F	G	H 1	I	J
		4 5 2		
		3		
K	L	M 1	N 1	O
		4 5 2	4 5 2	
		3	3	
P	Q	R	S	T
U	V	W	Z	Y 1
				4 5 2
				3

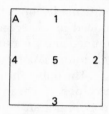

Figure XVII: Positioning of Coloremes inside the Grid

analysis describes 125 coloremes (there being five zones multiplied by 25 compartments) regularly dispersed across the pictorial plane. The parameters of description correspond to the ensemble of the visual variables, since they all are always implicated in any place of the centration of the gaze on the visual field. However, as the coloremes are not truly isolated by the grid of partition or the zones division, the description will include their relations with those coloremes which immediately surround them. This will involve the description of topological relations inside and on the borders of each compartment, the state of their boundaries, and so on.

Thus the description of coloreme A1 requires the consideration of its dynamic relations with A4, A5, A2, and B1. Similarly, for the others:

A2 → A1, A5, A3, B4, B1, and B3.
A3 → A5, A4, A2, B3, B4, and F1.
A5 → A1, A2, A3, and A4.
B1 → A1, B2, B5, B4, and C1.
M1 → M4, M5, M2, L1, G3, H3, I3, and N1.

and so forth.

One must note, moreover, that these compartments are not endowed with characteristics of equal energies since they are structurally diversified by their placement in the Basic Plane. Thus, the compartments A, E, U, and Y are animated by the potentialities of the energies of the corners; C, H, M, R, and W are sustained by the central vertical axiality, and K, L, M, N, and O by the horizontal axiality; A, G, M, S, and Y are integrated in the disharmonic diagonal; and U, Q, M, I, and E in the harmonic diagonal.

In the same way, the peripheral compartments envelop the central compartment M, and the compartments G, H, I, N, S, R, Q, and L are both enveloping and enveloped in relation to the others. However, it is at the level of subsequent syntactic regrouping of compartments that their interior energies will be assessed in relation to the energetic matrix of the Basic Plane, and not at the level of exploratory analysis. It will become quickly apparent, furthermore, that each compartment of the grid contributes the added energy of diagonal and cruciform axialities, given the gestaltian quality of peripheral decoupage which is attributed to them.

In effect, analysis of coloremes already requires a form of syntactic operation, in the sense that their interrelations are always established at the plane of the dynamic of the visual movements which constantly transform them. One cannot conceive of the visual variables or their integration in a coloreme as discrete units, previously cut out and identified in the internal/external experience, to be submitted to operators which would regroup them from the exterior without modifying their identity, as proposed by the logical schema: "$X = F(a,b,c,)$," where "F" represents a similar function acting on each variable.

If one compares this procedure of colorematic analysis with that used in formal grammar, one might observe that the analyst in the present case is not free to use only one or the other of visual variables in his description of visual language, but rather that he must use them all in modalities which are always, however, different and which cannot be determined a priori. In the context of a system of axiomatic description, one might say that the alphabet will always be constituted by the finite ensemble of six variables (texture (T), color/tonality (CT), dimension (D), vectoriality (V), implantation (I) and form (F)), but in instances of occurrence where each is always different from what it was on a previous occasion.

The coloremes are also described as symbols composed of certain types of visual variables capable of forming ensembles according to certain so-called syntactic rules.

Thus, we would have:

C1 : Ta, CTb, De, Vd, Ie, Ff . . .
C2 : Ta', CTb', De', Vd', Ie' Ef' . . .
C3 : Ta'', CTb'', De'', Vd'', Ie'', Ef'' . . .

One must point out that the topological relation of succession which identifies the order in which an ensemble of coloremes can be inscribed cannot be reduced to the function of concatenation, which is not applicable as such in the visual language, whereas it is fundamental in verbal, logical, or mathematical language. In effect, in a visual field, the simple relation of concatenation cannot exist, neither between the visual variables nor between two coloremes, in the sense of a simple adjunction or juxtaposition. The variables or coloremes cannot be added to one another without being mutually transformed. Thus, color, for example, is transformed according to its dimension or its texture, if the contours are different, as much as by the interrelations with close or farther positioned coloremes.

The syntactic rules are therefore "operators of integration" at the level of the coloreme as well as at the level of regrouping of the coloremes. They can be described in a nonterminal vocabulary as categorical components of grammar, whereas coloremes form a part of a terminal vocabulary accompanied by markers specifying certain of their characteristics, their immediate or distant environment, their position in the Basic Plane, and so on.

This analysis will ideally recover the entirety of the perceived visual field, step by step, in the heterogeneity of visual movements effectively produced by the visual variables used by the producer of the work. A list of distinctive traits, which can be observed among the visual variables grouped in a coloreme, as well as of the interrelations of adjacent coleremes, is presented in Appendix III.

In summary, the colorematic analysis takes account, for each centration, of the constituting elements of a coloreme. It will describe, therefore, the visual variables constituting the perceived coloreme, the types of liaisons or of interrelations of multiple variables in a coloreme, and the interrelations of these coloremes with adjacent coloremes. In addition, the first perceptive syntheses, especially those of the topological species, describe the predominant vectorialities in each of the zones.

If the analysis of coloremes can take account of the basic dynamic structure of the energetic elements that a given producer privileges over others in the construction of his particular representation, it cannot serve to demonstrate how these basic units are spatially brought together in a particular structure. The ensemble of these coloremes is regrouped in significant spatial sequences through syntactic rules which govern the infrastructure of the medium, as well as the colorematic interrelations at more and more dialectic and synthetic levels.

7.4. Syntactic Analysis

Syntactic analysis accounts for the application and the particular functioning of syntactic rules in a determinate visual text. In a manner analogous to the numerous syntactic rules of grammar of verbal language, the syntactic rules of visual grammar, which we have examined in Chapter Three, are juxtaposed in order to regularize and specify the functional potentialities of the liaisons/disjunctions of colorematic groups, to form specific spatial statements.

Owing to the state of ignorance we are still mired in today concerning the syntactic structures of visual language, more than two millennia after a constant practice of this discourse by all human societies, topological semiotics will establish steps in the apprehension/analysis of this discourse. The base units of visual language, of the phonological type, are not able to furnish the hypotheses of regroupment on the syntactic plane. Visual semiotics proposes as a preliminary hypothesis of segmentation necessary for any analytic approach, the segmentation of the visual field by scanning of the peripheral vision, in order to facilitate the observation of the syntactic mechanisms between large aggregates of coloremes.

The various intuitive modes, which have served until now to describe the enunciatory function of visual language, have involved extremely disparate syntactic consequences. Until now the most common model simply applied the operator of concatenation, typical of verbal language, to previously constructed iconic fragments in an aleatory order. Most often, this construction remains insensitive to stylistic differences in the process of iconization, capable of modifying the syntactic functions of elements. Moreover, this form of iconic segmentation seems to offer two defects. First, being indissociable from verbal lexicological units which are a guarantee of the completion of the process of iconization, the iconic units always present themselves already as a plane of content. This procedure does not maintain the separation between the plane of expression and the plane of content which appeared essential to Hjelmslev in any analysis of linguistic function. Second, this process conceals and rejects from the plane of expression the noniconizable zones of the visual field which form at times the largest part of it. Finally, it cannot integrate into the verbal meanings the effect of the various visual treatments to which these images have been submitted.

Instead of this operator of concatention, which rules in a linear and irreversible way the digital relations between discrete elements, such as numbers or morphematic units of verbal language, we propose the introduction of operators which can take account of the spatial, analogical and continuous function operating in visual language.

In recognizing the dynamic character of the variables constituting the material plane of visual expression, we propose a syntactic analysis which can account for the differentiated networks of energetic groupings produced by the topological and gestaltian perceptual operators. These groupings will be constituted by aggregates of informal visual variables as well as by iconizable fragments, interconnected not in some linear order but rather in the three dimensions of space itself.

However, in referring to the scanning of the peripheral vision to obtain a first reading—a first segmentation of the visual field—one has to be aware that this perceptual route takes into account only a restricted number of the elements of the visual field, leaving a larger number of other sections not perceived. In this scanning, the eye establishes general junctions/disjunctions outside of the dynamism of the chromatic elements, inaccessible to peripheral vision which is endowed with rods and not with cones. This preliminary segmentation serves as a scaffold for the analytical work and must be replaced, at the conclusion of the syntactic analysis, by a more adequate segmentation of the visual field.

This scanning, which is effected in a back and forth fashion from left to right and from bottom to top on the visual field, recognizes larger or smaller aggregates as units. They are quite similar to those which Ror-schach described as global responses (G), responses of great detail (GD), or responses of little detail (Dd). It may again regroup in a much larger ensemble a multiplicity of small regions, which more easily lend them-selves to a more enveloping form or gestalt. It is of relatively little im-portance that this decoupage is made in one given direction or another, provided that it takes account of the totality of the field. This decoupage serves only as an armature for a description of relations which are es-tablished between various regions of the field. These relations themselves, by syntactic analysis, will provide the appropriate model of adequate segmentation that semiotical perception must produce in the visual field.

To this primary peripheric level of reading, syntactic analysis adjoins the perceptual possibilities of foveal/macular vision in order to recognize the effective differentiations supported by all regions and subregions, being individualized through characteristics of their visual variables, even if these figures are presented under irregular or blurred forms, as bad gestalts or nonlexicalizable figures. Thus, the decoupage by peripheral vision of large previously seen regions permits the establishment of a mode of description and nomenclature of characteristics and relations linked to this potentiality of the process of perception, but does not prejudge any-thing about the syntactic functions of these regions before they have been submitted to a syntactic analysis.

Less suitable in reacting to chromatic energies, peripheral vision, however, maintains a primordial function in perception, since, in being opened to a larger angle on the visual field, it is the sole instrument of analysis and of grouping of regions of large dimensions. It never acts alone but always concurrently with foveal/macular vision, whereas these latter can, in a process of intensification of attention in the centration of the gaze, operate on the smaller regions of the visual field.

The perceptual mechanisms of peripheral vision provide two types of syntactic information on the visual field: 1) they determine the superre-gions, formed by an aggregate of coleremes which are amalgamated or differentiated through the laws of junction/disjunction of the gestaltian theory and which are capable of entering into relations with other superre-gions through the same mechanisms; and 2) they put into play or shed light on the energetic network constituted by the pictorial plane in its relation with the Basic Plane.

In the schema shown in figure XVIII, one could regroup these various rules, of which the boundaries not only are not airtight but also con-tinuously transport the energies of each level towards the others:

The central zone could be called "more connected" to the objective aspect of the visual field, and the other zones more linked to the subjective dimensions of perception. But one can only take account of visual language while conceiving it as a product of a continuous interaction of all these structural levels. Also, any description of the functioning of the language

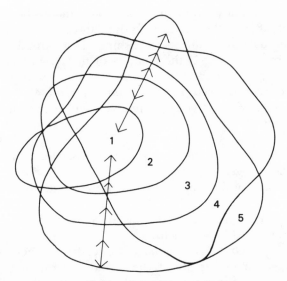

Figure XVIII: Five Structural Levels of Visual Grammar

at one of these levels results from an artificial distinction made to serve the ends of the analysis.

The syntactic analysis of visual language, which we call operative analysis, since it describes operations, but which can only know them in effectuating them, establishes the nature of the interrelations existing between those large, more or less autonomous regions, recognized by peripheral vision upon approaching of the work and their eventual subdivision into smaller regions.

It uses the ensemble of syntactic laws, and its topological and gestaltian operators, to disclose networks of liaisons/disjunctions between agglomerates of coloremes constituted by peripheral vision into totalities. These present themselves as series of regions reunited/separated from one another on two fundamental levels:

(1) In a bidimensional expansion, that is, groupings/separations deployed in height and in width;

(2) In a tridimensional expansion, that is, at various distances in depth through a variety of factors such as boundaries, vectorialities, chromatic contrasts, relations with the Basic Plane, effects of perspectives, and so on.

Before commenting further on these, we present in summary the fundamental steps of a syntactic semiological analysis that are required to account for the particular dynamisms of any field of visual representation:

I.   Differentiation of the visual field into regions by peripheral vision.

II.   Description of regions according to their preponderant visual variables by foveal/macular vision: chromatic poles and recognition of phenomena of interaction of colors, dimension, boundaries/forms, texture, vectoriality, bidimensional implantation. The visual variable of implantation in the plane of depth requires an important ensemble of perceptual trajectories, establishing: 1) a putting-in relation of regions by scanning; 2) the analysis of the type of vision solicited from the eye; 3) the points of view, sightings, and openings of the angles of vision used by the producer; and 4) the spatializing potentialities of the diverse systems of perspectives used.

III. Recognition of topological liaisons of each region with each of the others.

IV. Establishment of gestaltian interrelations between each region and recognition of gestaltian regroupings endowed with an iconic function; pressure of the 'good form', figure/ground productions, and so on.

V. Recognition of the main subregions in each region and description of their internal/external structures.

VI. Insertion of each of the regions and of certain of their subregions in the infrastructure of the Basic Plane determining a particular energization of the spatial curve of the pictorial plane. This description establishes: 1) actual differential energies; 2) potential and virtual differential energies; and 3) the production of specific continuous/ discontinuous spatial models.

VII. A regrouping of the visual field according to regions of stronger or weaker energies, accentuating or nonaccentuating their topological proximity or distance in depth.

VIII. In this energetic segmentation, recognition of dominant events (or statements) from their subordinates, of liaisons between them and with more separate regions.

IX. Recognition among regions and segmented subregions of the arrangements of visual variables linked to the structural spatialization of various organic spaces.

The syntactic analysis of a visual representation is no less detailed and complex than verbal syntactic analysis, requiring moreover the intervention of a less familiar conceptual instrumentation, inasmuch as it refers to dynamic processes in constant interaction.

The reader will find in Appendix IV a group of abridged notations facilitating the recording of visual variables, topological liaisons, and so on.

7.4.1. Topological liaisons

While assisting the integration of visual variables in a coloreme and inter-colorematic relations, topological relations will also be active in the apprehension of relations between larger aggregates of coloremes constituting regions circumscribed by peripheral vision and their interrelations.

One must not confuse the relations of neighboring, separation, or envelopment, with the topographical or geographic notions of adjacent juxtaposition or of distancing in bidimensionality. Instituted in the subjective dimension of the percept, they establish more fundamental links between the dynamic elements transformed by forces with which they enter into relation. The neighboring relation effects a strong bringing together of percepts offering tensions of attraction of equal intensities. In the same way, separation, which recognizes and valorizes the energetic variations in contiguous or foreign groups, maintains those regions in a juxtaposition, permitting their oppositions to remain active. Far from denoting an absence of relations between two elements, the perceptual separation is the locus of an awareness of reciprocal dynamic interrelations in depth.

Similarly the relation of envelopment, which plays a fundamental and paradigmatic role, since it represents the fundamental structure of the Basic Plane as the reservoir of energies which constitute the linguistic fiction in visual materials, becomes dialectic at all levels of analysis. It defines the structural schema of the coloreme as the relations between a central layer and the diversely surrounding peripheral layers. It also determines the fundamental relations between regions, their subregions and superregions, by means of continuous or discontinuous relations in the encasing, the embedding, and so on.

7.4.2. Infrastructure of the Basic Plane

We have described the infrastructure of the Basic Plane as: 1) The system of limits defining the spatial matrix of the pictorial or sculptural visual work and the foundation of their discursive autonomy; and 2) as the reservoir of energies permitting a spatial fiction to expand into the three dimensions and not remain in the bidimensionality of the material pictorial support.

The syntactic analysis of the visual work must, therefore, describe the way in which the pictorial plane, as produced by the artist, interrelates, that is, does or does not actualize the actual and potential energies of this infrastructure. In other words, the aggregates of the visual variables forming the pictorial plane will see their proper energies increased tenfold, transformed according to their type of implantation in the original matrix.

The syntactic structure depends, in the first place, on the dialectic and energetic exchange produced between regroupings of coloremes and the centers of energy of the Basic Plane, producing diverse spatial curves in the pictorial plane. These diversely spatialized regions are interrelated in view of the production of functional, organic, or practical spaces. They are amplified at the levels of increasing complexity calling for extremely subtle and mobile spatial curves. They may also coalesce into illusory spaces, usually more static, since these depend less upon the specific dynamics of reflected light as a privileged constitutive material and rely more upon collateral information.

Let us take as an example the grid of partition of 25 compartments described previously (see figure XIX), in which we have observed that the

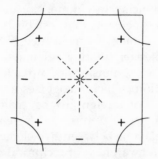

Figure XIX: Schema of the Spatial Energetic Structure of the Basic Plane

positioning of different compartments is equivalent to varied energetic levels.

The formative sides of the Basic Plane are indicated by the letters identifying the compartments, at their moment of origin and termination, being AE, AU, UY, and EY (see figure XX).

The corners identified as FAB, DEJ, PUV, and XYT constitute those regions which possess the maximum of actual energy, which decreases in the central section of the sides, more remote from the place where the angles meet.

By reverberation, the maximum potential energy will reside in the peripheral compartments, which are A, B, C, D, E, J, O, T, Y, X, W, V, U,

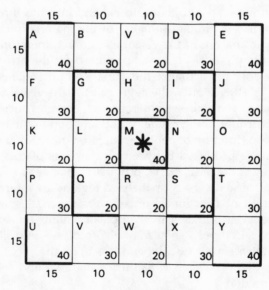

Figure XX: Actual and Potential Energetic Charges of Regions of the Basic Plane

P, K, and F, with a similar attenuation in the central compartments of each side. In the same way, the compartments of the central and intermediary region, which are M and G, H, I, N, S, R, Q, and L, possess a virtual linear energy of axial, diagonal, and cruciform coordinates which cross them.

The energetic system of the Basic Plane could be illustrated by a hypothetical quantification where the total of the actual energies of the corners and formative sides and the total of potential and virtual energies in the internal mass of the Basic Plane would be equivalent.

In other words, the actual energies of the angles are equivalent to the potential energies of diagonals; the energies of each of the sides are equivalent to the virtual energy of the central zone where the diagonal and cruciform axes meet:

Actual energy of angles in A, E, U, Y = 160
Potential energy generated diagonally = 160

Moreover, the actual linear energy (ALE) of the formative sides, is identified from A to E by the quantities 15, 10, 10, 10, 15 = 60 ALE.

It is equilibrated by the virtual energy of cruciform vectors calculated at half of the energies of mass: VLE = 60.

The equilibrium between the actual, potential and virtual charges involves a distribution of energies, different according to certain zones, producing three particular regions, and identified as follows:

(1) The compartment M regroups the virtual linear energies: 40.

(2) This region, formed by compartments G, H, I, N, S, R, Q, and L, possesses a minimal potential mass energy (20 for each compartment).

(3) The peripheral zone is more diversified, since the corner compartments possess a potential energy equal to 40, the intermediate compartments: 30, and the middle compartments: 20. These latter compartments will obtain an accrued charge, if we describe them as points of anchorage of virtual energy of the cruciform axes and of the internal diamond area (figure XIX).

The energetic elements which constitute the visual variables used in the constitution of the pictorial plane will be all the more powerful depending on whether or not they are conjoined with this specific reservoir of energy by an ensemble of mechanisms that syntactic analysis will describe.

In a general way, any actual reiteration of the vectors of the infrastructure of the Basic Plane, by the coloremes of the pictorial plane, multiplies their energies and their function in the whole of the work. Moreover, any activation of segments of the elements of the Basic Plane reinforces in a proportionate way the energy of the localized visual variables. This activation can be realized by a reiteration of sections of the matrix, by a lightly shifting rendering or by colorematic regroupings which punctuate their trajectory, producing a virtual vector of the pictorial plane upon the emplacement of a virtual vector in the Basic Plane.

The mechanisms which reactivate the energy of the corners and of the formative sides include the production in the pictorial plane of open forms in these regions, in strongly saturated chromaticities, or their repetition in proxemic shifting in what art theoreticians have called 'deductive structures' (Fried, 1966; 405).

The maximal peripheral energies are significantly attenuated by the inscription of coloremes offering tonalities, that is, an incorporation of black/white in the chromas, or by the inscription of a closed form which would establish the peripheral zone as a more or less distant background in relation to this figure.

The analysis must also account for the energetic transformation which results from the reiteration on the pictorial plane of the vertical and horizontal axes of the Basic Plane, or of their shifting duplication in the pictorial mass. The intensification of the central zone, in particular, in an attempt to focalize, often is accompanied by a decrease of the peripheral forces in the pictorial plane.

The reaffirmation of the infrastructure of the Basic Plane by the zones constructed by the pictorial plane attempts to integrate them in the spatial coordinates of the Basic Plane, that is, in the distance of depth proper to this topological mass. But this expression of neighboring can be thwarted by other characteristics which these zones possess and which will be explained at another stage.

7.4.3. Gestaltian regroupings/disjunctions

The analysis of regroupings/disjunctions between the elements of visual language constitutes primarily an analysis of visual movements in a specific field. However, contrary to what a certain interpretation of Gestaltian theory tends to hold, these visual movements are not uniquely and principally those establishing stable, simple, and regular forms (closed forms) from visual elements which lend themselves more or less easily to this end.

The application of gestaltian mechanisms in syntactic analysis concerns, first of all, the constitution of the regroupings of regions or superregions through factors of junction/disjunction which gestaltian theory has revealed and which we have treated earlier in this text. If the gestaltian factors tend to produce certain effects of regroupings of the coloremes in a unified form or of groups of coloremes in larger aggregates, they also contribute in an equal manner to the phenomena of separation, distancing, differentiation, distantiation, and isolation, which structure in a very fundamental way the mass of coloremes in the pictorial plane.

Syntactic analysis will proceed systematically in the examination of factors which bring together or separate elements in the three dimensions, through a functional application of gestaltian laws to the pictorial plane. The analysis will afterward establish those correlations which arise between regions through the factors of proximity, similarity, and complementarity.

The factor of proximity between two elements can stress distance as well as heterogeneity, since perception, which endeavors to bring together contiguous regions, will be hindered by the disparities between some of the visual variables, the structures of their boundaries, or other factors. In the case of an energetic homogeneity, the factor of proximity will lead to an effect of neighboring. But in the case of heterogeneity, perception will refer to more complex hypotheses resulting from other syntactic levels in order to diminish the separation between these elements.

The factor of similarity produces visual movements between elements separated by more or less important intervals. Syntactic analysis takes into account the links which are established between elements which are similar in color, texture, boundary, orientation, angularity, vectoriality, or form. By definition, this similarity established between one or more visual variables does not recover the whole ensemble of visual variables, thus creating particular tensions between regions which are brought closer by a certain similarity, but which are differentiated, separated, and diverted by other factors. Indeed, the similarities perceived between coloremes or groups of coloremes are not the properties of objective elements which would be attached to them as distinctive traits. They are the result rather of subjective gestaltian approximations, resulting from relations established by the operations of the perceiver on the basis of multiple visual trajectories in the field. These are applied to specific aspects of the visual variables, while deliberately ignoring some of their other dissimilarities (figure XXI).

Insofar as a similarity of properties, movements or functions has been established, one can conclude an operation of abstraction or distancing in

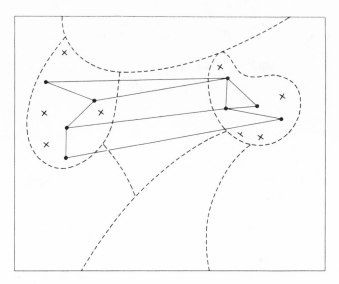

Figure XXI: Liaisons between Similar Elements in Separate Regions of the Visual Field

relation to the group of effective movements of coloremes or a regrouping of the same—a temporary cessation of perception of visual movements in certain regions to the benefit of the establishment of liaisons in others. However, a resumption of the trajectory of perception can lend to the elements or regions previously determined as similar a dissimilarity or heterogeneity and thus fracture the regrouping effected on the basis of similarity. This newly recognized dissimilarity will be the nucleus of another type of dynamic interrelation between these coloremes and the other regions now considered, leading to different regroupings and positionings in the three dimensions.

This perceptual and dialectical process does not carry any contradiction, but rather points to a simple coherence at the heart of the perceptual process, open to heterogeneity of the real and which recognizes that the establishment of relations between elements can only be the result of a perceptual, subjective, and perspectivist operation. Without the recognition of heterogeneity, no possibility of analysis and of regrouping is possible. This is recognized by typological analysis itself, when it "assumes that the population of objects is always heterogeneous, that is, that groups exist" (Chandon, 1981; 176). Certainly, only processes of abstraction, which retain only certain particulars of the real, permit the establishment of homogeneities setting up the very notion of ensembles or of sets among heterogeneous elements.

The effects of regrouping or of neighboring, produced by the factor of similarity, must be observed from all the visual variables, of which chromaticity and tonality appear particularly dynamic. However, the visual movements between coloremes carried out through gestaltian regulation will be again transformed, in the case of color/tonality by the laws of interaction of colors which possess their own structure.

The interrelation between regions which resemble each other by their characteristic of 'closure' usually entails the visual movement productive of a figure on a ground, just as regions do which seek an immediate recognition through a hypothesis of objects of external reality to which they can seemingly refer. But it is necessary to remember that syntactic analysis must proceed in the placing into relation of all the elements of the visual field. It is extremely rare that closed forms are more numerous in a given visual field and their syntactic function can only be defined by way of the structure of their variables and of their interrelations with other open regions in the visual field.

Moreover, the normal functioning of the eye, according to the three types of vision (including foveal, macular and peripheral), constantly gives rise to the appropriation of individual coloremes specific to foveal/macular vision which can interfere with the gestaltian process of the completion, that is, of the assimilation by peripheral vision of variables pushed toward their 'good form', in spite of their specific reality. The foveal/macular centration may systematically reinstitute the irregularity or opening of a form which one has closed or regularized, the discontinuity of texture, an opposite vectoriality in the ensemble, a more faithful chroma of a color which has been pulled toward its chromatic pole, and so on.

These perceptual contradictions, the sources of incessant movements and tensions, lead to the necessity for syntheses. By virtue of such syntheses, the homogenizing gestaltian productions can lose their organizing force to the benefit of more complex spatializations than that, for instance, of the simple mechanism of a form on a ground. If certain characteristics of the visual variables correspond very closely to the pressure for 'good form', the perceptual process at times attempts vainly to regroup them into more flexible and open structures.

7.4.4. Regroupings by interaction of colors

The junctions/disjunctions between visual areas by way of the laws of interaction of colors are, above all, the product of the foveal/macular centration. If peripheral vision is particularly sensitive to variations in tonalities and to the movements of mass which it institutes, foveal/macular vision reacts vividly also to clear and dark aspects of chromas which are subjected to the same tonal laws.

The chromatic contrasts termed 'simultaneous' or 'successive' are of a different order and contribute at an autonomous level to the regroupings/ disjunctions of regions in the pictorial plane by laws altogether different from those of gestaltian theory. As we have already described, the phenomenon of interaction of colors creates very particular visual movements which literally transform the material chromas placed on the pictorial plane. For example, by a centration effected by the fovea, to which chromatic percepts of the macula gather, the eye projects a percept of a complementary color to a given region, which will bring it closer or distance it from its surroundings.

A chromatic transformation of a region, through interactions of color, simultaneously modifies all the visual variables of this region and, consequently, the relations of this region with adjacent or more distant regions. Through their mobility and the instability of their effect, the interactions of color constitute extremely powerful, yet at the same time subtle, unstable, and unexpected visual movements. They permit the regrouping or the opposition of regions (while subtracting or multiplying their reciprocal chromas) and the joining of distant regions which are constituted as complementary. They introduce into distant regions forms, colors, vectorialities, and so on, which reiterate totally, partially, or inversely those which have been perceived elsewhere, in relation or not with the energies of the Basic Plane.

7.4.5. Modalities of perspectives

The modalities of perspectives belong properly to the syntactic structure of the field of visual representation. While they constitute instances of subjectivity in defining the point of view taken by the producer on the field of representation—as well as the experimental network of percepts that he puts into play in his work—they constitute ineluctable infrastructures of the pictorial plane. Moreover, they are always concretized in a specific treatment of visual variables and of their modes of regrouping, thus constituting observable elements in the visual work.

As explained in chapter 5, perspectives make explicit, above all else, the distance that the producer takes vis-à-vis his field of representation, the specific sighting of his point of view, and the distance that he puts between the objects which constitute his representation. These parameters are at first established by the recognition of the type of vision required or sought by the various aggregates of the visual variables on the whole surface of the pictorial plane.

The characteristics of the regroupings of coloremes give us data, in effect, according to their internal precision, the treatment of textures, the saturation or luminosity of chromas, the distinctiveness of boundaries, the contrasts of dimension, and so on, on the representation envisaged by the producer and on the type of discourse that he holds at a near, far, or medium distance. They equally reveal whether the percepts sought belong to proxemic spaces, indebted to a particular sensory experience with respect to spaces at a medium or a far distance.

Grammatically, the chosen distances, completed by sightings, angles, or different points of view taken on these fields, are established by programs of organization of the coloremes which cannot be modified without the given perspective being partially or completely transformed to the benefit of another.

However, certain regions of the pictorial plane are frequently treated according to a code of a certain perspective, whereas other regions are treated altogether differently, indicating in effect a transformation of the point of view, of the distance, and of the type of perceptual referents in play. This is why syntactic analysis of perspectives must not presume, on the faith of the perception of certain regions, that the ensemble of the pictorial plane belongs to the same perspectivist modality.

It is extremely important, to the contrary, that the analysis systematically examine the characteristics of diverse regions of the pictorial plane and recognize among the perceptual fields the type of perspectives that are constructed.

In so doing, the analysis establishes the types of spatialities that may be relatively disjointed from one another, both by the position in depth and by the dynamic of the treatment of the visual variables.

If the various proxemic perspectives, constituted by the very mechanisms of perception in the space constructed by the Basic Plane, present among them greater potentialities of regroupings—although they can offer numerous and divergent points of view and perceptual spaces—the illusory perspectives at a medium or a far distance present stronger disjunctions.

To the maximum extent, the areas treated according to modes of perspectives entirely heterogeneous in relation to those which organize other regions appear like gaps, ruptures of spatial tissue, or wedges, which no longer possess the elasticity needed to be incorporated into a wave which appears continuous.

In particular, the illusory perspectives often propose irreconcilable points of view to perception because they require a virtual ubiquity of the producer or the recourse to sightings which can only belong to several producers and not to the one that produces the discourse, since he cannot occupy at the same time two or more positions in space. These structures depend upon an abstract or imaginary trajectory which is not linked to the elaboration of a concrete space, but rather to allusions to the hypotheses or logical deductions derived from other discourses than that of visual language. Similarly to what happens in graphic language, they no longer function according to visual language dynamics and its proper creative potentialities. They are debased to illustrating themes already manufactured by other languages (Saint-Martin, 1989).

The different depths, established by the different modes of perspectives, can be described by means of a schema termed a 'grid of depths', which has been illustrated earlier (figures XIVe and XIVd). Representing a hypothetical profile of the pictorial plane under consideration, it establishes a series of numeric notations which account for an estimation of the various levels of depth where the observed regions seem to be situated.

Whereas the proxemic depths, which are registered inside the topological mass of the Basic Plane, are considered as ranging inside a maximal distance of one meter in relation to the position of the producer, the medium or far distances are evaluated in relation to the metric measurements used by the external world to which they allude. The distances of depth, therefore, may be registered from an intimate distance of several centimeters to a far distance leading to a point of infinity, interpreted as being situated at more than three hundred meters. The intermediate distances will be defined proportionally at the interior of these limits. It is important to point out again that the depths termed 'indefinite' belong by virtue of certain characteristics to a remote visual distance but are registered by other traits in the elasticity of the topological depth.

Moreover, in the representations known as 'nonfigurative', which do not make reference to metrically measurable remote distances but which are registered in the topological depths, different parameters will be developed where the various positionings in optic depth will be identified on a scale of one to ten. The dialectic interrelation in proxemic depths is as varied as that of intermediate and far perceptions of distances.

7.4.6. *Spatial continuity*

The production of more and more synthetic relations between heterogeneous elements produced by the visual variables tends toward the construction of a continuity. This term refers to a liaison or functional integration so close and proximal in nature that the field can be constituted as a unified space in spite of its internal, partial, and different types of spatial organizations.

A space (or a spatiality, a spatialization) is the product of a perceptual interconnection of elements in an unbroken level (or undulation) of depth. The inherent elastic potentiality of the topological regions is the paradigm of any aptitude to spatialization, since other geometrical types of regions may tend to break and generate different orders of levels of depth devoid of continuity.

This continuity can only be the result of an active interrelation between perceptive functions acting on previous disjunctions between the elements of the visual work. The coexistence of discontinuous elements in the visual field or the pictorial plane does not imply as such a continuity but, as its very name indicates, a simple coexistence or juxtaposition of elements, whose unification is undertaken according to hypotheses of spatialization capable of creating strong enough liaisons between them to constitute a unified space. In the latter, the function of the various regions is not negated, excluded, or concealed to the profit of others, but rather affirmed and assumed by the sensibility.

Without unification of the visual field in a given work, no awareness and knowledge of a visual discourse can be achieved. There only results a simple confrontation between partial elements, diversely heterogeneous and at worst, a confrontation leading to a chaos of unrelated percepts. Even the conscious intentionality of a speaker to construct a discourse full of discontinuities or heterogeneities, on the planes both of expression and content, can only be interpreted through a hypothesis which recovers and embraces these very disjunctions—a hypothesis that, in effect, unifies them in the appropriate dialectic continuity. Otherwise, these elements would not find a concrete ground for relations but would call for abstract interrelations produced by criteria external to visual language.

This function of continuity constructed by perception can never be interpreted as an objective trait, in the sense that the pictorial plane would produce it per se, or that the perception would succeed in homogenizing most of the dissimilarities between visual variables. As we have already explained, even a monochrome field without any variations in textures offers a specific spatial disjunction between its peripheral energy, strongly accentuated by the activation of the formative sides and corners and the nonstructured central regions, and only animated by chromatic aftereffects produced by perception. The static effect of similarity between its material constituents has to find ways of integration with the perceptual mobility, so as to be felt as parts of a unified field. If not analyzable in terms of organization, it cannot offer a visual counterweight to the actual energies of the periphery.

The description of regroupings/disjunctions, of vectorial tensions, of positioning of regions in topological or remote illusory depths, leads to the perceptual evaluation of a spatial curve specific to a given pictorial plane which represents the succession of the different levels of depth of the different regroupings of regions. When some regions cannot be perceptually integrated in a continued undulating spatial curve, they are qualified as "problematic." They play an important role in the syntactic and semantic structures of the work, both by their specificity and autonomy, and by the need they create to summon up for their interpretation super-syntheses, which may be more logical and dialectical than spatial.

This semiotical description can be realized by a variety of means, which make use of numeric functions or graphic representations. In effect, any curve of various surfaces can be represented by a numeric function. Through a division into regular units, the vectorial movement which animates the surface toward laterality and depth can be described by a sequence of numbers in which the position indicates the chosen parameter (figure XXII).

This spatial curve can be explained by the addition to the numbers of an alphabetic notation of ten elements (a, b, c, d, e . . .) in order to demarcate in the ensemble of a work the levels of depth occupied by the regions, from those closest to the perceiver to those farthest away (figure XXIII).

Other graphs based on numeric functions can be developed in order to represent regions of a stronger neighboring or disjunctions, of stronger

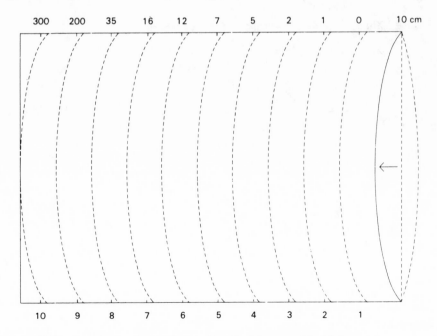

Figure XXII: Topological and Illusory Depths Measured in Meters

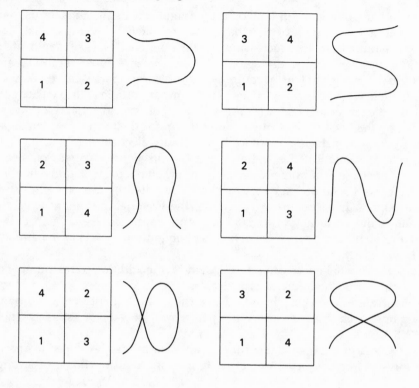

Figure XXIII: Linear Representation of the Vectorial Curve of Surfaces

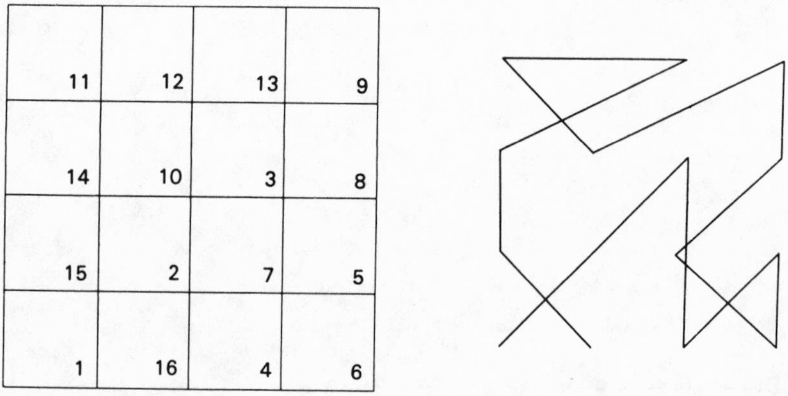

Figure XXIV: Linear Representation of Levels of Depth

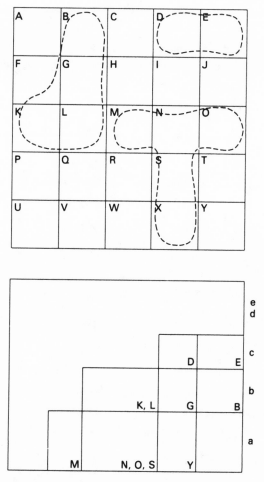

Figure XXV: Establishment of Three Frontiers

chromatic activities, of contrasts in perspectives, or else to show the interrelations between the potential and virtual structure of the Basic Plane in
relation to that of the pictorial plane.

Other types of graphs are developed for the characteristics common to
a certain number of compartments, determining a boundary around these
regions in which the different spatial curve is analyzed in relation to those
which are produced at the exterior. In the same way, in these descriptions,
textural and tonal indices can identify the places where particularly intense
energetic nodes polarize the principal vectorialities (figures XXV and
XXVI).

These and other graphs, which can be developed in response to
various needs, present essentially the undulation proper to a pictorial

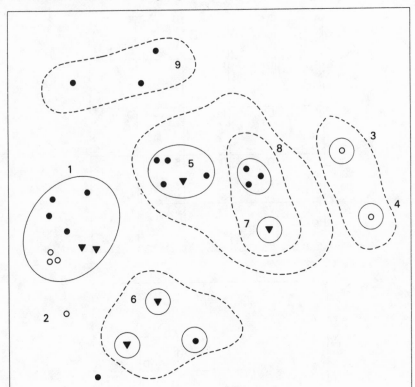

Figure XXVI: Boundaries Outlined to Regroup Regions into Superregions

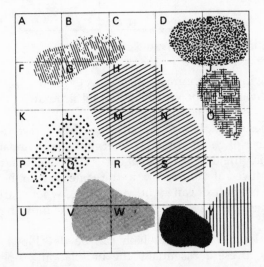

Figure XXVII: Graphs Evaluated Tonally and with Shadings

plane—but in a static way. They must be augmented or completed by other types of schemas symbolizing the vibratory movements which at times cause the pictorial plane to oscillate in a respiratory rotation or alternation regularly activated by the energetic equilibria of the visual work.

To evoke the highly developed energetic phenomena produced by certain contemporary visual works, it is necessary to borrow those vibratory schemas which the physical sciences use in their attempt to represent the experience of movement and organization of nonlinguistic matter. We allude to trajectories and rotations of the 'spin', vibrations of gaseous clouds, catastrophic curves or photonic fluxes, as well as to classical movements which animate, for instance, the nucleus of the atom, that is a global vibration of mass which alternately expands and contracts, which changes its shape by spontaneous reorganization of its energetic nodes and which oscillates irregularly in a lateral or vertical movement by a redistribution of its tensions and vectors (Bertch, 1983). Whether it concerns limited regions in a pictorial plane or the ensemble of its visual movements, it seems altogether impossible that nonspatial schemas, such as words, can in some way approximate the events which regularize the syntactic rules of visual language.

Thus, through the modes of relation between coloremes, regions, and various perspectives, the ensemble of these descriptions permits us to recognize and distinguish the various perceptual spaces which correspond to the specificity of these regroupings developed by the producer, offered to the eye, even if they correspond to spatial experiences relevant to different sensory fields. In this case, the so-called visual field of the pictorial plane, which offers the apparatus for the elaboration of different perceptual spaces within visible space, is used with a view to construct a representation of the organic spaces constituted by stimuli whose modes of interrelation and integration differ to a great degree from those which can regroup visual stimuli.

In a general fashion, the spaces organized in the zones close to the body itself may be said to refer to sensori-motor, emotive/conceptual experiences and interrelate tactile, thermic, postural, buccal, kinesthetic, and auditory spaces. The spaces constructed at a medium distance refer to kinesthetic, auditive, and visual experiences. The spaces evoked at a great distance refer to auditive experiences but especially to visual ones. All these spatial experiences are intermingled in representation as they are in reality.

The majority of the more traditional pictorial works in the occident are constructed by the disjunction/juxtaposition of tactile and postural spaces evoked at the first plane, kinesthetic spaces and their volumetric connotations at the intermediate plane, visual spaces mostly at the third plane.

These disjunctions between the perceptual spaces involve the construction of a spatial curve which encompasses the various depths and which will appear more or less chaotic or disjointed, according to the very potentiality of the ensemble to be reintegrated at a more synthetic level by certain of its structural characteristics.

In opposition to certain procedures of typological, probabilistic, or statistical analyses, semiotical analysis cannot brush aside, as a nonelement of the structure of the work, any of those regions which seem to be disjunctive, heterogenous, idiosyncratic, or not linked to a possible global perceptual space that can be constructed in a given pictorial plane. These oppositions/disjunctions form the very semiotic material of the visual discourse inasmuch as it is a cognitive and performative discourse, aiming at the production of a unified spatiality out of the very heterogeneous character of experience itself.

The purpose of semiotical analysis, by means of an actual experimentation with the tensions/contrasts/ruptures affecting the elements of the discourse, will be the construction of a spatialized representation permitting their perceptual integration. These mechanisms of integration, of which the guidelines are furnished by the particular treatment accorded by a producer to the visual variables, are based on the emotive and conceptual tensions of the perceiver himself. Actualized in various experiences of the work, this should lead to the elaboration of a unified construction and offer integration of the internal discontinuities. For want of this necessary leap in the production of a spatial model of the representation, the visual work itself remains nonunified, relatively chaotic, in other words, not known and not understood by the perceiver.

7.4.7. Syntactic articulations

The aim of syntactic analysis is the recognition of the specific articulation of the spatialities within a visual text based on positions in the third dimension. It must produce a final segmentation of the pictorial plane corresponding to the diversity of its spatialized regions; their components, functions, and intensities; their reciprocal interrelations; and the possible isolations of some of them. This representation establishes a few more or less autonomous or interdependent "propositions" within the whole that they articulate. Given the energetic character of these "propositions" whose sum will correspond to the performative statements realized in a visual representation, they would be better named by the term "events."

This final segmentation can present analogies with the division of the field already operated on by peripheral vision, since depth is a perceptual construction based on points of reference in the visual field. But the synthetic segmentation will diverge essentially in that, instead of isolating some larger superregions, it will distinguish among them an energetic hierarchy which discloses their liaisons and specific interrelations.

The last steps in the syntactic analysis of a visual representation consist in a perceptual assessment of the differences in depth between regions. This perusal will lead also to the recognition of the most important subdivisions of these large regions. These subregions can be as numerous as their characteristics are influential in the internal or external liaisons between regions for a given perceiver.

The tensions arising from the dissimilarities between the visual variables of boundaries or contours will lead to the analysis of the passages between the regions, establishing the quality of the frontiers (firm, blurred, degraded), their gestaltian quality (regularity, diffuseness, cohesion, figure/ground disparities, openness/closure). It is mainly through the visual variable of closed forms that regions or subregions lend themselves to the process of "iconization" through which they are interpreted as similar to the mnemonic percepts of objects belonging to external reality. On the other hand, chromaticity may be more active in the "recognition" of open forms (sky, earth, sea, forest, etc.). This iconization which is usually realized differently by several perceivers would require that a definitive list of iconic elements assigned to a visual representation be corroborated by an adequate group of observers (Saint-Martin, 1987, 1988).

While the syntactical function in the visual text establishes the spatial interrelationship between elements and their perceptual correlatives, the iconic regions, always linked to a verbal label, install thereby a "verbalized" level in the text whose semantic correlations are different from that of a spatialized language.

The analysis of the modes of insertion of the regions into the Basic Plane infrastructure will reveal higher levels of energetic intensities in parts or in the totality of the regions. The accrued intensities of regions anchored in various ways into this energetic system result in their movement toward the front in a more proxemic depth. Phenemona linked with the interaction of colors, mainly in relation to the simultaneous and successive contrasts of color and tonalities, will contribute to strong movement toward the front. The after-effects appear indeed like chromatic films hovering above the "surfaces" of the regions and intermingling with them, diminishing the distance between them and the perceiver that may be built from the other visual variables.

Disparities between the visual constituents will produce specific tensions between regions, when some are at the same time attracted and pushed away by different visual variables. These separative and distancing effects will first define the implantation in the two-dimensional plane, which is not equivalent to a topographical localization of regions in the field, but to the nature of the links which tie, contract, or expand them, contributing to the rhythmic expansion of space.

These disparities between regions will produce even more forcefully variations in the implantation in the depth or third dimension. But to these factors, localization in depth will add a certain amount of "deictic" information, referring to the producer and establishing his position in relation to his spatialized field of representation. This will be recognizable through: a) the type of vision according to which the visual variables are produced on the pictorial plane, the products of foveal vision being closer to the producer than those of macular or peripheral vision (This analysis is better achieved through the use of the grid over the whole field.); b) the overall distance from himself that the producer establishes for the ensemble of the representation; c) the angle of the position of his whole body in relation with the field (above, under, oblique, etc.); d) the angularities of specific sightings or directions of the gaze on the same regions; and e) added information is given about the producer through the various distances in depth he establishes between the objects themselves positioned in the field of representation.

These variations in depths, added to the recognition of specific traits in the visual variables, reveal the unified or contrasted use of modalities of perspectives, both expressive of a "syntactic meaning." The intimate relation between syntax and meaning was demonstrated by Tesnière in his analysis of the structural syntax of verbal language when he concludes that "the structural expresses the semantic," or more precisely: "To structural connections are superimposed semantic connections" (1976; 42). This is even more important in visual language as this form of language provides two levels of signifiers, one which can be termed "factual" or representing direct production of junctions/disjunctions or topological relations and another which remains linked with the verbal or iconological forms of representation. These two levels which carry different emotional and semantic contents are basic to syntactical constructs (Saint-Martin; 1987).

Graphs can be produced of the in-depth distribution of the regions and subregions with two entries: their effective distribution from left to right in the field and their estimated perceptual depths. Such a linear graph illustrates at once the leaps in depth which may exist between contiguous regions on the pictorial plane, some so abrupt as to break the spatial continuity and appear as problematic disjunctions in a discontinuous milieu (see figure XXVIII).

The energy and the interrelations of the various regions, multiplied by the intensification provided by the Basic Plane potential and actual energies, will finally define the different levels of events in the field, leading to

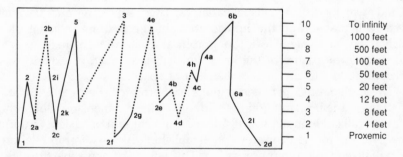

Figure XXVIII: Positioning in Depth of Some Regions and Subregions According to Syntactic Analysis

the proper syntactic segmentation and articulation of the parts in the spatial text. They will allow for the recognition of the rhythmic oscillations and vibrations in the field, leading to definition of its main perceptual referents.

In using the term 'text' to designate a visual work, such as painting, photography, or sculpture, etc. analogous to its use in the verbal domain, we wish to retain two characteristics. The first is the fact that a text possesses a certain structural autonomy by virtue of which the parts are understood as a function of the whole, though we do not pretend to determine what can be truly defined as an autonomous text in the verbal domain. In addition, we would like to evoke the synthetic and pluralistic connotation of the term, in opposition to a comparison of the visual work with a single propositional phrase as those which compose verbal prose.

On a belief in the possibility of the translation of visual language into verbal language, Umberto Eco already observed that the simple description of a silhouette of a horse drawn on a sheet of paper requires the cooperation of a large number of verbal statements (1978; 104). In this regard, the description of a more complex visual work would correspond to a very large number of statements indebted more to a textual grammar than to a propositional grammar.

But in all respects, it is more fitting to speak here of a grammer of the field, since no subensembles of the visual work can correspond to the structure of the verbal statements composing a text. These are commonly described as formed by the sequence of syntagms of noun, verb, and predicate (NS—VS—PS) at the interior of syntactic paradigms, such as gender, temporal modalities, and so on.

Unfortunately, the analysis of the visual field cannot find support in a general textual grammar, in fact nonexistent to this day, except for some narrative schemas linked to a theory of action, relatively foreign to the activity of representation put into play in artistic visual expression.

Despite several recent works, such as those of Ray Jackendoff (1983; 170–175) showing a growing concern with the cognitive and perceptual functions of language, most verbal grammars are founded on a radical omission of the spatial dimension in human experience to the benefit of temporal succession, in accord with the most tenacious tendencies of occidental philosophy (Frank; 1986).

To counteract this assimilation of dynamically interrelated regions in the visual field to verbal statements, and although both languages serve the same basic functions of mental representation, we call "events" the agglomerates of regions endowed with a specific and contrasting energy which "autonomizes" them as dynamic nodes in the field and positions them at sufficiently distinct levels on the scale of depths.

Inasmuch as these regions/events represent very strong condensations of energy and appear to occupy disparate positions, implying bifurcations and leaps in the field, they would not contradict the proposition of René

Thom (1972) to the effect that "any event is a catastrophe." They could eventually be describable by a grammar of catastrophes as we have already suggested for the poetic text (Saint-Martin, 1985b).

These visual events are presented, in effect, as complex, qualitative reorientations of energy, but always suitable to be interrelated by various mechanisms of envelopment, emboxing, optic attraction, to produce the rhythms of topological successions. In addition, they present, on an internal plane, subevents more or less integrated or discontinuous in their containing region, in active interrelation with other events of the field through their particular environmental position. Moreover, certain radical discontinuities in the three-dimensional liaison, often explained by systems of heterogeneous perspectives, institute problematic energetic nodes, forming antagonistic poles to the discourse of the surrounding regions.

In its progressive modeling of structural elements of the visual field, visual semiotics will be careful to avoid the obstacle that has constituted, for numerous verbal grammars, a mode of graphic representation using a discontinuous neutral trait to represent the relations between its principal terms. This graphic artifice, as demonstrated by J. Petitot-Cocorda (1985; 141), most frequently leads to a substantiation of terms, a fixed reification of the relation, and their subsequent assimilation by the logic of the identity. As suggested already by Kurt Lewin, it appears more heuristic to call on notions of topological and "ensemblist" wholes to represent, at more abstract levels, the dynamic liaisons between elements in transformation.

We propose, therefore, to substitute for the straight lines used in the 'stemma' schema proposed by Tesnière (1976; 162), the curves in helix, like corkscrews, capable of recalling the continuous and reciprocal interaction between regions (figure XXIX).

This form of graphic representation shows, moreover, that we generalize to all the interrelations between regions of the visual field, the "rubber-band" effect observed by Arnheim in many visual representations (1982; 240). It is the term he applied to the magnetic inter-tension which links the peripheral regions of a work to its focal region. This elastic tension exists, according to topological semiology, between all regions of the field, even those defined as separate or foreign with respect to certain of their characteristics, because the perceptive tension itself always generates movements bringing them closer or moving farther off in the three dimensions. In particular, this elastic tension is characteristic of the pulsating link between the regions of the pictorial plane which redouble or reiterate the structures of the Basic Plane and its energies.

The visual events can be represented by oblong shaped figures, of variable dimensions according to their energetic impact, on which will be positioned, by intersection, other events which are subordinated to them by encasing or embedding. The liaisons offered by the pictorial plane itself between the principal or subordinate events resulting from superimposi-

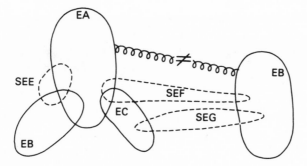

Figure XXIX: Graphic Model of a Syntactic Structure of a Visual Work

tions, optic links, effects of shadows, and so on, will be represented by dotted curves.

One could schematize the syntactic structure of a hypothetical visual work in the following manner, by regrouping the primary peripheral regions forming an event under a capital letter (EA, EB, EC . . .), and the subevents by these initials and an added capital letter.

In this illustration, the principal events EA and ED are interconnected by a strong disjunction. The regions EB and EC are the subordinates of EA by encasing and embedding. The subevent SEE links EA to EB; SEF links EA, EC and ED; SEG links EC to ED. While describing factual energetic liaisons, these systems of separation and dependency, quite different from the early peripheral segmentation of the field by peripheral vision, will be analyzed as to their perceptual space organizations, providing a basis for interpretation.

The magnitude of an actual application of syntactic analysis of a visual representation, which is a quite lengthy procedure, prevents its publication in this book. The reader may refer to a sample in another publication (Saint-Martin; 1986).

We are also entrusting to a future work the development of the semantic system of topological visual semiotics which constitutes its aim and last term. Any attempt at the interpretation of visual language can only rest on the analysis of the syntactic data it offers. But semantic hypotheses have been alluded to in the very study of syntactic theories. This is inevitable since any grammar consists of the set of linguistic methods by which meaning is conveyed by the intermediary of particular sensory materials and codes.

Appendix I

1. Dimensions of regions (assessed by scanning)

All very small
All medium size
All large
Small and medium
Small and large
Small, medium and large.

2. General division of the Pictorial Plane

a) *Horizontally* (from left to right):

Half and half

{ by the harmonic diagonal
by the dysharmonic diagonal
by a vertical
by a curve

One third/two thirds

{ by the harmonic diagonal
by the dysharmonic diagonal
by a vertical
by a curve

Two thirds/one third
$\left\{\begin{array}{l}\text{by the harmonic diagonal}\\\text{by the dysharmonic diagonal}\\\text{by a vertical}\\\text{by a curve}\end{array}\right.$

$\frac{1}{4}, \frac{1}{4}, \frac{1}{4}, \frac{1}{4}$
$\frac{1}{4}, \frac{1}{4}, \frac{1}{2}$
$\frac{1}{4}, \frac{1}{2}, \frac{1}{4}$
$\left\{\begin{array}{l}\text{by the harmonic diagonals}\\\text{by the dysharmonic diagonals}\\\text{by verticals}\\\text{by curves}\end{array}\right.$

b) *Vertically* (from top to bottom):

Half and half
$\left\{\begin{array}{l}\text{by an horizontal}\\\text{by a curve}\\\text{by a harmonic oblique}\\\text{by a dysharmonic oblique}\end{array}\right.$

One third/two thirds
$\left\{\begin{array}{l}\text{by an horizontal}\\\text{by a curve}\\\text{by a harmonic oblique}\\\text{by a dysharmonic oblique}\end{array}\right.$

Two thirds/one third
$\left\{\begin{array}{l}\text{by an horizontal}\\\text{by a curve}\\\text{by a harmonic oblique}\\\text{by a dysharmonic oblique}\end{array}\right.$

$\frac{1}{4}, \frac{1}{4}, \frac{1}{4}, \frac{1}{4}$
$\frac{1}{4}, \frac{1}{4}, \frac{1}{2}$
$\frac{1}{4}, \frac{1}{2}, \frac{1}{4}$
$\left\{\begin{array}{l}\text{by horizontals}\\\text{by curves}\\\text{by harmonic obliques}\\\text{by dysharmonic obliques}\end{array}\right.$

c) *Cruciform:*
Shifted cruciform
Implicit checkerboard
Explicit checkerboard
Concentric circularity

3. Sources of lighting in the Pictorial Plane

Pure chromatic luminosity
Light reflected from a painted object
Light reflected by many painted objects
Light produced by an object external to the painting
Various light effects produced by objects external to the painting
Presence of cast shadows
Chiaroscuro (from clear to dark in certain masses)

4. Grid analysis of types of vision solicited

	Foveal	Macular	Peripheric	
Compartment 1				
Compartment 2				
Compartment 3				
Compartment 4				
Compartment 5				

Appendix II

REPERTORY OF FORMS

A. ACTUAL FORMS

1) *Open forms:*
   Linear:
   Simple unidirectional:

   Double unidirectional:

   Simple bidirectional:
   angular: continuous
                  discontinuous

   curved: continuous
                  discontinuous

   curvi-angular:

Double bidirectional:
    angular: continuous
                      discontinuous

    curved: continuous
                      discontinuous

    curvi-angular:

Simple multidirectional:
a) angular:

    regular: joined
                  disjoined

    irregular: joined
                  disjoined

b) curved:

    regular: joined
                  disjoined

    irregular: joined
                  disjoined

c) curvi-angular:

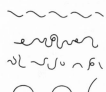

Double multidirectional:
a) angular:

    regular: joined
                  disjoined

    irregular: joined
                  disjoined

b) curved:

    regular: joined
                  disjoined

    irregular: joined
                  disjoined

c) curvi-angular:

2) *Closed forms:*
Simple forms:
Regular and symmetrical:
angular
curved
linear and curved

Regular and asymmetrical:
angular
curved
straight and curved

Irregular and symmetrical:
angular
curved
straight and curved

Irregular and asymmetrical:
angular
curved
straight and curved

Compound forms:
Circumscribed and symmetrical:
angular
curved
curved and angular

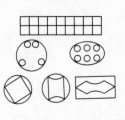

Circumscribed and asymmetrical:
angular
curved
curved and angular

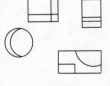

Forms compounded by adjunction or superposition
  Linear
Closed and angular
closed and curved
closed and curvi-angular

Masses are quantities which may have either closed or open frontiers, outlined or not by marked linear contours.

B - VIRTUAL FORMS
  Virtual forms may present any of the characteristics of actual forms and should be described accordingly.

Appendix III

ANALYSIS OF THE VISUAL VARIABLES FORMING
A COLOREME

1. *Texture*

a) Texture of the *support:*
   Fine granulation
   Medium granulation
   Coarse granulation
   Firm stretching
   Undulated/floating stretching
   Checkerboard, oblique weaving
   Disjointed support
   Slight reliefs
   Hollowed regions
   Frayed material
   Assemblage of materials
   Addition of contrasted material

b) Texture of the *Pictorial plane:*
   Stained canvas
   Flat and glossy
   Flat and mat
   Slight reliefs
   Medium reliefs
   Speckled brushworks
   Corrugated brushworks
   Juxtaposed brushworks
   Superposed brushworks

Hatchings
Droplets
Pasted
Drippings
Continuous brushworks
Dots in relief
Primed or unprimed canvas/support
Bulges by plaiting or sewing
Superposition by collages
Glazes
Mat varnish
Shining varnish

2. *Boundaries/Forms*

Hard-edge
Neat and firm
Contour line
Shading off
Dissolved frontiers
Opened on the superior side
Opened on the inferior side
Opened on the left side
Opened on the right side

The various forms can be described according to the Repertory of Forms (See Appendix II). The virtual forms are produced mainly by the vectorialities and interactions of colors. As numerous as the actual forms, the virtual forms are made up of the same visual variables and should be described by the same criteria.

3. *Colors*

a) Tonalities:

Regions	Very dark	Dark	Bright	Pale	Mixed chiaroscuro	Do not apply	
1							
2							
3							
4							

b) Chromatisms

Chromas	Clear	Dark	Red	Blue	Yellow	Saturation		Luminosity			
						Yes	No	Strong	Medium	Weak	
Red											
Blue											
Yellow											
Green											
Orange											
Violet											
Ochre											
Purple											
Brown											
Pink											
White											
Black											
Gray											

4. *Vectorialities*

Horizontal
Vertical
Harmonic oblique
Dysharmonic oblique
Centrifugal circular
Centripetal circular
Arcs of circle
Orthogonal
Focusing
Interlaces
Spiral
Undulated
Envelopment of the top by the bottom
Envelopment of the bottom by the top
Envelopment of the left by the right

Envelopment of the right by the left
Angularity
In spray
Some encasing/emboxing
Virtual movement in surrounding field
Movement stopped by frontier

5. Dimension

The dimensions of coloremes are described on the basis of their perceptual expansion inside a compartment and their possible expansion in neighboring compartments. If the criterion of five coloremes by compartment is chosen, each coloreme occupies $\frac{1}{5}$, $\frac{2}{5}$, $\frac{3}{5}$, $\frac{4}{5}$ or $\frac{5}{5}$ of it, and the same scale is applied in the neighboring compartments. The dimension of regions (or groups of coloremes) is appreciated by their occupancy of so many compartments following the use of the statistical grid.

6. Types of liaisons between adjacent coloremes

	Neighboring	Separation	Envelopment	Encasing	Repetition	Recurrence	Juxtaposition	Superposition	Chromatic contrasts effects
A1 → A2									
A2 → A3									
A3 → A4									
A1 → A5									
A4 → A5									
A5 → A3									
A5 → A4									
A1 → B1									
A2 → B4									
A3 → B3									
A3 → F1									

Or else, in the case of compartment "H" :

H1 ➤ H2										
H2 ➤ H3										
H3 ➤ H4										
H4 ➤ H5										
H1 ➤ H5										
H5 ➤ H2										
H5 ➤ H3										
H1 ➤ C3										
H2 ➤ I4										
H3 ➤ M1										
H4 ➤ G2										
H1 ➤ G1										
H3 ➤ G3										

7. *Vectorialities inside a compartment*

	Horizontal	Vertical	Harmonic oblique	Disharmonic oblique	Centrifugal circular	Centripetal circular	Arcs of circle	Orthogonal	Angular	In sprays	Envelopment L → R	Envelopment R → L	Envelopment T → B	Envelopment B → T	Movement stopped by frontier	Virtual movement
A																
B																
C																
D																
E																
F																
G																
H																
I																
J																
K																
L																
M																
N																
O																
P																
Q																
R																
S																
T																
U																
V																
W																
X																
Y																
Z																

Appendix IV

SYSTEMS OF NOTATIONS

1) Chromatic Poles

The terms designating the chromatic poles, namely, the saturated shade toward which a coloreme or region converge may be abbreviated as follows:

W	:	White
Bl	:	Black
Y	:	Yellow
R	:	Red
B	:	Blue
O	:	Orange
G	:	Green
V	:	Violet
Oc	:	Ochre
Br	:	Brown
Gr	:	Gray
P	:	Pink

2) Tonalities

Cl	:	Clear
D	:	Dark
Ch	:	Chiaroscuro

3) Vectorialities

Foc   : Focusing effect
Lat   : Lateralization effect
Cp - Cf : centripetal, centrifugal movement
V   : Vertical axiality
H   : Horizontal axiality
HD   : Harmonic Diagonal
DD   : Dysharmonic diagonal

4) Topological and gestaltian liaisons

U   : Envelopment
u   : Semi-envelopment
⌐⌐   : Encasing/emboxing
≠   : Separation
/   : Frontier/boundary
≪   : In front
≫   : In back
---   : Superposition
——   : Continuous

5) Identifications inside the statistical grid

A, B, C, D . . . Z   From left to right and top to bottom, each compartment is named by a capital letter of the alphabet.

A1, A2, A3, A5, B1,   Inside a compartment, a number added to the identifying letter locates the four cardinal and the center points.

Liaisons or vectorial links between two regions of the pictorial plane can be represented in two ways. Along the clock model, marked dashes connect specific regions positioned approximately at the hour numbers (1 o'clock, 4 o'clock, 10 o'clock . . .).

Or in a parallelepiped similar to the work's format and divided by a certain grid, a dart relates two compartments at their "hour" location. In illustration; From region F5 to D3.

References

Josef Albers (1963), *Interaction of Color*, New Haven, London, Yale University Press, 2d ed. 1971.

Carl Andre and Hollis Frampton (1980), *12 Dialogues*, Halifax, Press of Nova Scotia College of Art and Design and New York University Press.

Rudolf Arnheim (1954), *Art and Visual Perception*, Berkeley, Los Angeles, University of California Press.

———(1966), *Towards a Psychology of Art*, Berkeley, University of California Press.

———(1971), *Visual Thinking*, Berkeley, University of California Press.

———(1982), *The Power of the Center, A Study of Composition in the Visual Arts*, Berkeley, University of California Press.

Gaston Bachelard (1951), *L' Activité rationaliste de la physique contemporaine*, Paris, Presses universitaires de France.

H. Irvine Barret (1983), *The Syntax of Art, the Logical Form of Visual Language*, New York University, Ann Arbor, University Microfilms International.

Roland Barthes (1967), *Elements of Semiology*, London, Jonathan Cape.

G. Battcock (1968), *Minimal Art: A Critical Anthology*, New York, E. P. Dutton & Co.

Claude Berge (1966), *Espaces topologiques—Fonctions multivoques* (1959), Paris, Dunod.

B. Berlin and P. Kay (1969), *Basic Color Terms*, Berkeley, University of California Press.

G. F. Bertch (1983), "Vibrations of the Atomic Nucleus," *Scientific American*, May, vol. 248, no. 5, 62–73.

Jacques Bertin (1973), *Sémiologie graphique*, Paris, The Hague, Mouton.

Faber Birren (1969), *Principles of Colors*, New York, Van Nostrand Reinhold.

Charles Blanc (1880), *Grammaire des arts du dessin*, Paris, Hachette.

A. L. Blumenthal (1970), *Language and Psychology*, New York, Wiley.

U. Boccioni (1975), *Dynamisme plastique*, Lausanne, L'Age d'Homme.

M. Boll and J. Dourgnon (1946), "Echelle comparative des longueurs d'ondes et de fréquences dans le spectre visible," *Le Secret des couleurs*, Paris, P.U.F.

————(1962), *Le Secret des couleurs*, Paris, P.U.F.

P. E. Borduas (1978), *Ecrits/Writings, 1942–1958*, Halifax, Nova Scotia College of Art and Design & New York University Press.

P. Bouissac (1984), *Iconicity and Pertinence*, Toronto Semiotic Circle Prepublication Series, Victoria University, no. 1.

G. Braque (1969), cited by L. Aragon, *Les Incipit*, Geneva, Skira.

G. T. Buswell (1935), *How People Look at Pictures*, Chicago, University of Chicago Press.

James Cahill (1977), *La Peinture chinoise*, Geneva, Flammarion, Skira.

Ernst Cassirer (1955), *The Philosophy of Symbolic Forms*, (1923) New Haven, Yale University Press.

J. L. Chandon and S. Pinson (1981), *Analyse typologique*, Paris, New York, Mossan.

M. E. Chevreul (1981), *The Principles of Harmony and Contrast of Colors* (1839), New York, London, Van Nostrand Reinhold.

Noam Chomsky (1957), *Syntactic Structures*, The Hague, Mouton.

————(1980), *Rules and Representations*, New York, Columbia University Press.

Hubert Damisch (1972), *Théorie du nuage*, Paris, Seuil.

————(1974), "Huit Thèses pour (ou contre?) une sémiologie de la peinture," *Macula*, no. 2, 12–23.

————(1976), "Sémiotique et iconographie," *La Sociologie de l'art et sa vocation interdisciplinaire*, Paris, Denoël-Gonthier.

————(1979), "L'Origine de la perspective," *Macula*, no. 5/6, 113–37.

Gilles Deleuze (1988), *Le Pli, Leibniz et le Baroque*, Paris, Minuit.

Maurice Denis (1964), *Théories*, Paris, Hermann.

Umberto Eco (1965), *L'Oeuvre ouverte*, Paris, Seuil.

————(1970), "Sémiologie des messages visuels," *Communications*, no. 15, 11–51.

————(1976), *A Theory of Semiotics*, Bloomington, Indiana University Press.

————(1978), "Pour une Reformulation du concept de signe iconique," *Communications*, no. 29, 141–91.

Betty Edwards (1979), *Drawing on the Right Side of the Brain*, Los Angeles, J. P. Tarcher.

Anton Ehrenzweig (1967), *The Hidden Order of Art*, London, Routledge and Kegan Paul.

Jean-Marie Floch (1985), *Petites Mythologies de l'oeil et de l'esprit*, Paris, Hades-Benjamin.

M. Foucault (1968), "Ceci n'est pas une pipe," *Les Cahiers du chemin*, Paris, N.R.F., no. 2, January, 79–91.

P. Francastel (1965), *Peinture et société*, Paris, Gallimard.

R. Frances (1975), "La Perception des formes et des objets," *Traité de psychologie expérimentale, VI, La Perception*, 3d ed., Paris, P.U.F., 220–54.

Didier Franck (1986), *Heidegger et le problème de l'espace*, Paris, Minuit.

Sigmund Freud (1979), in *Les premiers psychanalystes*—Minutes de la Société psychanalytique de Vienne, H. Nunberg and E. Fedren, eds., III, 1910–1911, Paris, Gallimard (October 18, 1911).

M. Fried (1966), "Shapes as Form: Frank Stella's New Paintings," *Artforum*, vol V, no. 3, November, 404–409.

Wilhelm Fuchs (1967), "The Influence of Form in the Assimilation of Colors," *A Source Book of Gestalt Psychology*. London, Routledge and Kegan Paul, 95–103.

A. Gabar (1968), *Philosophic Foundations of Genetic Psychology and Gestalt Psychology*, The Hague, Martinus Nijhoff.

Naum Gabo (1964), "The Constructive Idea in Art," *Modern Artists on Art*, New Jersey, Prentice Hall.

Y. Galifret (1957), "Perception des sources lumineuses et des surfaces réfléchissantes," *Problèmes de la couleur*, Paris, S.E.V.E.N, 29–44.

A. Gelb (1967), "Color Constancy," *A Source Book of Gestalt Psychology*, London, Routledge and Kegan Paul, 196–209.

J. J. Gibson (1950), *The Perception of the Visual World*, Boston, Houghton Mifflin.

——(1966), *The Senses Considered as Perceptual Systems*, Boston, Houghton Mifflin.

J. Gips (1975), *Shape Grammars and Their Uses*, Basely Stuttgart, BirkHauser Verlag.

W. Goethe (1976), *Theory of Colors*, Cambridge, Mass., M.I.T. Press.

E. H. Gombrich (1960), *Art and Illusion*, Princeton, Princeton University Press.

——(1979), *The Sense of Order*, New York, Ithaca, Cornell University Press.

R. L. Gregory (1977), *Eye and Brain* (1966), New York, McGraw-Hill.

——(1980) *The Intelligent Eye* (1970), London, Weindenfeld and Nicolson.

A. J. Greimas (1966), *Sémantique structurale*, Paris, Hachette.

A. J. Greimas and P. Courtès (1979), *Sémiotique, Dictionnaire raisonné de la théorie du langage*, Paris, Hachette.

Groupe Mu (1979), "Iconique et plastique," *Rhétoriques sémiotiques*, Revue d'esthétique, 1–2, Paris, Union générale d'éditions, 173–92.

Marcel Guillot (1957a), "Variété des couleurs obtenues en peinture avec un seul pigment," *Problèmes de la couleur*, Paris, S.E.V.E.N.

——(1957b), "Discussion à la suite de la présentation de 'La Couleur dans l'architecture' par Fernand Léger," *Problèmes de la couleur*, Paris, S.E.V.E.N.

A. Gurvitsch (1957), *Théorie du champ de la conscience*, Paris, Desclée de Brouwer.

M. A. Hagen and G. J. Brisnahan (1984), "Computer Graphics and Visual Perception; the State of the Art," *Visual Arts Research*, Spring, vol. 10, no. 1, 32–41.

Edward T. Hall (1966), *The Hidden Dimension*, New York, Doubleday and Anchor Books.

——(1972), "Sistema per la notazione del comportamento prossemico," *VS*, January–April, 67–91.

A. Herbin (1949), *L'Art non-figuratif non-objectif*, Paris, Lydia Canti.

A. von Hildebrand (1907), *The Problems of Form*, New York, Stechart.

Louis Hjelmslev (1963), *Prolegomena to a Theory of Language* (1943), Madison, University of Wisconsin Press.

Hans Hofmann (1948), *Search for the Real*, Cambridge, Mass., M.I.T. Press.

J. Itten (1970), *The Elements of Color* (1961), New York, London, Van Nostrand Reinhold.

R. Jackendoff (1983), *Semantics and Cognition*, Cambridge, Mass., M.I.T. Press.

E. Jacobson (1948), *Basic Color*, Chicago, Paul Theobald.

R. Jakobson and K. Pomorska (1980), *Dialogues*, Paris, Flammarion.

Julian Jaynes (1976), *The Origin of Consciousness in the Breakdown of the Bicameral Mind*, Boston, Houghton Mifflin.

Don Judd (1964), "Black, White and Grey," *Arts Magazine*, vol. 38, March, 36–38.

W. Kandinsky (1964), "Reminiscences" (1913), in *Modern Artists on Art*, New Jersey, Prentice Hall.

——(1970), "Conférence de Cologne," in *Ecrits complets*, t. 2, Paris, Denoël-Gonthier.

——(1975), *Cours du Bauhaus* (1929), Paris, Denoël-Gonthier.

——(1976), *Point, Line and Plane* (1926), New York, Dover.

——(1977), *Concerning the Spiritual in Art*, New York, Dover.

G. Kanizsa (1957), "Gradient marginal et perception chromatique," *Problèmes de la couleur*, Paris, S.E.V.E.N, 107–14.

——(1980), *Organization in Vision*, New York, Praeger.

D. Katz (1935), *The World of Colour*, London, Kegan Paul, Trench, Trubner.

D. Katz (1955), Introduction to *Psychologie de la forme*, by P. Guillaume, Paris, Marcel Denière.

P. Kaufmann (1968), *Kurt Lewin, Une Théorie du champ dans les sciences humaines*, Paris, Vrin.

R. Klein (1970), *La Forme et l'intelligible*, Paris, Gallimard.

W. Köhler (1940), *Dynamics in Psychology*, New York, Liveright.

———(1967), "Physical Gestalten" (1920), *A Source Book of Gestalt Psychology*, London, Routledge and Kegan Paul, 3d ed. 1967.

———(1969), *The Task of Gestalt Psychology*, Princeton, N.J., Princeton University Press.

R. Krauss (1977), *Passages in Modern Sculpture*, New York, Viking Press.

———(1986), "The Originality of the Avant-Garde, a Postmodernist Repetition," *October*, no. 37, 47–66.

Julia Kristeva (1972), "L'Espace Giotto," *Peinture/Cahiers théoriques*, 2/3, January.

Harald Küppers (1975), *La Couleur*, Fribourg, Office du livre.

N. de Largillierre (1981), Catalogue *Largillierre*, Montreal Museum of Fine Arts.

Y. LeGrand (1957), "Variations dans la vision des couleurs," *Problèmes de la couleur*, Paris, S.E.V.E.N. 75–91.

C. Lévi-Strauss (1973), *Tristes Tropiques*, New York, Washington Square Press.

Jerre Levy (1974), "Psychological Implications of Bilateral Asymmetry," in *Hemisphere Function in the Human Brain*, S. J. Dimond & J. G. Beaumont, eds, New York, John Wiley & Sons.

Kurt Lewin (1935), "The Conflict between Aristotelian and Galilean Modes of Thought in Contemporary Psychology," *A Dynamic Theory of Personality*, New York, McGraw-Hill.

———(1936), *Principles of Topological Psychology*, New York, McGraw-Hill.

———(1938), "The Conceptual Representation and Measurement of Psychological Forces," in *Field Theory in Social Sciences*, New York, Harper and Brothers, 1951.

———(1941), "Regression, Retrogression and Development," in *Field Theory in Social Sciences*, New York, Harper and Brothers, 1951, 87–129.

———(1951), *Field Theory in Social Sciences*, New York, Harper and Brothers.

André Lhote (1967), *Les Invariants plastiques*, Paris, Hermann.

René Lindekens (1971), *Eléments pour une sémiotique de la photographie*, Brussels, AIMAV, Paris, Didier.

El Lissitzky (1968), "Art and Pangeometry," in Sophie Lissitzky-Küppers, *El Lissitzky*, London, Thames and Hudson, 2d ed. 1980, 352–58.

Iouri Lotman (1973), *La Structure du texte artistique*, Paris, N.R.F.

Louis Marin (1976), "Eléments pour une sémiologie," *Les Sciences humaines et l'histoire de l'art*, Brussels, La Connaissance, 109–42.

M. McLuhan (1962), *The Gutenberg Galaxy*, Toronto, University of Toronto Press.

J. Mehler (1981), *Language Disposition in the Infant, Studies in Cerebral Asymmetry*, Toronto Semiotic Circle, Victoria University, nos. 2–3, 25–48.

M. Merleau-Ponty (1968), *The Visible and the Invisible*, Evanston, Northwestern University Press.

Christian Metz (1977), "Le Perçu et le nommé," *Essais sémiotiques*, Paris, Klincksieck.

L. Moholy-Nagy (1947), *Vision in Motion*, Chicago, Paul Theobald.

Guido Molinari (1980), *Lecture Notes*, Unedited.

J. Molino (1973), "Structure et littérature," *Archives européennes de sociologie*.

F. Molnar (1966), "Aspect temporel de la perception de l'oeuvre picturale," *Sciences de l'art*, vol. III, 136–44.

Piet Mondrian (1967a), "De Stijl" (1918), in *De Stijl*, Hans L. C. Jaffé, ed., New York, Harry N. Abrams.

———(1967b), "The Plastic Means," in *De Stijl*, Hans L. C. Jaffé, ed., New York, Harry N. Abrams.

A. M. Monnier (1957), "Elaboration du message lumineux au niveau de la rétine," *Problèmes de la couleur*, Paris, S.E.V.E.N, 15–27.

Jacques Monod (1970), *Le Hasard et la nécessité*, Paris, Seuil.

Noël Mouloud (1964), *La Peinture et l'espace*, Paris, P.U.F.

Jan Mukarovsky (1976), "The Essence of the Visual Arts" (1944), *Semiotics of Art, Prague School Contribution*, L. Matejka and J. T. Titunik, eds., Cambridge, Mass., M.I.T. Press, 229–44.

A. H. Munsel (1969), *A Grammar of Color*, New York, Van Nostrand Reinhold.

C. Musatti (1957), "Les Phénomènes d'égalisation entre surfaces chromatiques," *Problèmes de la couleur*, Paris, S.E.V.E.N, 93–104.

Hans Namuth (1978), "L'Atelier de Jackson Pollock," Paris, Editions Macula.

Erwin Panofsky (1915), "Le Problème du style dans les arts plastiques," in Panofsky (1975), 183–97.

————(1972), *Studies in Iconology*, New York, Harper and Row.

————(1975), *La Perspective comme forme symbolique* (1929), Paris, Minuit.

René Passeron (1962), *L'Oeuvre picturale et les fonctions de l'apparence*, Paris, Vrin.

W. Penfield and L. Roberts (1959), *Speech and Brain Mechanisms*, Princeton N.J., Princeton University Press.

Jan M. Peters (1981), *Pictorial Signs and the Language of Film*, Amsterdam, Rodopi, N.V.

J. Petitot-Cocorda (1985), *Morphogenèse du sens I*, Paris, P.U.F.

Jean Piaget (1952), *The Origins of Intelligence in Children*, New York, New York University Press.

Jean Piaget (1980), *Les Formes élémentaires de la dialectique*, Paris, Gallimard.

Jean Piaget and B. Inhelder (1956), *The Child's Construction of Space*, London, Routledge and Kegan Paul.

Jean Piaget, B. Inhelder, and I. Szemenska (1960), *The Child's Conception of Geometry*, New York, Harper Torch Books.

Karl Pribram (1971), *Language of the Brain*, Englewood Cliffs, New Jersey, Prentice Hall.

Luis J. Prieto (1964), *Principes de noologie*, London, The Hague, Paris, Mouton.

————(1966), *Messages et signaux*, Paris, P.U.F.

————(1975), *Etudes de linguistique et de sémiologie générales*, Genève-Paris, Librairie Droz.

————(1976), *Pertinence et pratique*, Paris, Minuit.

W. V. O. Quine (1969), *Ontological Relativity and Other Essays*, New York, Columbia University Press.

H. Rabati (1957), "Peintures pour artistes," *Problèmes de la couleur*, Paris, S.E.V.E.N. 155–65.

Herbert Read (1964), *The Art of Sculpture* (1956), Penguin Books, Bolliger Series XXXV—3, 3d ed.

F. Recanati (1981), *Les Énoncés performatifs*, Paris, Minuit.

A. Riegl (1978), *Grammaire historique des arts plastiques*, Paris, Klincksieck.

Irwin Rock (1975), *An Introduction to Perception*, New York, Macmillan.

Hermann Rorschach (1947), *Psychodiagnostics: A Diagnostic Test Based on Perception*, Bern, Huber, New York, Grune and Stratton.

Barbara Rose (1967), *American Art since 1800*, New York, Prager.

R. Rosenblum (1976), *Cubism and Twentieth-Century Art*, New York, Harry N. Abram.

M. N. Rosenfeld (1981), *Largillierre, an 18th Century Portraitist*, Museum of Fine Arts of Montreal, Annex A.

Fernande de Saint-Martin (1968), *Structures de l'espace pictural*, Montreal, HMH-Hurtubise.

————(1980), *Les Fondements topologiques de la peinture*, Montréal, HMH-Hurtubise.

————(1985a), "Le Lien critique: Des Images visuelles aux images mentales," *Protée*, vol. 13, no. 3, Autumn, 91–104.

————(1985b), *La Fiction du réel, poèmes 1953–1975*, Montréal, l'Hexagone.

————(1986), "Analyse syntaxique de Mascarade de Pellan," *Protée*, Université du Québec à Chicoutimi, vol. 14, no. 3, Autumn, 27–40.

————(1987), "L'Insertion du verbal dans le discours visuel de Pellan," *Canadian Literature*, nos. 113–14, Summer-Fall, 28–45.

————(1988), "La Fonction perceptive dans la constitution du texte visuel," *Protée*, vol. 16, no. 1–2, Winter-Spring, 202–13.

————(1989), "From Visible to Visual Language: Artificial Intelligence and Visual Semiology," *Semiotica* 77-1/3, 303–16.

————(1990), *La Théorie de la Gestalt et l'art visuel*, Sillery, Presses de l'Université du Québec (in press).

M. Salomé-Lagrange (1971), "Un Aspect du traitement des images, les codes analytiques élaborés au Centre d'analyse documentaire pour l'archéologie du C.N.R.S." *Interphotothèque*, Numéro spécial.

————(1973), *Analyse sémiologique et histoire de l'art*, Paris, Klincksieck.

Meyer Schapiro (1969), "On Some Problems in the Semiotics of Visual Art: Field and Vehicle in Image Sign" (1966), *Semiotica*, vol. 1, no. 3.

J. R. Searle (1970), *Speech Acts*, Cambridge, Cambridge University Press.

Philippe Sers (1970), "Présentation du texte," W. Kandinsky, *Ecrits complets*, vol. 2, Paris, Denoel-Gonthier.

W. Strzeminski and S. Syrkus (1973), "The Present in Architecture and Painting" (1928), *Constructivism in Poland, 1923–1936*, Lodz, Museum Sztuki.

W. Strzeminski and K. Kobro (1977), *L'Espace uniste*, Lausanne, L'Age d'Homme.

J.-J. Sweeney (1961), "Mondrian, the Dutch and De Stijl," in *Art News*, Summer.

N. Taraboukine (1972), "Pour Une Théorie de la couleur" (1923), in *Le Dernier tableau*, Paris, Champ libre.

Lucien Tesnière (1976), *Eléments de syntaxe structurale*, Paris, Klincksieck.

René Thom (1972), *Stabilité structurelle et morphogénese*, New York, W. A. Benjamin.

————(1980), "L'Espace et les signes," *Semiotica*, 29, 3/4.

————(1981), "Morphologie du sémiotique," *RS/SI*, vol. 1, no. 4, 301–309.

Félix Thürlemann (1982), *Paul Klee, Analyse sémiotique de trois peintures*, Lausanne, L'Age d'Homme.

W. P. Thurston and J. R. Weeks (1984), The Mathematics of Three-Dimensional Manifolds, *Scientific American*, vol. 251, no. 1, July.

A. Tomatis (1978), *L'Oreille et le langage*, Paris, Seuil.

M. Turvey (1974), "Constructive Theory, Perceptual Systems and Tacit Knowledge," *Cognition and Symbolic Processes*, W. B. Weimer and D. S. Palermo, eds., Hillsdale, New Jersey, Lawrence Erlbaum, 165–80.

Dora Vallier (1979), "Le Problème du vert dans le système perceptif," *Semiotica*, 26/1–2, 1–14.

V. Vasarely (1970), *Notes Brutes*, Venice, Alfieri.

Jiri Veltrusky (1976), "Some Aspects of the Pictorial Sign" (1973), in *Semiotics of Art, Prague School Contribution*, L. Matejka and J. T. Titunik, eds., Cambridge, Mass., M.I.T. Press, 245–61.

H. Wallach (1961), "Brightness Constancy and the Nature of Achromatic Colors," *Documents of Gestalt Psychology*, Mary Heule, ed., Berkeley, Los Angeles, University of California Press.

M. Wertheimer (1925), "Gestalt Theory," *A Source Book of Gestalt Psychology*, 1967, London, Routledge and Kegan Paul.

Hermann Weyl (1952), *Symmetry*, Princeton, N.J., Princeton University Press.

Olive Whicher (1971), *Projective Geometry*, London, Rudolf Steiner Press.

John White (1972), *The Birth and Rebirth of Pictorial Space*, London, Faber and Faber.

L. Wittgenstein (1958), *Philosophical Investigations*, Oxford, Basil Blackwell.

————(1978), *Remarks on Color* (1950–51), Berkeley, Los Angeles, University of California Press.

H. Wölfflin (1950), *Principles of Art History* (1915), transl. by M. D. Hottinger, 7th ed., New York, Dover.

————(1961), *Renaissance et Baroque* (1888), Paris, Le Livre de poche.

W. Wörringer (1953), *Abstraction and Empathy*, New York, International Universities Press.

H. Yilmaz (1969), Quoted in W. V. O. Quine, *Ontological Relativity and Other Essays*, New York, Columbia University Press.

Index

FERNANDE SAINT-MARTIN, poet, essayist, and art
theoretician, has been Director of the Musée d'art
contemporain in Montreal and is now professor of
contemporary art history and visual semiotics at the
Université du Québec à Montréal.